WRECK OF THE *CARL D.*

Reasons to Believe: New Voices in American Fiction

Creative Conversations: The Writer's Complete Guide to Conducting Interviews

Dharma Lion: A Biography of Allen Ginsberg

Crossroads: The Life and Music of Eric Clapton

There but for Fortune: The Life of Phil Ochs

Francis Ford Coppola: A Filmmaker's Life

Mighty Fitz: The Sinking of the Edmund Fitzgerald

Mr. Basketball: George Mikan, the Minneapolis Lakers, and the Birth of the NBA

WRECK OF THE *CARL D.*

A TRUE STORY OF LOSS, SURVIVAL, AND RESCUE AT SEA

—— MICHAEL SCHUMACHER ——

BLOOMSBURY

New York   Berlin   London

Published by Bloomsbury USA, New York

Title page photo courtesy Presque Island Historical Museum

Map by Patrick McDonald

All papers used by Bloomsbury USA are natural, recyclable products
made from wood grown in well-managed forests. The manufacturing processes
conform to the environmental regulations of the country of origin.

LIBRARY OF CONGRESS CATALOGING-IN-PUBLICATION DATA

Schumacher, Michael.
    Wreck of the Carl D. : a true story of loss, survival, and rescue at
    sea / Michael Schumacher.—1st U.S. ed.
        p.   cm.
    Includes bibliographical references and index.
    ISBN-13: 978-1-59691-484-1 (hardcover)
    ISBN-10: 1-59691-484-X (hardcover)
    1. Carl D. Bradley (Ship) 2. Shipwrecks—Michigan, Lake.
3. Survival after airplane accidents, shipwrecks, etc.—Michigan,
Lake. I. Title.
G530.C2958S38 2008
917.74—dc22   2008014242

First U.S. Edition 2008

1 3 5 7 9 10 8 6 4 2

Typeset by Westchester Book Group
Printed in the United States of America by Quebecor World Fairfield

To the crew of the *Carl D. Bradley*

and

to those who knew and loved them

CONTENTS

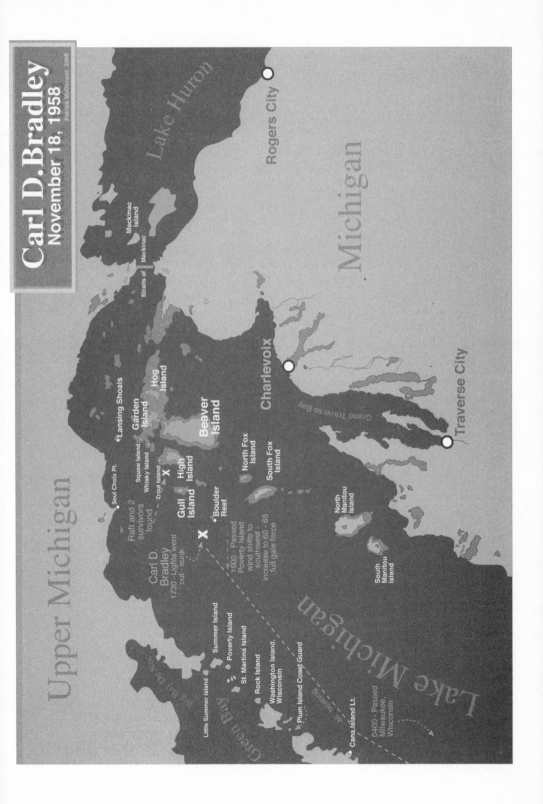

PROLOGUE

Tuesday, November 18, 1958

The wind, strong and out of the southwest, blows in, and temperatures start to fall.

The people of the small town of Rogers City, Michigan—or at least those who give this kind of thing a second thought—regard the change in weather with mixed feelings. Deer-hunting season is only in its fifth day, and the predicted colder temperatures, along with the possibility of snow, are more than welcome to those wielding shotguns and rifles. They trudge around the heavily wooded area behind the massive limestone quarry that is Rogers City's identity and livelihood. Snow, no stranger to the area this time of year, will make the deer much easier to track. In these parts, deer hunting transcends the idea of sport and recreation; bringing down an eight-point buck is the first sentence of a story that will be embellished and retold until someone comes up with something better.

Nature has created a region for outdoor sports, and the residents of Rogers City regard their surrounding beauty the way most Europeans admire the frescoes in surrounding cathedrals and basilicas. The lakes and woods provide them with their livelihoods and recreation; people here hunt and fish the way people in downstate Michigan might attend a concert or go to the opera, head out to Briggs Stadium for a ball game, spend an afternoon or evening at the movies, or gather at nightclubs. And why not? This is the region where downstaters retreat, where they take summer vacations to escape the boundaries of the city. Rogers City has Lake Huron for its northern boundary.

There are days when the lake is the most beautiful place on Earth, when you can stand near the shoreline and the water seems to move toward you like a welcoming gesture. The midmorning sun, overhead and reflected on the water, is such that you have to squint just to look straight ahead. Sometimes you might hear birds, geese or gulls or others, moving with disinterest over the water, or you might hear sounds of the wind, coming from as if inside your head, but if it's really quiet, you can make yourself believe you're hearing the sound of a promise. And you take it to heart. This is what the residents of Rogers City understand.

The hunters are out today. Their prey, normally in such plentiful supply as to provide entertainment to families driving out to the woods during the summertime and making a game of spotting and counting them, now know better than to wander into view; they won't feed until dusk. The day is warm enough that the men and women looking for them work up a sweat as they make their way through the woods. Every so often, someone squeezes off a shot.

A layer of fresh snow—a good couple of inches of it—would help . . .

Maybe the weather is about to cooperate.

Rogers City, located in the northern tip of lower Michigan, is a clean, quiet city, far removed from the concerns of such larger cities as Lansing, Flint, Ann Arbor, Grand Rapids, or Detroit. The people in those places live in ways that are foreign to the folks in Rogers City or any of the other tiny communities along the shore of Lake Huron. Rogers City has all of one stoplight; a main drag displaying almost all of the city's businesses; and neat, tidy houses lining neat, tidy streets. Residents here can go to bed without locking themselves into their houses or worrying about strange sounds outside their windows. They're friends with the butcher trimming their steaks at the corner store, neighbors of the guys delivering their mail or cutting their hair. Everybody knows everybody, and the prospects of gossip are probably as responsible for keeping people on the level as any law passed downstate in the Capitol building.

The 3,873 residents of Rogers City can thank the Michigan Limestone and Chemical Company, a division of the U. S. Steel Corporation, and, by extension, the Bradley Transportation Company, for their comfort. The limestone quarry, the world's largest, sprawls out for miles at the city's southern border, and among the workers mining the stone, crushing and processing it at the plant, and moving it to ports around the Great Lakes, almost everyone in town is connected, in one way or another, to the business. Hundreds work at the plant, while nearly 350 others work on the fleet of nine massive self-unloading boats hauling the product. Aside from going into the service or attending college in another town, a young man graduating from City High has two basic choices for the future: he can work at the plant, or he can go sailing on the boats.

To those families with loved ones working on the stone boats, today's changing weather pattern is cause for notice. It's late in the shipping season, with Thanksgiving only nine days away. Most of the boats will be laid up for the winter in days, and the men will be home for some long-overdue time with their families. As far as anyone in Rogers City is concerned, a little snow is one thing, but there is no good reason for a late-season storm's complicating shipping schedules, or causing delays or anxiety.

Betty Kowalski, wife of one sailor and sister of four others, can't help but notice and be slightly irritated by the wind.

The day started out breezy and warm, with temperatures climbing to a balmy sixty-six degrees, and Betty used the unseasonably mild conditions to hang her laundry on lines outdoors. Now the wind is twisting her carefully pinned clothes into a bollixed-up mess, which is precisely the kind of distraction she can do without. Less than a week shy of her twenty-first birthday, Betty already has two tiny kids to keep her busy, and with her

husband Bob's boat, the *T. W. Robinson*, due later in the evening, she needs
to finish a number of household chores and get the kids cleaned up and
over to her parents' house before she drives out to pick him up.

Like any other sailor's wife, Betty has learned to take her husband's ab-
sences in stride. It's part of the job. The men take off early in the year, as soon
as the ice on the Great Lakes has broken sufficiently enough to allow safe
passage for the ships. From early spring until late fall, the wives will raise
their children, handle all the household chores, take care of the bills, and address any emergencies that might demand a quick, unilateral decision. Some
of the wives hang out together in their own social circle; they meet and greet
one another every time their husbands' boats are due, when they pack their
kids into cars and head down to the docks.

Working for the Bradley boats offers the sailors from Rogers City one
enormous advantage over other shipping companies: since the Bradley
Transportation boats are picking up nearly all of their limestone from the
Michigan Lime plant, the boats are home far more often than you might find
elsewhere. A boat full of limestone might leave the Port of Calcite near
Rogers City on a Monday; dump its shipment in Gary, Indiana, the following
evening; maybe head to another port for a load of coal and have it dropped
off in, say, Traverse City, Michigan, by Thursday night; and be back in Rogers
City by Friday. Boats from other companies might be out for weeks on end;
the Bradley boats always seem to be around.

The visits between the sailors and their families last only as long as it
takes to load up for another haul. Sometimes this translates into just six to
eight hours. At other times, if you're lucky and there are other boats in line
ahead of you, you might get an overnight stay. Regardless, the hours are
precious. Husbands and wives catch up on household business and any
pressing matters demanding attention; school-age children show their fathers their schoolwork and discuss their classes. Some families will steal
away to the Swan River, which cuts through the Michigan Lime property,
where they might have a picnic, go fishing, or just stand near the riverbank,
talking and leisurely allowing the time to pass quietly.

But time always passes too quickly. The families watch the boats pull out on the breakwater, and they'll go fatherless or husbandless for a few more days. It's just the way things are.

Today is Cecilia Krawczak's birthday, and as in the past, her husband, Joe, won't be around for it. Joe works as a wheelsman on the *Carl D. Bradley*, a limestone carrier now out somewhere on the lakes. Cecilia and Joe both have birthdays that fall during the shipping season, and they've gotten used to celebrating them before or after the actual date—whenever Joe is in town. No one gives it a second thought.

This year was an exception. With business down and the *Bradley* laid up for much of the summer, Joe was around for his thirty-fifth birthday in July—the first time he'd been home on his own birthday since he began working on the stone boats. For the rest of her life, Cecilia would regard this as one of her fondest memories of her husband: just the thought of the entire family—her, Joe, and their five kids—sitting down at a table and enjoying cake together.

A card arrives in the day's mail.

Krawczak, known as "Crawford" by his shipmates, had picked it up and dropped it in the mail the day before yesterday, when the *Bradley*, docked in Cedarville, Michigan, was taking on a load of dolomite to be delivered to a port in Gary, Indiana.

From the guy who seldom shows it, but knows his wife is a whiz.

The printed lines on the card are strictly corn, about as sentimental as a guy like Joe Krawczak permits himself to be. After considering the greeting card's message, he had handwritten a couple of lines of his own.

Here's a card that fits you just right, I guess, he wrote, adding what, in years to come, would seem like an ominous postscript. *We were at Cedarville. Man, did we have a roll coming over.*

* * *

The wind builds throughout the afternoon—enough to uproot a few trees and send dirt, fallen leaves, and other debris flying through the air. The hunting is miserable, especially for those not wise enough to bring an extra layer of clothing. For some hunters, the deteriorating weather is enough to persuade them to pack it in for a day. It gets dark early this time of year, anyway.

Bob Hein is one of those hunters. He and his father, George, haven't had any luck out in back of the quarry, and they decide it might be best to head back into town, toss down a beer or two at the Rainbow Garden, and gas up for a drive out to the woods tomorrow morning.

Bob worked for a few years on the stone boats, but when he married, and he and his wife started a family, he decided to give up the time away from home in favor of a job onshore. He'd been through a few storms on the lakes while he was sailing, and as he and his dad drive back into town, they wonder aloud about how the winds, now howling from the southwest, are going to play on the open water. Whitecaps top the choppy waves near the Lake Huron shoreline; it will be exponentially worse the farther you stray from land, where the waves build and pack a punch that landlubbers can't begin to imagine. The Heins are looking at waves that might capsize a rowboat or give a twenty-five-foot fishing boat some trouble; fifteen miles out on the lake, the waves are powerful enough to roll a big ship onto its side.

"Boy," George Hein remarks to his son, "the guys on the lake are going to get a bouncing around tonight."

WRECK OF THE *CARL D.*

When a boat is well built, properly trimmed, and not deep laden, the waves in a strong gale, when she is going large, seem always to slip from beneath her—which appears strange to a landsman—and this is what is called riding, in sea phrase.

Well, so far we had ridden the swells very cleverly, but presently a gigantic sea happened to take us right under the counter, and bore us with it as it rose—up—up—as if into the sky. I would not have believed that any wave could rise so high. And then down we came with a sweep, a slide, and a plunge that made me feel sick and dizzy, as if I was falling from some lofty mountain-top in a dream. And while we were up I had thrown a quick glance around—and that one glance was all-sufficient . . .

—Edgar Allan Poe, "A Descent into the Maelstrom"

THE THIRTY-FIVE MEN ON BOARD THE *CARL D. BRADLEY* HAVE NO way of knowing that their ship, at one time the largest vessel on the Great Lakes and the flagship of the Bradley Transportation Company fleet, will be plunging to the bottom of Lake Michigan in half an hour. As far as anyone on the 638-foot limestone carrier can tell, the *Bradley* is sailing as smoothly as can be expected, given the late-autumn storm that's been lashing the lake and intensifying by the hour.

It's 5:00 P.M., Tuesday, November 18, 1958. The *Bradley* has been out on the lake all day, edging its way northward along the Wisconsin coastline. Its destination: Rogers City, Michigan. According to the planned course, the boat will continue up the coast until it reaches the top of Lake Michigan. It will then turn east, move along the northern shore of lower Michigan, slip through the Straits of Mackinac and into Lake Huron, and eventually arrive at the Port of Calcite in the wee hours of the morning—later than originally projected, but not all that bad, given the circumstances.

Dusk has settled over the lake, and it will be totally dark very soon. Thick, dark clouds hang low overhead, offering a strong hint of rain or, maybe later, when temperatures fall, snow. The wind has picked up substantially over the past hour, and the sound it makes, as it screams through the *Bradley*'s wires and railings, is deafening. Sea spray assaults anyone who happens to be on deck. Huge waves roll up under the ship, twisting it and lifting it in sections. The men on board the *Bradley* take note of all this, but they're not concerned. They've been in storms before, and they'll deal with this one. The ship is laboring, but it's working exactly as it's been designed to do.

When the *Bradley* left Gary, Indiana, the night before, it had been greeted by winds of twenty-five to thirty-five miles per hour blowing out of the southwest, but at that point the seas hadn't built into anything noteworthy. Weather forecasters called for gale-force winds and thunderstorms the following day, but Captain Roland Bryan, the *Bradley*'s skipper, reasoned that the *Bradley* would be well on its way before the really heavy weather set in.

So far, everything has gone according to plan. Rather than take the *Bradley*'s usual course from Gary to Rogers City, which would have placed the boat closer to the Michigan side of the lake and saved time, but which, in this instance, also would have exposed the vessel to heavier seas, Bryan has positioned the *Bradley* within five to twelve miles of the Wisconsin shore, where waves won't have as much room to build. The course is standard operating procedure for boats heading north on Lake Michigan when a storm is coming out of the southwest.

Another option would have been to take the *Bradley* into a harbor and wait for the storm to blow itself out. The storm is moving much faster than the original forecasts had anticipated; in all likelihood it will be out of the area within the next twenty-four hours.

Bryan, though, is not a commander given to dropping anchor and waiting out a storm in safe harbor. The fifty-two-year-old captain prides himself on delivering his cargo on schedule. Every dockside hour can be measured in dollars—thousands of them—and at this point in time, a couple grand represents a sizable percentage of the average worker's annual income. Company officials can grow impatient with timid captains. They would never admit to placing commerce above safety, but they also have subtle ways of letting their skippers know that they aren't being paid to sit around.

Ed Partyka, who worked on nearly all of the Bradley fleet boats, including the *Carl D. Bradley*, during a thirty-one-year career that saw him advance as high as first mate, remembers the kind of pressure the companies could put on the boats' captains.

"They claim it's up to the captain, but that isn't always true," he says. "I've seen some nasty letters coming from the office, stating the fact that, last month, there were ten boats running and you're the only one that had twelve-hour delays. None of the others had them. Well, that doesn't necessarily mean anything. You might have been in a spot where you had to take those delays. The other boats were down on Lake Erie someplace, hauling coal, where the weather was nice. Some skippers got some snotty letters from the office."

John Czcerowsky served for forty-three and a half years, including a number as captain. He had little patience for corporate officials inquiring about when his boat was going to pull anchor when the officials were safe and sound while he was facing the prospects of going out in a storm.

"When you go to anchor," he says, "you call in and tell them where you are. An hour later, they'll call you and say, 'When are you gonna get going?' If I went to anchor, I'd call and tell them where I was anchored. I'd say, 'Don't bother calling. I'll let you know when I get going.' I cut them off because most of the time when they're calling you, they're down in their basement, looking out a window, and they don't know if it's blowing or what the hell's going on. I used to tell them, 'You don't know what it's like out here. That's why you're paying me out here. So don't bother calling.' They didn't call, either."

Captain Roland Bryan, a consummate company man, knows all this, but he also knows the *Bradley*. He's been with the Bradley fleet for seventeen years, had his master's license since 1949, and has commanded the *Bradley* for the past four seasons. He's seen enough in Great Lakes storms during his thirty-eight overall years of sailing to know what a ship can and cannot handle.

In the language of the sailors, he's a "heavy-weather captain."

"Bryan was always in a hurry," one lifetime sailor commented many years later. This was the case when the *Bradley* left Gary at about ten o'clock the previous evening. The Gary run was originally slated to be the *Bradley*'s last trip of the season. After dropping off his cargo in the Indiana port, Bryan was to take his ship to a Manitowoc, Wisconsin, shipyard, where the *Bradley* was scheduled to sit in dry dock all winter and undergo significant repairs and upgrades, including installation of a new $800,000 cargo hold. The company had tacked on another trip at the last minute. Now, instead of heading to Manitowoc, Bryan is directing his ship back to Rogers City for another load of stone.

Bryan can't be any more pleased about this turn of events than the men serving under him. Unlike most of the *Bradley* crew, who make Rogers City their home, Bryan, a bachelor originally from Collingwood, Ontario, re-sides in Loudonville, New York. With Thanksgiving just around the corner, he's undoubtedly eager to get home and put what's turned out to be a dis-appointing shipping season behind him.

Normally one of the busiest ships in the Bradley fleet, the *Carl D. Bradley* had not been overwhelmed with work during this particular sea-son. The steel industry, suffering a downturn in business, hadn't needed all the Bradley boats, and the *Carl D.*, as the ship is affectionately known by those working on her, had been laid up for much of the season. She spent her July 1 to October 1 downtime in Rogers City, and her crew had been forced to find work on other boats. The crew returned when the *Bradley* was fitted out for a couple of months of fall work, but it was hardly enough to salvage the year's production. Prior to this trip to Gary, the *Bradley* had made only forty-three round trips during the 1958 shipping season. This doesn't make its master happy. It's been an unpredictable year, and Bryan would just as soon get it over with.

Then there's the matter of the *Bradley*'s overall condition. Although it isn't at all old by stone boat standards, the *Bradley* is showing signs of the bat-tering it has taken over thirty years in the punishing limestone business. All the loading and unloading, the accumulation of immense cargoes adding up to millions of tons over the years, the banging against the docks, the occa-sional groundings in shallow water, the bending and twisting in storms— time and heavy lifting have conspired to weaken the ship's hull, if not its determination.

As far as Roland Bryan is concerned, the *Bradley* won't be laid up in Manitowoc a minute too soon. Its cargo hold has seen better days—many years ago—and a common joke among those working on the boat is that rust is about all that's holding the *Bradley* together. In some places it's rusted out so badly that you can see from one compartment into another. The hold leaks like hell after a load of wet stone is dropped in, and crew-men are constantly sumping water out of the long tunnel extending from the front to the back of the boat. If the *Bradley* is running without cargo and has been ballasted to keep its propeller and rudder low in the water, the excess water will roll down the tunnel to the back of the ship, occa-sionally forming a pool, requiring boots for those sumping it out or moving about in the area.

More significantly, in terms of the sailing in rough weather, the *Bradley* has the well-earned reputation of being very "limber," as sailors like to call it, meaning that in storms it will bend and twist excessively in heavy seas. The elongated ore and stone boats are designed to be flexible, to avoid cracking when they're not at even keel, but even so, the *Bradley* snakes much more than any of the other big boats. If you were in a good storm and the winds were whipping up fifteen-to-twenty-foot seas, you could stand at the back of the pilothouse, look down the length of the ship, and not see the back end of the boat. You'd have a wave under the bow, while the stern, without any support from the wave, dropped down. It would reappear moments later, as if by magic. This was normal enough, but it could rattle you nonetheless.

"Many times, when you go down in the tunnel and you look forward, it almost looks like the stanchions are marching, it's moving that much," says Jerry Badgero, who put in forty-four years on the stone boats. "When you start rolling and you go to put your right foot down, the deck isn't there."

"You could see her moving," says Norm Quaine, who worked as a deck-hand on the *Bradley* from 1945 to 1949. "We used to kid about being down in the tunnel, sumping out, and the back door to the engine room would go out of sight. The bigger ships do that."

Quaine, who eventually capped his thirty-five-year career as skipper on several boats, including the *Rogers City* and the *Irvin L. Clymer*, believes the *Bradley*'s construction had a lot to do with the way she worked in heavy seas.

"The *Bradley* had a different type of framing. She had what they called an Isherwood type of framing. That meant she was built longitudinally for strength. That meant fore and aft framing. They did that for two reasons: they used less steel and she could haul more cargo. She had a different ride than the other ships with vertical framing. When I was getting my license, I was talking to one of the guys who had been on her, and he said, 'God, she's got more sounds than a new bride.'"

The snaking action is murder on the already overburdened cargo hold. At the time of the *Bradley*'s construction, the hulls and holds were riveted rather than welded, and in especially harsh conditions, the twisting will sheer off rivets by the bucketload. They'll snap and go flying belowdecks like so many spent shell casings and, depending on where they're being lost and how much water might be leaking in, crew members might have to scramble to make temporary repairs. Pieces of broom handles are a popular method of plugging the holes. The rivets will be replaced later, during the ship's winter layup, but this hasn't happened during the *Bradley*'s most recent winter downtime. Over the 1957–58 layup, workers, reasoning that there was no point in putting in new rivets if the cargo hold was going to be replaced, had substituted carriage bolts for the missing rivets.

The *Bradley* has other issues. A couple of years earlier, on April 3, 1956, the *Bradley* had collided with the *White Rose*, a Canadian vessel, in the St. Clair River near Detroit. The *Bradley* had suffered some damage below the waterline, but it wasn't considered serious, and the ship had been temporarily patched and put back on the lakes. Later, in dry dock for permanent repairs, workers detected a number of hairline fractures in eight of the *Bradley*'s bottom plates. These were repaired by cutting out and replacing the damaged sections.

Then, earlier in this current season, on a spring trip, the *Bradley* had touched bottom in shallow water near Cedarville, sustaining damage so minor that repairs weren't even called for. Six months later, only a couple of weeks before the *Bradley* set out on this trip to Gary, the ship had bottomed out near Cedarville again, but with more serious consequences. A fourteen-inch crack had ruptured one of the hull plates, leading to repairs back in Rogers City. Repairmen welded a patch over the crack, and the *Bradley* was given a clean bill of health.

Neither of these groundings or repairs was reported to the Coast Guard, as required by law.

The Coast Guard inspected the *Bradley* twice during the 1958 season, once in the spring for its in-depth annual inspection, and then again, briefly, on October 30, when inspectors had observed the *Bradley* crew conducting lifeboat and fire drills. The spring inspection began on January 30, when Coast Guard Lieutenant Frank M. Sperry visited the *Bradley* and thoroughly inspected the interior of the boat's hull, and it continued on February 25, when Commander Mark L. Hocking checked the engine room. The inspection was completed on April 16–17, ending with a going-over of the *Bradley*'s life-saving equipment. Sperry had watched repairmen burning out old, worn rivets and replacing them, as well as missing rivets, with carriage bolts. The long, thick bolts were pounded through the rivet holes and fitted with nuts in the back. This wasn't a standard repair, but Sperry was willing to allow it, since the *Bradley* was already scheduled for major repair work on the side ballast tanks and cargo hold after the current season. He wasn't satisfied, however, with the missing rivets he'd seen. Hocking noted that the *Bradley*'s Chadburn—the communications device connecting the pilothouse and engine room—was malfunctioning, but the boilers, turboelectric power system, and steering system were all in good working condition. At the end of the day on April 17, the Coast Guard issued a certificate of inspection to the *Carl D. Bradley* on condition that its owners make three required repairs:

1. *Make necessary repairs to electric engine order telegraph to comply with section 113.35-40(e);*

2. Install lagging or other suitable protection for persons in way of hot piping in exposed areas; [and]

3. Renew wasted side tank plating and replace rivets where missing at first available yard date during the 1958 season.

The *Bradley* repairmen performed the first two on the list, but when she made her first trip of the season five days later, the plating and rivets had not been touched. That would be done during the off-season.

These inspections might have signified an official endorsement of the *Bradley's* seaworthiness, but on at least two occasions earlier in the year, Captain Bryan had privately expressed reservations about his ship's condition. The boat might have seemed seaworthy when it was being inspected while tied to a dock in calm waters, but Bryan wondered how it might handle a storm.

"The boat is getting pretty ripe for too much weather," he confided in a letter to his girlfriend in Port Huron, Michigan. "I'll be glad when they get her fixed up. Supposed to go to Manitowoc this Fall to lay up. They say it won't be until the 10th of Dec. I hope it's before that. It's been a screwy season all the way through."

He was more specific in detailing his worries in a letter to his best friend.

"The hull is not good," he complained, noting that he had been ordered by company officials to "nurse" the *Bradley* along in bad weather, that he was to "take it easy" on the ship. Not that it took a lot of convincing. Bryan still worried about the groundings earlier in the year.

"The hull was badly damaged at Cedarville," he concluded.

In its day, the *Carl D. Bradley* was strong, healthy, immortal—much like any young kid so confident of his future that he never gives it a thought. The *Bradley* was as fine a ship as you'd find anywhere on the lakes—the "Queen of the Stone-Carrying Fleet," as she was called—the longest and strongest of the working boats, as well turned out as you'd see this side of a passenger liner.*

Since it was the Bradley Transportation Company's flagship and often carried corporate officials and other notables in her staterooms, the *Bradley* received special attention not normally afforded to other company ships. The paint was always fresh, the decks freshly hosed down, and the crew a little larger than you'd find on the other boats. One old salt, remembering the *Bradley*'s physical appearance, commented that her looks might have exceeded her abilities, certainly by the end, and that she might have been better off functioning as a showboat.

Perhaps, but when work began in 1926 on Hull 797 at the American Shipbuilding Company in Loraine, Ohio, the boat was designed for a lifetime of heavy lifting. Michigan Limestone had a lucrative contract with a cement firm in Gary, Indiana, and the *Bradley*, sleek and long (638 feet 9 inches in length, 65 feet in width), with a powerful 5,000-horsepower propulsion system, was expected to haul a lot of crushed limestone, and quickly, between the Port of Calcite and Gary. Throughout her career, she moved different grades of limestone from Lake Huron to deepwater ports along Lakes Michigan and Erie, with occasional excursions to Lake Superior.

The Rogers City townspeople greeted the arrival of the new boat with the kind of enthusiasm generally reserved for major political figures. The boat's massive hull was lowered into the water at Lorain on April 9, 1927, and after spending another three-plus months being outfitted with her fore and aft housings, the *Bradley* streamed into the Port of Calcite harbor at 8:00 A.M. on July 28. Michigan Lime shut down operations for several hours so its employees could head down to the dock and watch the ship come in. Hundreds of

---

*This was actually the second stone boat to be named after the Michigan Limestone president, Bradley Transportation founder, and Rogers City benefactor. The first, still in operation at the time of the second *Bradley*'s launching, was renamed the *John G. Munson*; it would be renamed yet again—the *Irvin L. Clymer*—when a new, 660-foot boat was built and assigned the *Munson* name in 1952.

citizens showed up as well, the Rogers City Community Band played on, and dignitaries, including village president Rudolph Dueltgen and Carl Bradley himself, gave speeches. Spectators were invited to tour the boat.

The crew quarters were beautiful, with individual rooms for the captain, mates, chief steward, and engine room officers, and comfortable dormitory-style rooms for the rest of the deck, galley, and engine room crews. The galley was state-of-the-art, housing huge refrigeration units and storage pantries. The engine room—the heart of any boat's operations—housed not only the huge generator capable of moving the *Bradley* along at a top-end speed of fourteen miles per hour; it also contained two Foster-Wheeler boilers, which fed steam to the generator. Unlike all but a couple of other boats, the *Bradley* was fully electric: the generator produced power controlling everything on board the *Bradley*, from propeller to running lights. Not surprisingly, the *Bradley* instantly became the boat that every Bradley Transportation worker wanted to sail on.

Big things were expected of the biggest ship on the Great Lakes, and the *Bradley* didn't disappoint. She delivered on her promise from her very first voyage, on August 3, 1927, when she hauled 16,562 tons of limestone from the Port of Calcite to Gary, setting a tonnage record that would last all of a week. Sixteen-thousand-ton loads of limestone had never been attempted prior to the *Bradley*'s maiden voyage, but the boat set the bar even higher on its second big run the following week, when she hit 17,030 tons.

The following season she hit 18,113 tons—a record that would stand for the next thirteen years. Great Lakes historian William Ratigan put the size of that particular load in perspective when he noted that the haul required "three complete freight trains each fitted out with a string of one hundred railroad cars to move overland."

The gigantic cargoes might have amounted to huge company earnings and bragging rights to go along with them, but they also were questioned by some of those working on the boats, by men who wondered if the *Bradley* might be paying a steep price for the beating it was taking in the limestone trade. The self-unloaders scheduled more trips per season than the conven-

tional straight-deckers, which was good for the company but tough on the boats. What might all this work be doing to the *Bradley's* hull?

"They would overload that *Carl D. Bradley*," remembers Kenneth Friedrich, who served as a deck watch on the boat for two seasons. "They had so much stone on it one time they couldn't close the hatches. I can remember a time when we took a load of coal out of Toledo. They wanted to set a record. They didn't have to go far on the lake—just from Toledo to the Detroit River—but they had coal on the deck, eight feet high. None of the hatches were closed."

"When I first went on the *Bradley* as a deckhand," says Leonard Gabrysiak, who spent his entire sailing career on the limestone carriers, "we would load stone that was two to three inches in diameter. They used it in blast furnaces in making steel, to purify it. I can remember they'd load the hatches so full we'd have to pick stones and throw it on deck to get the hatch covers closed. We'd get out on the lake and send that excess stone over. [The captain] got his tonnage."

In the early days of the limestone shipping business, the boats' skippers were paid a bonus, based on total tonnage hauled, at the end of the season. The company supposedly dropped the practice at about the beginning of World War II, but rumors persisted that the captains were still receiving premiums for overloading their ships.

Fred Dagner spent two years on the *Bradley*, and he can't remember her ever being overloaded—at least not to the point where the boat exceeded the legal, established load line limits. Coal, he explains, is lighter than stone, and you could fill the cargo hold to the top without placing the *Bradley* any lower in the water than she was permitted to go. The *Bradley* was a huge vessel, and the company wanted as much out of it as possible, whether it was hauling stone or coal.

If anything, Dagner offers, the boat's cargo was determined by the port it was visiting.

"She'd load right to the nuts," he says of the *Bradley*, "down to as deep a draft as they're allowed. But not overload. With some ports, you couldn't get it down that deep. It all depended on where you're going. Gary was a deepwater port. Buffington and Outer Cleveland were deepwater ports. They'd put her down twenty-two feet, and as they loaded, the deck watch would be up forward and look at the marks that they had on the bow. There were marks on the rudder—how far you were down. And they would communicate with the guy loading. They had it down to a science. The mate would go to the dock office and they'd put your draft on record so they wouldn't get in any trouble. When they left port, the draft was okay. But they loaded her right to capacity every time."

The *Bradley's* size also meant early opening to the shipping season, of-ten when ice on the lakes prohibited smaller vessels from leaving port. The *Bradley* was traditionally the first boat through the Straits of Mackinac. Dag-ner remembers her being used as an icebreaker for other ships.

"She was the number one icebreaker on the lakes at the time," he recalls. "They used a lot of the old car ferries to break ice, but the *Bradley* was the biggest boat on the lakes then, and they filled her forepeak full of cement and away they'd go. It was a rough ride, but she would go through. They'd either go to Gary with open-hearth or Indiana with cement. They'd take her back light, all the way down to the shipyard in Lorain. They'd clean her out, take the busted plates off, and have new plates for her. They'd put the new plates on and she'd be ready for the season."

And there were many of them—thirty full seasons in all. Due to her size and speed, the *Bradley* outperformed the other lake vessels and, prior to the 1956 collision with the *White Rose*, the ship's history had been blissfully uneventful. She had received a new propeller and rudder in 1940 and radar in 1947, and her boom had been extended from 165 to 205 feet. The com-pany sank plenty of money into the *Bradley's* upkeep, but the one thing it could not do is keep her from aging. Ships built before 1948 were con-structed with less flexible metals than those built after that year, and the older vessels' metals could be more brittle in icy water. There was no way of measuring how this, along with all the twisting and bending in heavy weather, affected the *Bradley's* structural integrity. Ironically, the cargo hold renewal planned for the winter of 1958–59 would have added strength to the middle of the boat.

These are not issues that overly concern the men working on the *Bradley*; they believe in the boat. In Great Lakes shipping, so much depends on faith—in the boat, the captain, and the capabilities of the crew. It's a faith, like the belief that one is going to wake up after a good night's sleep, that's taken for granted. Boats are repaired, bad captains and crewmen are weeded out. The faith remains.

Until, of course, it is severely tested.

No captain, regardless of pressure from the top, would ever consider taking a boat out if he felt that doing so would be endangering the safety of his crew. Roland Bryan is no exception. For all her faults, the *Bradley* is still a strong ship. All Bryan has to do is nurse her along on this last trip or two. She'll go to the shipyard, get repaired, and be back in great shape by the time he reports back to work in spring 1959.

So far his faith has been rewarded. The *Bradley* is running smoothly— "like an old shoe," as sailors like to say. Within a couple of hours they will have crossed what promises to be the roughest part of the trip—the stretch of lake between Wisconsin and lower Michigan—and it should be fairly easy going the rest of the way. Less than two hours ago, Bryan had conferred with First Mate Elmer Fleming and Second Mate John Fogelsonger, and they'd drawn up a course to take them from Cana Island, near Wisconsin's shore, to Lansing Shoals, just beyond the Beaver Island group. The boat will probably take a rolling, but nothing it can't handle.

Bryan prefers to take a cautious approach. Since the *Bradley* has already dropped off its limestone, she is running light—sailing without cargo—in the storm, which presents a new set of hazards. In calm seas, the lack of cargo can be beneficial in terms of meeting a schedule. A lighter ship moves more quickly, and while company officials would prefer profitable cargo in the belly of a boat—"you don't make money hauling nothing"—speed is crucial to those with their eyes on the clock. All this changes in stormy weather. A loaded boat rides lower in the water and doesn't work as much. Captains will order their crews to pump seawater into a ship's ballast tanks to add weight to a vessel traveling light in a storm, though it's never as effective as a load of cargo. In Gary, after hearing the weather forecasts, Elmer Fleming had supervised the ballasting of the *Bradley*'s side and aft tanks.

These precautions usually help when a ship is caught on a lake in a storm, but as Roland Bryan is discovering with each passing minute, this is not your average Great Lakes storm. The U.S. Weather Bureau, now busy tracking its trail of destruction, is already predicting that this is "a storm which will make weather history for its large extent and unusually severe conditions."

NO TIME IS MORE TREACHEROUS FOR SAILING ON THE GREAT Lakes than the thirty days of November. The weather can change dramatically with very little warning, especially when cold air from Canada, pushed south by high-pressure cells, slams up against warmer, moister air brought up by low-pressure systems from the south or the west. A ship can leave port in calm water, only to face a freshwater maelstrom a few hours later. Captains have learned, through experience and the lessons of history, to pay close attention to weather advisories. More Great Lakes vessels have met their doom in November than in any other month.

The *Bradley* is moving right into two separate weather patterns that, over the past day, have merged and become one especially lethal storm. A cold air mass, originating in the Gulf of Alaska, moved down through Canada and into the western part of the United States, dipping through Nevada into Arizona and socking the region with bitterly cold temperatures. At the same time, warm, moist air moved north from Mexico.

The results were devastating. Snowstorms blew through Arizona, including a 6.4-inch snowfall recorded in Tucson—the earliest snowfall in the city on record, and only the second time since 1885 that Tucson had seen snow at any time in November. Three Boy Scouts, on an excursion to the Santa Rita Mountains, were trapped in the storm; their bodies would be found two weeks later. Temperatures plummeted to record lows, with portions of Nevada plunging to subzero readings.

The storm moved into Texas, setting off nearly three dozen recorded tornadoes in a line extending from Texas to as far north as Illinois. In the northern part of the country, nearly two feet of snow fell in Wyoming, while a foot or more dropped on North and South Dakota. A weak low-pressure system over North Dakota teamed with the massive low-pressure system in Texas, creating one huge storm that seemed to cut the country in half. It rushed eastward, gaining strength by the time it reached the Great Lakes region. When the *Bradley* was leaving Gary on Monday evening, the Chicago Forecast Center was posting gale warnings for Lake Michigan for the next day. According to the forecasts, boats on Lake Michigan could expect showers and thundershowers, with fifty- to sixty-five-mile-per-hour winds out of the southwest, eventually shifting to winds out of the west.

Under these conditions, Lake Michigan is about the last place you want to be. If you're a captain and your ship is heading south, you'll be pointing your vessel almost directly into the storm. If you are heading north, you'll be pounded from behind by following seas, which usually means your boat will be working more than usual. In extreme cases a huge wave might lift the stern of a ship out of the water. Chief engineers fear this occurrence. If the propeller comes out of the water, overspins, and is then slammed back down, it will send a terrible vibration throughout the ship; in the worst-case scenario, it can stop the engine. A ship without an engine in the middle of a storm is dead in the water. At that point all you can do, unless you manage to get the engines going again, is sit back and watch the seas pound your boat into pieces.

As a body of water running north and south, Lake Michigan can be pitiless in this kind of storm. Waves have the entire length of the lake to build up, and if you're in the northern portion of the lake in a storm out of the south or southwest, you could be looking at huge walls of water—fifteen-to-twenty-foot waves if you are lucky, twenty-five to thirty feet if you aren't. You've ventured into the point of no return. You can't even think about turning your ship around and heading to shelter. You'd risk putting your boat on its side.

Every sailor who's ever faced a turn in a nasty storm seems to have a story about the harrowing experience.

Bob Bellmore, one of four Bellmore brothers working on the stone boats, can remember a time when the ship he was on, downbound on Lake Michigan for Chicago, dealt with twenty-five-foot waves piling up near the Windy City's dock. According to Bellmore, the ship rolled like crazy when the captain tried to bring her into the port. The captain decided that if he wasn't going to make it into Chicago, he might as well cut across to Gary, Indiana, drop anchor, and wait out the storm. The decision proved to be an almost fatal one.

"She took one big wall [of water] and went down," Bellmore recalls. "She almost lay on her side. Then she came back. We went another little bit and it started again. We went over again, came back, and went over again. Then the tugs came out to get us. The captain on the tug said that was the first time he'd ever seen the bottom of a boat. That's how far over we were."*

Len Gabrysiak, who served briefly on the *Bradley* and later survived the wreck of the *Cedarville*, sounds almost reverential when he talks about the power generated by storms. He sailed on all five of the Great Lakes at one point or another, and he saw all kinds of storms. One in particular stays with him.

"We had left Port Huron, Michigan, and Lake Huron was smooth," he remembers. "We got up by Point Aux Barques, heading into Saginaw Bay, and in fifteen minutes we were in a full gale. I was down in my room, reading. I was on the four-to-eight watch, and I had about an hour to go before I relieved the wheelsman. The next thing I knew, I looked out the porthole and I could see sky one minute, water the next. The chairs and wastebaskets were sliding outboard to inboard, back and forth."

Gabrysiak grabbed a life jacket and headed out into the hallway. Nobody was around. Outside, the vessel was losing its struggle to remain upright in the storm. The aftercabin was getting buried in water. The boat was rolling to such an extent that Gabrysiak reasoned that he'd be better off heading to the wheelhouse, where he figured he'd report early to work and at least know

---

*Over the years that he served on the lakes, Bellmore saw enough tragedy to appreciate his good fortune. His brother, Doug, was on the *Bradley* during its final trip, and seventeen years after the loss of the *Bradley*, while working on the *William Clay Ford*, he went out on a storm-ravaged Lake Superior in search for the *Edmund Fitzgerald*.

what was going on. The front of the boat, when he finally reached it, was a mess. The boat had rolled so heavily that everything not tied down had been sent flying. Gabrysiak had to step over books and chairs and other tossed-around possessions just to get up the stairwell to the wheelhouse. Once there, he found the captain in the front window and the second mate at the wheel. The ship, he learned, had dropped into a trough and nearly gone over.

"One wave caught her and it got away from the wheelsman," he says. "Then the next wave caught her. There were *two* of them. They ripped her port to starboard, starboard to port, and when she finally swung around, we were heading back to Port Huron. It swung us completely around."

Of course, there are storms, and then there are the ones that attain legendary status. These monsters seem to come around every decade or so, cutting down everything in their paths, on land or in the water. The old-timers speak of these storms in quiet tones.

A November 27–29, 1905, storm on Lake Superior was just such a storm, claiming the lives of dozens of men and destroying thirty ships, all but wiping out U. S. Steel's Pittsburgh Steamship line; other boats had been severely damaged. Eight years later, another killer storm—indisputably the worst ever to hit the Great Lakes—nailed all five lakes on November 9–12, sinking ten ships, damaging thirty others, and taking the lives of 235 men. Lake Huron was hit hardest, with Lake Superior coming in a close second. Ships out in the storm stood no chance. High winds blew some off course and into rocky shoals, while other ships found their superstructures completely blown away. Two ships went missing, never to be heard from again.

Lake Michigan endured its most memorable storm in November 1940. For two days and nights, the "Armistice Day Storm," as it came to be known, blew into the upper Midwest with unexpected ferocity. The weather had been uncommonly warm throughout that autumn, and people were caught off-guard by forecasts calling for falling temperatures and snow flurries.

The storm blew into Minnesota in the middle of the day. Temperatures dropped drastically, and a wild precipitation cycle followed. Hard rain switched to sleet, which turned into heavy snows that, blown by fierce, seventy-mile-per-hour winds out of the west, led to whiteout blizzard conditions. Duck hunters, out en masse on the holiday and unprepared for the sudden changes in weather, faced life-threatening situations as their boats were swamped and sunk by waters now raging on the smaller, inland lakes. Some of the hunters drowned, while others, stranded on tiny islands, froze to death in the wind and bitter cold. All told, the storm, which continued the next day and covered almost all of the Midwest, claimed 49 lives in Minnesota alone, and 150 across the Midwest.

Sixty-six of the fatalities were sailors. Nor surprisingly, the winds kicked up massive waves on Lake Michigan and the other lakes. Three freighters and two smaller vessels went down, while others were blown off course, grounded, smashed on the rocks, or otherwise damaged by what one meteorologist called "an inland hurricane."

The other Great Lakes took a beating as well. On Lake Huron, twelve ships grounded and two ore carriers sank. As painter and former sailor Kenneth Friedrich recalled, "The wind blew all the water out of the Saginaw River and for miles out into the bay. People walked on the dry river and bay bottom, picking up tubs full of stranded fish."

The *Bradley*'s older crewmen—Roland Bryan, Ray Buehler, and Elmer Fleming—had been sailing at the time and could remember the storm. If pressed, each could tell a story of his own of a particularly nasty storm that made him wonder if he would step on dry land again.

Ray "Dizzy" Buehler, the *Bradley*'s fifty-nine-year-old chief engineer, has been on the lakes through some really heavy weather over the course of a career that began in 1919, including a storm on Lake Huron that nearly sank his ship. The storm, recalled by Great Lakes historian Don Davenport, "left the engine room waist deep in water" and blew the ship two hundred miles off course. Buehler had been a twenty-year-old kid then, in his first year of sailing, and since that time, including nearly thirty years on the *Bradley*, he'd seen just about everything.

The storm he's looking at now ranks up there with the worst of them.

STORMS TERRIFY CHICK VALLEE. THE *BRADLEY*'S FORTY-NINE-YEAR-old conveyorman finds it impossible to sleep whenever heavy waves start rolling a boat and water washes over the decks. He'll stay up all night if the storm is severe, and he's rarely far from his life jacket when the seas get really rough. Some of his crewmates have wondered why he puts himself through all this when he could probably find a good job on land, but if truth be known, Vallee is hardly alone. The boats carry all kinds of sailors with seemingly contradictory relationships with the element that provides them their livelihoods. Pete Horn, an oiler on the *Bradley*, is scared to death of water. Watchman Mel Orr and stokerman Marty Enos are among the crewmen who can't swim a stroke. These men differ from Vallee in one critical area: they don't even consider the idea that one of these massive vessels might sink. They're well aware that other boats—thousands of them, in fact—lie broken on the floors of the Great Lakes, but that's something that happens to other people. The *Bradley* might need a little work, but it's not going anywhere except port to port.

Vallee has spent some time thinking about the *Bradley*, pondering its condition, how it's affected by storms, and what he should do if anything ever went wrong. His uncle, Bill Chain, a skipper on the lakes, has all but begged him and Keith Schuler, Vallee's nephew and the *Bradley*'s second engineer, to find another boat. The *Bradley*, Chain insists, isn't safe. This isn't something Vallee cares to hear, especially in front of his wife, who shares his fear of storms. He doesn't switch ships as advised, but Chain's concerns are never far from his mind when a storm is brewing.

Barry Vallee, Chick's oldest son, worked for one summer with his father on the *Bradley*, and he will never forget the time his father pulled him aside for a serious talk about what to do if it ever looked as if the *Bradley* was going to sink. He pointed to the huge A-frame near the back of the forward cabins. The unloading boom was connected to the frame, but that's also where the *Bradley*'s pontoon-style life raft was stowed. "If it ever looks like we're really in trouble and going down, that's where you hit," Vallee told his son, "because that's where I'm going."

Despite his fears, and the reality that sailing keeps him from his family much longer than he'd like, Vallee stays on the *Bradley* because he likes the job. A sailor's pay is as good as he's likely to earn around Rogers City, and he earns a little more than most of his crewmates because he is in charge of the unloading when the *Bradley*'s in port and the other guys are out on the town, and this pays overtime. The conveyorman's job is a good one, and Vallee, like the conveyormen on the older boats, spent years working up the job ladder to get it. He'll gut out the storms.

Like any veteran of Great Lakes sailing, Vallee has been bounced around in a memorable storm or two. Some of the old-timers, in fact, love to regale newcomers with stories of the big ones they've encountered, always intimating to the seasick novice that the storm they've presently braving is absolutely small-time in comparison to this storm or that storm of the past. By the time the story is told, the wide-eyed deckhand, barely holding down his lunch in the rolling boat, will be mentally checking off his job options on terra firma.

The huge, self-unloading vessels are one of the Bradley Transportation Company's trademarks, dating back to 1912, when the Michigan Limestone and Chemical Company began operating and the 436-foot *Calcite* was constructed. The self-unloaders offered advantages that made them ideal for the limestone trade. The traditional straight-deckers used for hauling iron ore, coal, grain, and other freight required larger crews for unloading, and it took much longer to unload. This, of course, translated into additional costs. The self-unloaders essentially utilized a system of conveyor belts that moved the stone from gates in the bottom of the cargo holds, down a tunnel in the bowels of the ship to a bucket elevator that ultimately delivered the cargo to a huge conveyor boom mounted on the deck. The boom could swing over either side of the boat and deliver product to dockside storage bins or even directly into boxcars. The Bradley boats became as recognizable for their distinctive unloading booms, located behind the foredecks, as they were for their gray and red paint.

Chick Vallee and his assistant, Leo Promo Jr., use caution when unloading the *Bradley*. Like all of the long, gangly Great Lakes freighters, the *Bradley* has a lot of weight at either end, with very little in the middle. While unloading, you have to keep her as close to even keel as possible, which means loading and unloading cargo holds in a designated sequence that involves taking a little cargo from one portion of the ship, then taking some from another portion—all in an effort to maintain a balance. The self-unloaders add another wrinkle not seen in the straight-deckers: the booms are extremely heavy, especially when they're unloading stone, so another kind of balance— across the beam—is necessary during the unloading. Adding water to the ballast tanks on the side of the ship opposite the boom usually does the trick.

In storms such as this one, Vallee has to check and double-check the boom to make certain that it hasn't worked loose from its stays. It doesn't take much of an imagination to picture what might happen if the boom came loose on a rolling ship. The shifting weight and the momentum of the rolling ship would be enough to capsize the boat. With the *Bradley* about to venture into the roughest waves of the trip to this point, Vallee inspects the boom and is satisfied that it is still secure. In fact, the *Bradley* is still riding really well for the conditions it's in. This doesn't mean that Vallee is going to get any sleep tonight, especially with the *Bradley* getting into Calcite late in the evening or early in the morning, but at least he might not have to worry as much.

Captain Roland Bryan knows what the *Bradley* is heading into, and with the ship due to hit really heavy seas right about the time dinner is usually served, he asks steward John Zoho to serve the evening meal a little earlier than usual. Bryan can see no reason to risk having everything in the galley flying around if the *Bradley* starts rolling. Better to have everyone fed, the place cleaned up, and everything put away before that happens. Zoho couldn't agree more. The sixty-three-year-old cook has mopped up many a mess over the years.

Zoho loves working on the *Bradley*. He's been with the boat since 1934. He put in time on other Bradley Transportation Company boats, including the *T. W. Robinson* earlier in the year, when the *Bradley* was laid up over the summer, but he always preferred the *Carl D*. He made a point of bumping for his old position when the *Bradley* was fitting out for its fall run. Art Gapczynski, a thirteen-year veteran temporarily assigned to take Zoho's place on the *Bradley*, was relieved when informed that Zoho wanted his old job back. "He can have this damn boat," Gapczynski told the company official delivering the news. Gapczynski didn't think much of the *Bradley*. As he saw it, the boat "bent like hell"—too much so—in rough weather, and he'd heard enough from others who'd sailed on her to know that he'd probably be better off on his usual station, the much newer *Cedarville*.

The *Bradley* crew likes the short and stocky Zoho, who looks every bit the part of a ship's cook. A lifelong bachelor, Zoho lives with his aging mother in a small town near Pittsburgh, and when the shipping season ends, he likes to take off for a winter in Florida, where he'll drop a bundle betting on the dogs. Like most men filling his position, he can bullshit with the best of them, mete out gossip when it's harmless and hold his tongue when it's not, and most important of all, lay out a tasty spread of food. The Bradley boats have the reputation of feeding their workers well. The steward's job is to get this accomplished within a tight budget.

No one's better at it than Zoho. The stewards on the Bradley boats are required to submit monthly expense reports to company officials, and every month Zoho comes in with the lowest expenditures. Zoho views this as a kind of competition, and it grates on him on those rare occasions when someone else registers a lower figure. Part of his success can be attributed to his ability to balance the higher-end meals, such as steaks, with lower-priced meals, such as hamburgers or hot dogs. It's also helpful that he knows the markets with the lowest prices, not only in Rogers City but also in all the ports the *Bradley* visits. When you're trying to feed a crew member for sixty or sixty-five cents a meal, every penny adds up. Zoho can remember the World War II years, when meat was rationed and expensive, and the Bradley boats would make runs to Canada, where he would buy meat by the truckload.

Tonight's offering is one of the less expensive meals: hamburgers, French fries, tomatoes, peaches, and sponge cake. Crew members file into the dining room and take a seat, four, five, six to a table. The deck crew, coming from the front of the boat, had to walk the length of the deck in raw weather, so they're all wearing coats, sweatshirts, and other heavy-weather gear, which they shrug off when they take their seats. The galley crew has taken the precaution of putting sideboards on the tables to keep cups and plates from sliding off in rough seas, but the *Bradley* is riding smoothly enough that they're quickly removed. As always, the men are hungry. Zoho mixes with them, trading barbs and kibitzing on bits of conversation.

There has always been a fraternity among Great Lakes sailors, but those working for the Bradley Transportation Company are especially tight. Since most are from Rogers City, they not only work and live together on the boats, they're also friends, neighbors, and, in some cases, related to one another. On the *Carl D. Bradley* alone, twenty-six of the thirty-five officers and crew members reside in Rogers City, with another four hailing from such nearby cities as Onaway, Posen, Cheboygan, and Metz Township. Watchman Alvy Budnick and deck watch Frank Mays are second cousins; wheelsman Ray Kowalski is married to deck watchman Gary Strzelecki's sister. Keith Schuler, the *Bradley*'s third assistant engineer, is Chick Vallee's nephew. The crews on the Bradley ships are so tight, and their ties to Rogers City so strong, that they jokingly refer to outsiders—particularly officers and engineers, who tend to come from Ohio—as "flatlanders."

Most figure to be working together after the current shipping season ends and the holiday season passes, when they do winter work on the ships laid up on the Frog Pond, a huge docking area built near the Michigan Limestone plant, just outside the regular loading docks. They'll clean, scrape, paint, weld, replace broken rivets, and perform other repairs, all in preparation for the next season. Sailing is a continuous cycle, passed from generation to generation, often within the same family. A kid, fresh out of school, starts out as a deckhand or porter and works his way up the ranks, just as his older brother did before him, or his father and uncles did before them. To the old-timers, winter work serves as a reminder of how long they've been on the lakes. Like the boats they're working on, the sailors are getting creaky and rusty; it seems impossible that the seasons have passed so quickly. The kids say they're only going to stick around for a few years, earn some big money and move on, maybe to college, maybe to shore jobs. But they stay. So many of them stay.

Carl Bartell is not one of those likely to stay. Bright and ambitious, Bartell has advanced up the ladder quickly, achieving third mate status by his twenty-fifth birthday. But unlike Roland Bryan, who started out in sailing at fourteen, and who will live and die on the lakes, Bartell has his sights trained elsewhere. One of only a handful of *Bradley* crewmen not from Rogers City or neighboring cities, the Kalkaska, Michigan, resident would like to work outdoors, maybe as a park ranger, or maybe in the constantly expanding horizons of conservation. This could be his last season on the lakes.

Jim Selke is another of those unlikely to hang around for long. His father, Alex "Shine" Selke, is a lifer on the lakes—he'll have spent forty-five years of his life on the boats by the time he calls it quits—and Jim wants no part of that. The work is hard and occasionally dangerous, and Jim has heard stories about storms from his father, who's one of those sailors who's scared to death of them. No; he'll go to school, get a college education, and find something on land, maybe as an accountant in a warm, dry office.

That's where the boats enter the picture. Jim graduated from City High School in June. He has nowhere near the money needed to go away to school, so he's taken a job with the Bradley Transportation Company, figuring he'll work as a substitute on the boats and maybe earn enough to attend school at the beginning of the second semester.

This is his first trip on the *Bradley*. He signed on to replace a porter named George Sobeck, whose father just passed away. The porter's job is the lowest rung on the galley ladder. You wait tables, wash dishes, mop floors, clean cabins, help load groceries, and do any other kind of grunt work that needs to be done. Company officials want their boats—the *Bradley* in particular—to be well turned out, and the porters, along with the lower seniority members of the deck and engine room crews, are largely responsible for seeing that everything looks good. As a substitute, Jim gets the worst of the dirty deeds.

Not that he's averse to any kind of work. All through high school, Jim got up early in the morning, often before sunrise, in rain and bitter cold, to deliver the Detroit papers to subscribers in Rogers City. You don't squirrel away a lot of money on the kind of money a paper route—even a good-size one—pays, but it's been enough to get around, pick up a few things here and there, and pay for dates with Geraldine "Getz" Tulgetske, the girl he's been seeing off and on (but mostly on) throughout high school. Getz isn't too thrilled about Jim's being away on the *Bradley*—a few days seems like forever, she'll remember—but when it turns out that Jim doesn't have anything to carry his clothing in, she loans him a piece of luggage from the set she received as a graduation gift. They'll pick up where they left off when he gets back.

At eighteen, Jim Selke is the youngest crew member on the *Bradley*, although two of his former high school classmates, Mike Joppich and Ben Schefke, also are on the boat. Like Selke, Mike Joppich followed his father's lead in taking a job with the Bradley Transportation Company. William Joppich currently serves as second mate on the *Foye*, but his son doesn't share his enthusiasm for the work. Mike plans to finish out the current shipping year, take it easy over the holiday season, and despite his mother's objections, join the air force. Maybe he'll figure out his future while he's there.

Ben Schefke's future, on the other hand, has always been about the present. His three older brothers sail, and he dropped out of high school to do the same. He likes the money, he likes what he can buy with it, and he's in no hurry to sacrifice any of it by getting off the boats. His mother can't quite understand why her sons don't find another type of work. She's terrified of water and worries for their safety. Bernard—she refuses to call him by his nickname—is her baby boy, and on one occasion, down at the Frog Pond, she watched him flirt with drowning.

"He was on a boat," Ben's sister Betty remembers, "and they were unloading something. He slipped off the ladder when he was coming down. All of a sudden, he fell in the water. My mother and a couple of the kids were in the car, waiting for him to come down, and my mother wouldn't get out of the car because she's deathly afraid of water. So I got out. A couple of guys were saying, 'Is he gonna come up? Is he gonna come up?' He finally came back up. They threw him a life ring and got him out of there. I thought to myself, 'Ben, this should be an omen to you.' But it wasn't."

ELMER FLEMING, THE *CARL D. BRADLEY*'S FORTY-THREE-YEAR-OLD first mate—a "spit-and-polish kind of guy," according to one of his former subordinates—insists on a ship's being run by the book. Every crewman has a job to do, and it had better be done properly and on time. If not, Fleming is likely to get loud when he talks to him about it. Some of the crew see him as serious, others as dour and standoffish. His constant frown and clenched jaw have earned him the nickname "Hatchet Jaw."

His demeanor is legendary among those who have worked under him.

"He never smiled much," Ed Brewster, a wheelsman who worked with Fleming, recalls. "The people who went to school with him used to say his lower lip hung so low that he might trip over it." Brewster, however, had no problems with Fleming. "He treated me like gold. He put me on his watch, he liked me real well, and I learned to wheel under him. If he liked you, he really treated you well. He would go all out for you. A lot of people didn't care for him because he didn't like everybody."

Art Gapczynski, who served with Fleming on the *Rogers City*, can only laugh when he remembers Fleming's "sourpuss" disposition.

"He'd walk down the deck and somebody would say, 'Morning, Elmer.' Elmer would just put his head down. He wouldn't say a word. Then, about the third time the guy said 'Good morning' and Elmer didn't say anything, the guy would say, 'Good morning, Herman.' That was his middle name: Elmer Herman Fleming. And Elmer would say, 'Kiss Herman's ass.'"

Others, who knew Fleming better, were more sympathetic. "He was a different type of guy, a very moody guy," says Ed Partyka. "Elmer and I lived right across the hall from each other, and we got along real good. He had a lot of family problems, and at times he would like to talk about it. We'd go in each other's room and shoot the breeze."

John Czcerowsky, who, like Partyka, wound up as a captain on the Bradley fleet, agrees that part of Fleming's sour disposition might be accredited to his home life. "He didn't have a good life at home," Czcerowsky says. "He had a chip on his shoulder. We had a wheelsman here, a real character named Sparky, and when they'd leave Calcite, Elmer would say, 'Well, Sparky, how'd you make out tonight?' And Sparky would say, 'Oh, all right.' And Elmer would say, 'Shit, when I got home, there's no rose in the flower vase.' That was the signal: if he was going to get anything, there'd be a rose in the flower vase on the kitchen table. If there was no rose, don't bother waking her up. Sparky says, 'Elmer, you're doing things wrong. If it's payday and you get what you want, don't pay her until next trip. At least the rose will be there again.'"

Fleming's home problems, known to any number of crewmen on the *Bradley*, draw both sympathy and derision. Fleming's tried to make his marriage work, but it's not going well. Fleming won't accept this. By nature he's a scrapper, a guy unafraid of taking on even the longest of odds. As a teenager he'd played high school football until doctors discovered a heart condition and advised him to quit. He probably wouldn't live a long life— maybe only into his twenties, they told him. Well, he'd beaten those odds, and he's just as determined to find a way to make his marriage work. But no matter what he does, it's never enough.

Mary Fleming is from the Upper Peninsula. A friend had introduced the two of them, and Elmer was smitten from the get-go. Mary was pretty, strong-willed, and smart—about everything he could have hoped for in a woman. She'd borne him a son, Douglas, and if their family isn't a textbook example of the happy, late-1950s American home, at least it is functional. To someone like Elmer Fleming, function is all-important, the foundation of happiness and success.

But there's one major hitch: Mary is restless, never content with the status quo. Elmer knows this, and it bothers him. Despite his officer's pay, he's never earned enough to satisfy his wife. She likes the finer things that Elmer's money can't buy—or, if he stretches it, can *barely* buy—and she likes to party. Rogers City is a lightning rod for gossip, and Elmer has heard stories of some of it, about how Mary likes to step out for the evening when he's out on the lakes. While others on the boat privately wonder why he puts up with it, Elmer bears up. It's either that or lose his family. Besides, he really *does* love her.

So, as it is for so many others, work becomes the center of his life. It defines him, fulfills him. He might bring some of his problems to the boat with him, but he's never let them interfere with his drive to achieve his one main goal: command of his own ship. The Bradley line has a limited number of captain positions, full-time or substitute, and Fleming fears that one wrong turn might hold him back. As a result, he pushes himself as hard as he pushes his subordinates. He cannot tolerate any kind of failure, or the thought that he, as first mate, has let his captain down.

Fleming, despite his icy demeanor, is as skilled a first mate as you'll find on the Great Lakes. He's been working on the stone boats since September 15, 1935, when he took a job as a porter, and for the next twenty-three years he worked his way up the ranks, excelling at every post along the way. He switched to the deck crew at the beginning of his second year, eventually serving five years as a wheelsman, and after that, as third, second, and finally first mate on different ships in the Bradley fleet.

Fleming wants to succeed, but perhaps even more than that, he fears the prospects of failing—or looking bad. Captains make him nervous, and whenever one beckons for him, his initial reaction, more often than not, is something along the line of, "What the hell does he want? What did I do wrong?" He and Roland Bryan get along fine, probably because Bryan is a by-the-book kind of leader himself and because Fleming has worked with Bryan long enough that the Old Man trusts his knowledge and instincts. In a storm such as the one they're facing now, Fleming is just the kind of officer Bryan wants in the pilothouse.

*   *   *

The storm has picked up significantly over the past half hour or so. Shortly before five o'clock, when he had walked down the spar deck on his way to dinner, Elmer Fleming had been pushing directly into the wind. The weather was freshening, as mariners like to say, but it wasn't serious enough for any concern.

By the time he finishes his meal and heads back to the pilothouse, the storm has intensified. The waves, in the ten-to-fifteen-foot range a short time ago, are building steadily now, twenty feet and higher. So far you're only getting hit with spray, but that could change quickly enough. The way the temperatures are dropping now, there might even be some snow before the night is over.

The wind, cold and raw and damp, hits him with a kind of lacerating power; on exposed flesh, it feels like the tips of countless needles barely penetrating the skin. It's not painful, but it hurts enough to be annoying. It's a damp wind known all too well by commercial fishermen, whose un-gloved hands turn an angry rash-colored red in no time, adding another layer of misery to the hard labor of setting and pulling nets. The men on the stone and ore boats know it as well, especially in November. In another month this wind will hasten the freezing over of the lakes.

Fleming, wearing a heavy coat, sweatshirt, cap, heavy pants, and boots, is outfitted for his brief, occasional excursions into the stormy weather. It will be warm enough in the pilothouse as long as the doors stay shut—and there's no reason they shouldn't—but you don't need to be a meteorologist to imagine the effects these winds will have on the building waves in the hours to come.

It would be a good idea, Fleming decides, to have the deck crew give the boat a thorough inspection, just to make sure everything is secure and tied down.

Fleming has the 4:00 P.M. to 8:00 P.M. watch in the pilothouse. Ray Kowalski is at the wheel and watchman Mel Orr is on hand, as is second mate John Fogelsonger, who had relieved Fleming so he could go to dinner. Roland Bryan also is hanging around, keeping an eye on how the *Bradley* is handling the storm.

So far they have nothing to complain about. No one will ever mistake this for a smooth ride, but it's unremarkable sailing, which suits everyone in the wheelhouse just fine. The *Bradley* is responding well to the conditions. They'll be docking in Rogers City a little later than hoped, but in plenty of time to load and leave by late morning or early afternoon tomorrow.

The men in the pilothouse are satisfied that all precautions have been taken. Earlier in the day, Fleming had ordered additional water to the ballast tanks, giving the boat as much stability as it could muster while running light in the storm; he'd also ordered chief engineer Ray Buehler to check down the engine speed by ten revolutions per minute, affording the *Bradley* a smoother ride in the increasingly heavy seas. The charted course had kept the *Bradley* in the lee of the Wisconsin shoreline all day, and now, as they headed toward Lansing Shoals and prepared to turn east, Captain Bryan, Fogelsonger, and Fleming agreed on a course that would keep them a healthy distance from Boulder Reef and the potential hazards in the area. Boats could be rocked pretty heavily in the shallower water surrounding reefs and islands, where seas were especially turbulent during storms. While Fleming was away at dinner, Captain Bryan had called Rogers City and informed the office that due to the storm, all bets were off regarding the *Bradley*'s arrival time. There was no use having a lot of people waiting around the dock for an indefinite time, all wondering when the boat was going to pull in. The *Bradley* could radio ahead in the hours to come, when they had a better estimated time of arrival.

With the exception of a single downbound ship a safe distance away, the *Bradley* is alone on the water. Fleming notes the bright green blip on the radar screen indicating the other vessel heading toward them, but he doesn't give it much thought. The two will pass one another safely enough, probably within the next half hour. At the moment, everything is exactly as it should be.

BELOW THE *BRADLEY'S* DECKS, IN THE TUNNEL RUNNING FROM the front to the back of the ship below the cargo hold, Frank Mays carries out the tasks he'd been assigned by Elmer Fleming only a few minutes earlier. Mays, a deckhand six days shy of his twenty-seventh birthday, had run into Fleming when the first mate was returning from dinner, and Fleming had ordered him to check the coal bunker and make sure it was properly dogged down. If the clamps weren't secured, the watertight integrity of the coal bunker would be compromised, which could be a problem if, as anticipated, some of the larger waves broke over the deck.

By now, Mays has grown accustomed to the menial yet important jobs of the deck crew, whether they involve dogging down and undoing hatch clamps after loading and unloading, moving the boom cables, hosing down decks, sumping water out of the tunnel, painting when times were slow, or performing any number of other tasks necessary for keeping operations running smoothly. Mays's two older brothers sail, and Mays, a Rogers City native, found his first job on the boats in June 1950, a week after he graduated from high school. He doesn't mind the work, but he has just enough wanderlust in him to keep him from swearing that he'll dedicate his life to it. For the time being, the job feeds his wife and three young sons.

Mays has spent most of his adult life drifting from job to job, and by his own admission he was "never in the habit of sitting still too long." In high school he couldn't wait to get out on the boats—he picked up his sailing card before he graduated—yet after a season of working on the *Adam E. Cornelius*, Mays decided to move on. He worked for about two months for a small manufacturing company in Detroit before enlisting in the navy, where he stayed for four years, three of which were spent on shore duty. He met and married Marlys Bush, the niece of a navy buddy and, after his discharge, moved to Waterloo, Iowa, his wife's hometown, where he worked a string of jobs that included a brief stint in a machine shop for John Deere, driving a truck on a route for Wonder Bread, and working for a beer distributor. When he heard that the Bradley Transportation Company was hiring sailors, he packed up his wife, two sons, and their possessions and headed back to Rogers City.

By nature, Mays is the kind of guy who fits in. He has a gift of gab that makes him well liked by the people working with him, and he's smart enough to pick up new jobs easily. He'd probably be an ideal worker on the assembly line at an auto plant in Detroit: point him to a job on the line and he'll stand there all day, doing a good, efficient job, cracking jokes with the guys on the line around him, staying friendly with both the supervisor and the union steward, and, after punching his time card at the end of the day, downing a few beers with the guys at the corner bar. He's a good guy to have around.

He'd bounced from ship to ship during the 1958 season, starting as a substitute on the *Calcite*, moving on to the *Clymer* for a brief period, and finally settling on the *Cedarville*. Just when he was getting used to the *Cedarville*, the *Bradley* was fitted out for her fall run, and he was bumped off the *Cedarville* by a man with more seniority. Mays wasn't happy about moving to still another ship, but the job was a permanent position, giving him more security than he'd ever had on the stone boats. Besides, it was only for a couple of months. He'd have the off-season to consider his future options.

After checking the coal bunker, Mays retreats to the warmth of the ship. The wind cuts through you, and the way the waves are piling up, the Old Man will probably order everyone off the deck before too long. Darkness, a rolling ship, and water sweeping over the sides of the ship will make the spar deck a dangerous place, and you'd be better off using the tunnel if you wanted to go from one end of the ship to the other.

Safety has always been a priority with the Michigan Limestone and Bradley Transportation companies. The quarry and crushing plants demand constant vigilance from their workers, as do the big vessels carrying the stone. From its very first issue, *Calcite Screenings*, the quarterly magazine published by Michigan Lime and distributed to its employees, has pushed the importance of safety consciousness, tracking the safety records in the plant and on the boats. There have been occasional serious and even fatal accidents, but the companies are proud of their overall numbers. The Bradley fleet has never lost a ship, and only a few months ago, in March, the Bradley Transportation Company set a world's record for becoming the first company of its kind to go one thousand days without a disabling injury.

Mays continues his rounds in the after end of the ship. He ducks into the engine and stoker rooms for a few minutes and talks to second assistant engineer Al Boehmer and stokerman Paul Heller. Even in the storm, everyone is relaxed. Mays and the forty-five-year-old Heller are neighbors; they met and became friends shortly after Mays returned to Rogers City following his move back from Iowa. At forty-five, Heller is one of the *Bradley*'s older crew members. He'd prefer to earn his living onshore—and he did, for a few years, when he left the boats and opened a grocery store with his wife, but that hadn't worked out. With a family to support, including a son ready to enter college within a year, Heller has resigned himself to the probability that he'll spend the rest of his working life on the boats.

Back on his rounds, Frank Mays spends a few minutes sumping out a couple of feet of water that's collected at the aft end of the tunnel. There always seems to be water leaking from somewhere on the *Bradley*, whether it's from the ballast tanks and the holes created by missing rivets, or from the cargo hold. A new cargo hold and winter repairs will take care of a lot of this.

There's one place—the dunnage room, at the forward end of the tunnel—that Mays figures to visit. The room stores the *Bradley*'s paint cans, and Mays wants to be certain they are secure, with lids tightened down, before the *Bradley* starts rolling in the storm. Gary Price, another deckhand and Mays's roommate on the *Bradley*, must have had the same idea. He and Mays meet in the room.

Mays likes Price. At six-and-a-half feet, Price is easily the tallest crew member on the *Bradley*, and he learned, early in the game, to duck in a ship's low-ceilinged areas. He'd weighed twelve pounds at birth, and he never seemed to quit growing. He spent his early years on a 160-acre farm in Onaway, a small, rural town a short drive from Rogers City. His father, Jud Price, had been crushed to death while doing winter work on one of the ships, when a load of steel being lowered into the ship broke loose and dropped on him. With seven kids to raise, Leo Maye Price, Gary's mother, found work with a grocery store. Money was scarce, and everyone had to contribute. Gary held down a number of jobs, including delivering milk in Onaway, working as a farmhand on another family-owned farm, and taking an assembly-line job in a car plant in Detroit. With a wife and small son to support, he presently earns extra money by working overtime on the boats when they're docked, filling in for others who'd rather be out on the town than working. Sailing, to Gary Price, is a job, not a vocation.

In the dunnage room, Mays and Price find a spot to rest among the shovels, brooms, ladders, paint cans, and other deck equipment stored there. Mays lights a cigar and Price a cigarette, and they chew the fat about the storm and how it might affect their arrival time in Rogers City. Both will be getting off their watches in a few hours, at eight o'clock. This probably means they'll be sound asleep in their bunks when the *Bradley* finally ties up at the Calcite dock in the early-morning hours. The *Cedarville* is due to arrive in Calcite at approximately the same time, and since both ships are scheduled to take on and deliver another load of stone, there is a sense of urgency about getting to the dock first. The first to arrive will be the first to load and consequently the first to take off. During the summer months, this isn't an issue: if you had to wait around to load, you had just that much more time to spend with your loved ones. The skippers might want to move things along, but you were in no hurry. It's different, though, at this time of year, when crews are ready to call an end to the season and get back home for the winter.

A deafening boom, coming from somewhere in the back of the ship, interrupts their conversation. The *Bradley* shudders, the way ships do when, in the midst of especially rough seas, their sterns are lifted out of the water and dropped forcefully back down. Within seconds of the vibration, Mays and Price hear the ship's alarm bell. Whatever happened has left the *Bradley* in grave danger . . .

The two men hightail it out of the tunnel and up two flights of stairs to the main deck, stopping only to grab their life jackets out of their room. In no time they are on deck, looking to see what happened. What they see shocks them: the *Bradley* has snapped somewhere near the tenth hatch. A huge, rapidly widening crack has cut across the spar deck. At a later time, Mays will marvel that he and Price moved as quickly as they did. If they had delayed at all, they would have drowned in the water now rushing into the very tunnel they'd been standing in only a few minutes earlier.

For Mays, it's a moment when fear and resignation collide and become one dreadful state. He knows that it's only a matter of very little time before he'll be in the lake, trying to keep his head above twenty-foot waves or, if he's extremely lucky, struggling to keep a lifeboat from capsizing in seas strong enough to break a 638-foot ship into two pieces. It's a moment when your mind locks on the present, on survival, but that same mind is trying to convince you that this isn't really happening, that this is all an illusion, that if you close your eyes and turn back the clock ten or fifteen minutes, the story will turn out differently.

When Roland Bryan, Elmer Fleming, and Ray Kowalski hear the strange-sounding thud coming from the back of the ship, Kowalski stays at the wheel while Fleming and Bryan rush to the pilothouse's port door to see what it could be. They stare at the back of the ship—or, more accurately, the area where the back is supposed to be. Both men are accustomed to the *Bradley*'s snaking in heavy seas, but not like this. The stern isn't just sagging, it's *flapping*. The *Bradley*'s deck lights run in a nice, straight line until they inexplicably drop off just behind the giant conveyor boom.

The lights suddenly reappear when a huge wave rolls beneath the ship's stern, lifting it up and bringing it again level to the forward portion of the ship. With each rise and fall of a wave, the *Bradley*'s stern sags and returns, sags and returns, the main deck bending and straightening until a giant crack, running the entire width of the ship, splits the surface of the deck.

The *Bradley* is ripping in two.

Only a few minutes ago, at 5:26 P.M., Fleming had been on the radio with Frank Sager, a radio operator from Central Radio and Telegraph in Rogers City. It had been a brief, mundane exchange. Fleming had no idea that anything was wrong—not during the conversation, not in the minute or so afterward, when he and Bryan were going over the charts to modify the course the *Bradley* would be taking in the hours ahead.

Now, from the looks of the split deck, they might have only minutes left on the surface.

Both men react instantly. Fleming sprints to the radiotelephone, while Bryan slams the boat's telegraph to "Stop Engines" and sounds the *Bradley*'s alarm bell. As the ship breaks apart and the two sections begin to separate, the stern now flapping up and down in the heavy waves "like the whipping of a dog's tail," as Mays will later recall, Bryan recognizes the hopelessness of the situation. The *Bradley* is lost.

Inside the pilothouse, Elmer Fleming grabs the handset of the *Bradley*'s radiophone and sends out an urgent message over marine channel 51:

"Mayday! Mayday! Mayday! This is the *Carl D. Bradley*. Our position is approximately twelve miles southwest of Gull Island. We are breaking in two and sinking. Any ships in the vicinity, please come to our aid!"

No one immediately responds. Fleming walks the radio's handset to the pilothouse's port door, stretching the cord over his shoulder. He has no life jacket and, for the time being, he is tethered to the radiophone; he needs to see what's going on.

Members of the deck crew rush out onto the deck behind the wheel-house. The *Bradley*'s living quarters are split up, fore and aft, with the officers' and deck crew's quarters up front, the engine room and galley crews' rooms in the back. The storm has made the division total and final: the deck of the *Bradley* has split apart, and the two sections of the boat come together only when a wave lifts the stern and slams it into the bow section. The grating sound is sickening, competing with the shrieking of the wind and the roaring of Lake Michigan. Every time the two sections of the ship pound together, sparks shower the darkness enveloping the *Bradley*. The lifeboats are in the back of the ship. No one in the forward end will be able to reach them.

Elmer Fleming desperately repeats his Mayday message into the howling winds of Lake Michigan; someone has to hear this.

RAY BRUNETTE, A RADIO OPERATOR AT THE WAD MARINE RADIO station in Port Washington, Wisconsin, hears Elmer Fleming's distress call. The station keeps channel 51 connected twenty-four hours a day, although Brunette is used to hearing very little other than a lot of meaningless chitchat, usually between riverboats on the Mississippi. Channel 51 handles communications traffic on the Pacific and Atlantic oceans as well as on the Mississippi and Ohio rivers and the Gulf of Mexico. Ships are supposed to use the channel only for distress messages or brief but urgent communications, but it's a policy that's constantly abused. It's irked Brunette in the past, when nothing notable was going on, and he's especially bothered by it now, when he's facing the most urgent distress call in his eight years at the station.

He grabs the microphone and hits the talk button.

"This is an emergency!" he shouts at anyone listening in or talking on the channel. "This is an emergency! Clear the channel!"

He then directs his attention to the stricken ship.

"What's your position, *Bradley?*" he asks, hoping that amid the bedlam on a sinking ship, his message is getting through.

"Twelve miles southwest of Gull Island!" a voice shouts back. "The ship is breaking up and going down!"

Brunette writes down the ship's position and scrambles to a map on a nearby wall. There are any number of islands on northern Lake Michigan. Most of them are tiny, desolate, uninhabited spits of land that seem to serve no purpose but to create potential hazards to boats in the area. Some of them, such as Plum Island at Wisconsin's Door County Peninsula, or Beaver

Island, in the group of islands farther north, have lifeboat stations. No one in Port Washington, a city about twenty-five miles north of Milwaukee, is in position to provide any immediate assistance—not at such a distance, or in a storm of this nature. Brunette's job, then, is to alert other ships—if there are any in the area—of the sinking, and contact Coast Guard stations that might coordinate search and rescue efforts.

Brunette can only envision what's happening on the sinking ship. Even as he tries to piece together a course of action, he can hear the *Bradley* continuing to transmit increasingly frantic Mayday messages to anyone, on-shore or at sea, within radio range. For Brunette, these are moments that make you feel utterly helpless. There are human beings connected to the voices coming in, and these men are in the struggle of their lives. "Run! Get the life jackets!" a voice—belonging to Captain Roland Bryan, Brunette will learn later—screams in the background of one of the Mayday transmissions. "We're breaking in half! Get the life jackets! We're sinking!"

Brunette radios the Milwaukee Coast Guard station. When he gets no re-sponse, he calls them on the telephone. They're farther away from the *Bradley* than the Port Washington radio station, but at least Brunette has another group spreading the word and trying to drum up help. From what Brunette was able to determine from the map, the Coast Guard station in Charlevoix, a town in western Michigan, is the station nearest to where the *Bradley* is sinking. The station, he learns when he contacts it, has just picked up Elmer Fleming's distress call.

At the Coast Guard station in Charlevoix, Chief Boatswain Joe Etienne hears only one of Elmer Fleming's calls for help, but it's one he will never forget.

"Mayday! Mayday Mayday!" a voice cries out. "This is the *Carl D. Bradley.* Our position is approximately twelve miles southwest of Gull Island. May-day! Mayday! May——"

And, with that, the voice falls silent.

Etienne tries to contact the *Bradley*. No answer.

Fearing the worst, Etienne considers his options for a search-and-rescue mission. The storm is as intense as any he's ever witnessed, and the Coast Guard has only limited resources capable of battling these weather conditions. Most of the vessels, in Charlevoix and elsewhere, are equipped to tow small craft broken down on calm seas, or to pick up fishermen stranded on one of the islands, but aiding an enormous stone boat like the *Bradley*, or contending with the storm that brought it down, are entirely different matters. The Coast Guard's standard thirty-six-foot motor lifeboats will be so overmatched by the heavy seas—if, in fact, they can even cut through them—that it will take God only knows how many hours to get to the site of the sinking. The closest of these boats to the site—the one on Beaver Island—isn't even an option: the three-man crew on duty there has very little experience in rescue missions, and none in seas of this nature, so there's no way Etienne will risk their lives by sending them out to look for survivors in winds that are reaching seventy miles per hour and seas that probably are cresting at thirty to thirty-five feet.

He's not doing much better in his own Charlevoix station. He has a 160-foot cutter, the *Sundew*, anchored in Round Lake, but the buoy tender is in Bravo-12 status, meaning that its crew is probably on shore leave. If he's lucky, Etienne can expect to assemble a skeleton crew, but even that might take an hour or two. By then, anyone from the *Bradley* unfortunate enough to be in the water will probably have expired from hypothermia.

Etienne can't figure what happened to the *Bradley*. He'd spoken to Elmer Fleming only a short time ago, and Fleming said that when he'd recently gone back to the galley for a couple of sandwiches, the ship was sailing very well. On the other hand, as Etienne knows from experience, Lake Michigan can present perils that sailors sometimes fail to recognize. For all its size, the lake can shrink considerably when vessels hit the area around the Beaver Island group in a storm. On top of that, the winds can be testy. They change direction very quickly and unexpectedly, creating serious hazards for ships caught out in storms.

"It confuses the masters of the ships," Etienne says of the shifting winds.

"They try to find a lee during a storm, they head in one direction to get some relief, and then they arrive at their destination and are caught in a worse position than they were in before."

Etienne has served on all five of the Great Lakes, as well as on the Atlantic and Pacific oceans. In his youthful days in the Coast Guard, he sailed on the North Atlantic, transporting scientists studying iceberg conditions near Greenland and sampling minerals at the ocean bottom. He's seen the enormous swells on the oceans and the choppy waves on the Great Lakes. This storm tonight ranks near the top of his list of the worst storms he's ever encountered.

Within minutes of the *Bradley*'s Mayday transmission, Etienne and his colleagues have come up with a plan. They will dispatch the Charlevoix station's thirty-six-foot lifeboat to the scene of the sinking, and then contact Lieutenant Commander Harold Muth, skipper of the *Sundew*. They'll send the *Sundew* out as soon as they can put together a crew.

Etienne calls the Coast Guard's Great Lakes headquarters, the Rescue Co-ordination Center in Cleveland, hoping for further instructions and assistance. In these conditions it will take any boat leaving Charlevoix an excruciatingly long time, probably in the five-to-six-hour range, to reach the area where the *Bradley* went down. That's far too long. They need to get aircraft in the area to search for wreckage and survivors. They're running out of time.

At WHAK, a tiny radio station on a hill about five miles west of Rogers City, Harvey and Janice Klann prepare to shut down operations for another day. At 5,000 watts, the station boasts the greatest wattage north of Bay City. However, the station is licensed to operate only during the daytime hours, which, at this time of year, means going off the air earlier and earlier. From now until December 21, each day will be shorter than the previous one. Sunset today officially took place at 5:10 P.M., leaving Harvey and Janice in an empty radio station, with little to do other than Harvey's reviewing some programming notes.

The station's wire service machine ticks away whenever a news item is transmitted. During the station's normal operating hours, the sheets with news stories are torn off and read over the air; at night, they pile up until the morning crew arrives and can examine them.

The machine is transmitting a news item now, and the Klanns, more out of habit than anything else, check it out.

Neither can believe what they're reading. A limestone carrier, the *Carl D. Bradley*, has broken in two and is sinking in northern Lake Michigan. Harvey, a Rogers City native, grew up with a number of the *Bradley*'s crew; he graduated from high school with Frank Mays. Although she was raised in Alpena and moved to Rogers City after she and Harvey were married, Janice knows the families of some of the crew members; Elmer Fleming lives just a few houses down the block.

The Klanns make an immediate decision. The station, by FCC regulations, can stay on the air after sunset in an emergency. This, Harvey and Janice agree, definitely qualifies as an emergency.

Harvey calls the Michigan Limestone plant. He needs information. If he's going to broadcast something of this magnitude to the people whose lives are about to change as a result of the events of this one night, he needs to be able to tell them something, and it had better be accurate.

Both of the Klanns realize that they're facing a very long night ahead.

Elmer Fleming's desperate call comes through clearly over the radios on the other Bradley fleet boats. Very few are actually out on the lakes. The *John G. Munson*, which, at 666 feet, replaced the *Bradley* as the largest boat in the fleet, is on Lake Huron, running light and bound for Rogers City. The boat had problems of its own in the storm, though nothing in comparison to the *Bradley*. According to John Czcerowsky, then a member of the *Munson* crew, the boat had "rolled to beat hell" until it finally placed the seas on its stern. The *Munson* is only a half hour or so out of the Port of Calcite when the *Bradley*'s Mayday call comes through.

Two men in the *Munson*'s engine room—second assistant engineer Charlie Horn and oiler George Meredith—have brothers on the *Bradley*.

Charlie's younger brother, Pete, is an oiler. Pete likes sailing, more than he anticipated when he signed on, and it looks as if he'll be following his older brother into a career in the engine room. He hopes to attend classes and test for his third assistant engineer's license during the winter layup.

George Meredith's brother, Dennis, is a deckhand on the *Bradley*. Although, at twenty-one, George is four years younger than his brother, he has more experience on the boats. In fact, he set up Dennis's job for him earlier in the year, when Dennis was getting out of the army and needed work. Dennis was talking about going away to business school, but George talked him out of enrolling for that fall's semester. Better to earn a little money first, he advised.

This isn't all that haunts George Meredith when he hears about the *Bradley*. Exactly one week ago to the day, on November 11, Dennis had bought George his first legal drink at the Rainbow Garden in Rogers City. The two were nursing their beers and talking quietly when Dennis startled George with a couple of totally unexpected questions.

"Do you think the *Bradley* is seaworthy?" Dennis wanted to know.

His next question, posed immediately on the heels of the first, was even more disturbing.

"Do you think it'll break in half?" he asked.

"Why?" was all George could think to answer.

Dennis went on to explain that the *Bradley* seemed to twist and bend an awful lot in the waves. After a recent trip, Dennis told his brother, they had picked up buckets of rivets in the tunnel—rivets that had popped out during just that one trip.

Dennis never said as much, but George would later wonder if that had been the talk on the ship.

George shrugged off his brother's questions.

"I don't know nothing about boats," he told Dennis. "How would a big boat like that sink?"

Other Bradley boats have crew members with brothers on the *Bradley*. The *Cedarville* is out in the middle of Saginaw Bay, fighting through some nasty headwinds, when news of the *Bradley*'s plight breaks on the pilot-house radio. The *Cedarville* and the *Bradley* had crossed paths yesterday morning, when both were loading at the Port of Dolomite near Cedarville. The *Bradley* had loaded first and shoved off for Gary, and the *Cedarville* had taken off later in the day for Detroit. Both vessels were due back at the Port of Calcite the same time tonight.

"To make a long story short," Bob Bellmore, a crewman on the *Cedarville*, would remark bitterly many years later, "we beat her there."

Bob's brother, Doug, is a porter on the *Bradley*. At thirty-four, Doug is a little old for an entry-level position, but he's only been on the boats for the past two seasons. For Doug, it's a matter of trying to rebuild a life that, to this point, has been a mess. Some years back, in what seems like another lifetime, he'd taken a job at Michigan Lime, married, and fathered three children. He'd run up some debts, skipped town without giving any notice to his family, and taken a job at a car plant in Detroit. That hadn't worked out, either. He eventually returned to Rogers City and found a job with the Bradley fleet. He met and befriended the young son of Flora Ellenberger, a woman he'd married only a few weeks ago. At least it was a step toward getting his life together.

While Bob Bellmore listens for updates on the *Bradley*, Bob Kowalski does the same on another boat, the *T. W. Robinson*, which has dropped anchor and is waiting out the storm in Menomonee, Wisconsin. Bob's brother-in-law, Ben Schefke, is on the *Bradley*, and Kowalski's first thought, upon hearing about the *Bradley*, is to get in touch with his wife. The ship-to-shore communications and radio stations will be working overtime tonight, with sailors calling loved ones to tell them they're safe, and with an overload of calls about the *Bradley*. There's no way the *Robinson* is going anywhere until at least tomorrow morning. Earlier in the day, the *Robinson* had tried to head back out, but the winds were so heavy that the bridge attendants near the dock refused to lift the bridge and let the *Robinson* through. Even now, there's a rumor that the captain might try to talk the operators into opening the bridge so the *Robinson* can go out and search for the *Bradley*. To the silent relief of those on board the ship, that's not going to happen.

Kowalski takes the only action he's in the position to take at the time: he calls home.

The *John J. Boland*, an American Flagship steamer loaded with cargo, has been waiting out the storm at a Port Island dock. The seas around the docks have been so rugged that the boat's crew has had to stay extra vigilant just to assure that the rolling vessel isn't slammed into the loading dock. Under the usual circumstances, the men on board would be getting antsy about leaving port and dropping off their cargo. Tonight, they're happy to stay put.

Bill Elliott, the *Bradley*'s twenty-six-year-old repairman, has two older brothers, Bernie and Albert, on board the *Boland*: Bernie serving as the vessel's second mate, Albert as her wheelsman. Both are down in the mess room, playing poker with a few other crewmates, when the *Boland*'s first mate rushes in with news of the *Bradley*. The two drop their cards and hurry to the pilothouse, where they take a place and listen to the radio for further word about their brother's boat.

Bill has a twenty-year-old wife and two kids, ages one-and-a-half and three months, and he's planning to move his entire family from Rogers City to his old hometown, Wausau, Wisconsin, for the winter. His wife and kids will stay with his parents while he does winter work on the *Bradley* while she's in the Manitowoc shipyard.

A veteran of the Korean War, the short, compact Bill Elliott had been a fleet champion boxer in the navy, and he found that he liked working on the water. When his service was up he decided to continue sailing, this time with his brothers on the Great Lakes. He switched to the Bradley line after meeting and falling in love with the former Sandra Leveck, who worked with her four sisters in a Rogers City restaurant owned by their father. Bill had stopped by when his boat was in Rogers City. Before long, he was leaving his Wisconsin roots for life on the shores of Lake Huron.

All kinds of thoughts pass through his brothers' minds as they listen for news updates on the *Bradley*. Bernie is a sailor through and through, destined to become captain of his own ship. As horrifying as the news about the *Bradley* is, Bernie views this turn of events as a freak occurrence that, as nature has it, happens to be playing out on his brother's boat. Albert sees it differently. Bill wasn't even supposed to be on the *Bradley*; he was only there because he'd been bumped by someone with more seniority. The boat shouldn't have been out in this kind of weather, in any event.

Badly shaken, Albert makes a decision that will affect the rest of his life: when the *Boland* completes its run and returns to port, Albert intends to step off the ship for the last time. He will never sail again.

In the wheelhouse of the *Christian Sartori*, a 256-foot German freighter, Captain Paul Mueller and Second Mate Jergen Schwand watch an incredible scene through their binoculars. A large vessel, about three and a half miles distant, appears to be sinking.

The other vessel has been on the *Sartori*'s radar for some time, but the *Sartori*'s crew has seen or heard nothing to indicate a problem. There's been an overload of chatter and static coming from the radio, but nothing about a ship being in trouble.*

Of course, the men on the German salty have other things on their minds. The storm hammers away at the *Sartori*, rolling the ship and sending green water over its decks. Spray hits the pilothouse and flecks the windows on the bridge with water. They've been fighting the storm for the better part of the day, from the time they slipped through the Straits of Mackinac and moved along the northern coast of upper Michigan, to the past couple of dreadful hours, when the *Sartori* was relentlessly battered as

*For whatever reason, the *Sartori* never heard any of Elmer Fleming's Mayday calls.

it negotiated some heavier weather near Lansing Shoals. Captain Mueller has never seen anything like it in his six years of sailing on the Great Lakes. The sailing has been horrendous, with the *Sartori* managing barely more than two or three miles an hour for the past few hours—and this is supposed to be the less difficult part of the trip. Heading down Lake Michigan to reach their destination—Chicago—promises to be a nightmare. They'll be sailing into the teeth of the storm.

Taking shelter and waiting for the storm to dissipate are not options available to Mueller and his crew. The *Sartori*, part of the Hamburg–Chicago line, must make a number of stops around the Great Lakes, including Chicago, Milwaukee, Detroit, and Cleveland, before making its way back to the St. Lawrence Seaway and, eventually, the Atlantic. Mueller, a U-boat officer during World War II, knows he's up against a very tight schedule if he has any chance to beat the December 6 closing date of the St. Lawrence Seaway locks. A painfully slow crawl down the lake is shaving valuable hours from that schedule.

Captain Mueller recognizes the boat in the distance as one of the long iron ore or limestone carriers so common on the Great lakes; its lights stand out in the encroaching darkness. Mueller has observed several similar boats earlier in the day, anchored in the lee of Garden Island. This boat, however, commands more attention. The *Sartori* should be passing it within the hour, and Mueller wants to give it plenty of room. He orders a slight course adjustment, assuring a safe port-to-port passage, then turns his thoughts to other matters.

Jergen Schwand's shout breaks his train of thought.

"Captain! The lights are going out on the forward part of the ship!"

Mueller grabs his binoculars and peers out through the storm. Indeed, the lights on the front portion of the ship, from the pilothouse back to the engine room, have gone out. The after end remains lit. Then, just as suddenly, the lights on that end go out as well. The ship's silhouette, barely visible against the twilight sky, gives no indication of any additional or serious problems. The ship, Mueller can tell, is rolling heavily on the seas, but then again, so is the *Sartori*. A short time ago, in his ship's log, Mueller had noted waves of twenty-five to thirty feet, whipped up by sixty-mile-per-hour winds—certainly enough to cause any ship to roll. The *Sartori* has been rolling to beat hell, occasionally at an alarming forty-two-degree angle.

The other boat's loss of lights is especially troubling to Mueller. You don't want to lose total power under the best conditions; it could be fatal in a storm. A ship without an engine is a ship that cannot steer. It's helpless against the forces of nature.

The sound of an explosion breaks through the din of the storm. Mueller and Schwand watch in horror as a gigantic red, yellow, and white column of flame erupts from the back of the boat in the distance. Smoke billows in the air, obliterating sight of the ship. When the smoke finally clears, the ship is gone.

Mueller checks the radar. No sign of it there, either.

He immediately orders his helmsman to direct the *Sartori* toward the area of the missing vessel.

IT TAKES ONLY MINUTES FOR THE *CARL D. BRADLEY* TO SINK.

As soon as he realizes the hopelessness of his ship's plight, Captain Roland Bryan sounds the abandon ship signal—seven short blasts and one long one on the whistle. If they move quickly enough, Chief Engineer Ray Buehler and his crew won't be trapped at their stations belowdecks when the ship goes down.

The *Bradley* has been breaking apart very swiftly in the past four or five minutes, since the initial thud was heard throughout the ship. Other thuds followed whenever a huge wave rolled under the boat and heaved its midsection upward, buckling the deck in the middle and pushing the buckled section upward ten, twenty feet in the air. When the wave passed, the stern dropped, further splitting the deck.

Roland Bryan, in what are undoubtedly his final minutes in command of the *Carl D. Bradley*, tries to offer directions in the midst of chaos.

"Run! Get your life jackets!" he shouts to any crew members arriving on the deck without them. He's already slipped on his own life jacket, though he can only guess as to how beneficial it will be in the kind of seas that await him. Still, a slim chance is better than no chance at all. "Get your life jackets!" he screams.

For the captain, this is an extraordinarily peculiar moment. Thirty-four men on board the *Carl D. Bradley* are looking to him for guidance and, because of his rank and experience, a sense, however remote, of security. Nature and a sinking ship have stolen his command. Bryan can no longer offer reassurance of any kind. Captains recognize and adhere to the unwritten rule that they can never show fear. Concern, perhaps, but never fear. That rule, however, applies to a safe, dry pilothouse, for men in control of their ship's destiny. Bryan is still enough of an officer to remain reasonably calm when shouting directions to his crew, but what he cannot do is make his men feel safe. He is no different than a military officer exhorting his troops to charge into greater enemy numbers and heavier ammunition. Hope is doled out on an individual basis, and it certainly isn't issued by the commander.

Water floods into the *Bradley*'s cargo hold. The split in the ship has now extended to below the waterline. The *Bradley* was constructed so its heavy equipment was placed at either end of the ship. The battle now is between that equipment and the weight of the water rushing into the *Bradley*'s cargo hold. The stern section, with the engine and boilers well belowdecks, holds its own, remaining at an even keel. The bow, with its heavy boom (and the A-frame supporting it) mounted on the deck, is top-heavy, with less counterbalance below the decks; as a result, it's filling with water at a quicker pace. Water now washes over the spar deck. It's only a matter of time—maybe only a minute or two—before the weight of the water will capsize the bow.

Men continue to rush out from their quarters and workstations, fore and aft. Some, caught sleeping in their bunks when the general alarm sounded, are poorly dressed for any open-air activity, let alone the possibility of being submerged in frigid water while they await a rescue vessel. Others wear heavy jackets and coats, sweatshirts, work boots, hats—whatever they could grab in a hurry. The crew on the stern section goes to work on the lifeboats. There's an efficiency to their efforts that belies the gravity of the moment: they've been well trained, and they handle their tasks the way they've been taught. They are resigned to the *Bradley*'s fate, to the inevitability of its sinking, and they can now only fight to save themselves.

On the deck behind the *Bradley*'s pilothouse, Frank Mays works frantically to free the life raft from the stays holding it in place. He braces himself against the powerful and cold spray that's made the air thick with water. The darkness settling in may be the greatest enemy the thirty-five souls on board the *Bradley* have yet to face—if, that is, they find a way to get off the ship and survive. Somebody out there must have heard Elmer Fleming's Mayday call, but how could anyone see them in such high seas and in total darkness?

That's an entirely different issue. Right now Mays and his shipmates have to figure out a means of abandoning ship and, as dreadful as it seems, braving the seas now roiling around them.

Mays and the others have been through the lifeboat drills. They know what they're supposed to be doing. But drills don't prepare you for the real event, largely because there is no standard way for a ship to sink. The *Bradley* is going down very rapidly, negating some of the crew's earlier training. When the crew lowered the lifeboats during the Coast Guard drill, it had been under ideal weather conditions. It had taken five minutes to get the lifeboats in the water. They don't have that kind of time now.

At the back of the ship, Hardy Felax, Al Boehmer, and Pete Horn, all crewmen from the engine room, attempt to lower one of the twenty-two-foot, twenty-five-man lifeboats, but it's tangled up in cable. The men chop at the steel cable with an ax, but they can't break through. The other lifeboat, although loosened from its stays, is totally useless. The stern is sinking in such a way that the lifeboat is dangling at an impossible angle for boarding or launching. If they're unable to launch a lifeboat, the poor guys on the stern will be stuck with a raft from the bow section—*if* they manage to locate it on the waves in the darkness, swim to it, and climb on board. There's also the grim reality that the raft cannot possibly accommodate everyone needing it. The eight-by-ten-foot raft only holds fifteen.

These are only a couple of the frightening prospects the men face in the minutes ahead. The *Bradley* is enormous, more than two football fields in length, and when it sinks, there will be a tremendous suction trying to pull people under. Men could be trapped belowdecks, or a few unfortunates might get entangled in wreckage and be dragged down with the ship.

Death is inevitable. Some of the crew will drown quickly, with little or no suffering. Others will confront Lake Michigan's icy water and hypothermia.

At the moment, no one's sure what to do. About half a dozen men have clustered on the pilothouse deck, awaiting instructions from Captain Bryan. Between the noise of the storm and the sounds of the *Bradley* tearing apart, the din is deafening. The crack in the ship widens until, with one massive hogging motion buckling the deck, the two sections separate. The stern pulls away from the bow, only to be lifted and driven forward by the waves and slammed back into it. Severed electrical cables send off a shower of blue and red sparks. The bow loses power, and its running lights go dark. In the midst of the turmoil, Second Mate John Fogelsonger dashes for the back of the ship. He tries to leap over the widening gulf between the bow and stern sections, but he doesn't make it. Instead, he drops into eternity.

As soon as the *Bradley*'s power lines are severed, all communication equipment goes dead. Elmer Fleming tosses his mic aside and looks around for a life jacket. To his dismay, all of the extra jackets are gone. Someone hands him a life ring, but there's no way this will be of any use once he hits the water. Fleming has a life jacket in his room, two decks below the wheelhouse. He wonders if he has enough time to retrieve it.

He races down the two flights of stairs to his room. The *Bradley* is totally dark. Fleming prays for more time.

The *Bradley*'s bow section, almost filled with water, lists to its port side. Captain Bryan urges those around him to move to the highest point of the ship. They pull themselves along the rail, working their way forward and upward toward the *Bradley*'s stem. They'll wait to abandon ship until the last possible moment.

Lake Michigan has other designs. It sends a massive wave at the crippled ship, overwhelming the bow section. The bow rolls suddenly and violently, hurling everyone into the water.

Frank Mays is sitting on the raft when the bow rolls. He's hoping that when the ship goes down, the raft will automatically break free, as it's been designed to do, and that he will be safely on board the raft when the ship slips to the depths of Lake Michigan. Instead, he and the raft are tossed off the *Bradley* with the other crew members. Mays is driven deep into the water. The sudden shock of cold water makes him want to gasp for air, but he knows he doesn't dare. He instinctively flails toward the surface. Beneath the waves and the storm, all sound has been cut off except the sound of water rushing into his ears. Time freezes and everything moves in slow motion.

Mays finally breaks surface. Water rushes into his open mouth. He can hear other men in the water, shouting in the darkness, but in high seas, they could be very close or they could be a long distance away. He can't tell. In this turbulence, twenty feet might as well be twenty miles.

By the time Mays finds his way back to the surface, the *Bradley*'s bow has disappeared. The stern section is still afloat, its running lights still on. It towers over Mays, rolling in the waves but holding the surface. Mays can see directly into the cargo hold, even as it fills with water; the *Bradley* looks like it's been sheared right down the middle—which, in fact, it has. It's a terrifying, awesome sight.

Mays is buoyed by his cork-filled life jacket, but the action of the waves keeps pushing it upward at such a force that he has to hold it down just to keep it on. He will need something to hold on to, some piece of floating debris, if he's to have any chance of surviving until a rescue vessel arrives. He can see nothing nearby. Miraculously, just as he's lowered his head and begun his swim in search of something afloat, he comes across the raft he'd been working on just before he was thrown overboard. The pontoon-style raft is a welcome sight but not the easiest thing to mount. Mays works at it until he's finally out of the water.

The raft is a mixed blessing, at least as far as Mays can tell. He's out of the water, which will spare him some time in the battle against hypothermia, and a lot of effort in trying to stay afloat, but the raft has no oars. The lake will take him wherever it chooses.

Another man—Elmer Fleming—makes his way to the raft. Mays leans over and, pulling on Fleming's life jacket, helps him aboard.

The past two minutes of Fleming's life have rocketed by. After racing from the pilothouse and down two flights of stairs to his room, he'd groped around in the darkness until he located his life jacket. He threw it on and rushed back to the wheelhouse deck, only to find the *Bradley*'s bow section in its final struggle for buoyancy. Water covered the spar deck, and the bow was rolling to its port side. Bryan and a handful of others were pulling themselves up the sinking bow by the railing—"actually good seamanship, but it didn't work out for them," Fleming would remark later. As much as Fleming tried to do the same, the deck sloped at too steep an angle for him to reach the top. When the bow suddenly lurched over, Fleming was tossed twenty feet into the air and into the water. By the time he'd popped back to the surface, the raft was only a couple of feet away.

Fleming and Mays shout out into the darkness, trying to let the others in the water know where they are. They can hear shouting everywhere around them, but they don't see anyone. Waves carry the raft up to dizzying heights before dropping it to the depths of troughs, and for all Fleming and Mays know, one of their fellow crewmen could be as close as the other side of a wave. It's too dark, though, and the seas too rough, to tell. They spot almost no debris from the ship. Lighted buoy rings float aimlessly in the water, and one of the ship's lifeboats, now filling with water, quickly passes by.

In real time, it's been only minutes since the first thud served notice that the *Bradley* was fatally wounded; to the men on the raft, however, it seems much longer. The stern, now rolling to its port side, has very little time left.

The two men on the raft see another crewman, Gary Strzelecki, swimming toward them. That Strzelecki, a scrappy, powerfully built deck watch-

man, would find a way to the raft is of no surprise to either Mays or Fleming: he's as tough as they come, and by far the best swimmer of the *Bradley*
crew. Years after the loss of the *Carl D. Bradley*, more than one person
familiar with Strzelecki's fiery determination would note, "If anybody was
going to make it through, it would be Gary." Mays and Fleming assist him
onto the raft, and they immediately struggle to keep the anxious crew
member on board.

Strzelecki's brother-in-law, wheelsman Ray Kowalski, is out there in the
darkness. Gary thinks he knows where Kowalski might be, and insists that
he should swim back out to look for him. He can't fathom the prospects of
facing his sister if he survives and her husband doesn't.

Fleming has already assumed leadership on the raft, and he urges Strzelecki to stay on the raft.

"You'll never find him out there!" he shouts. "If you go out, you might not
make it back."

After a brief exchange, Strzelecki reluctantly agrees.

One other crewman, deckhand Dennis Meredith, known as "Bud" by
many of his shipmates, manages to struggle his way to the raft, although by
the time he gets there, he's more drifting than swimming. He's already in
shock, and he's unresponsive when the others pull him aboard and try to
talk to him. Unlike the other three, who are wearing heavy coats and clothing, Meredith is poorly outfitted and, as the others can tell, won't last long
under these conditions. Meredith was sleeping when the abandon ship
whistle was blown, and he'd raced to the *Bradley*'s deck without throwing
on any additional clothing. He's wearing a white sweatshirt and light pants;
he has no shoes or socks. He shivers violently, and the others huddle
around him to block the wind and offer as much body warmth as possible.

The shouts of the men in the water around them are heartbreaking. It
would be tragic enough it they were just coworkers, but some of these men
are also neighbors and friends and, in Mays's and Strzelecki's cases, relatives. Fleming, Strzelecki, and Mays continue to shout out to them, but no
one else appears near the raft. The only other crew member anyone sees is

wheelsman Mel Orr, who appears briefly at the crest of a wave, totally help-less, his arms raised over his head. He's quickly swept away by a wave.

The stern section of the *Carl D. Bradley* loses its fight against the in-evitable. The damaged hull lets in water until the weight upends the stern. The forward portion sinks first, swinging the after portion out of the water, lifting its rudder and propeller upward, high in the air. The men on the raft watch in silence as the last remnant of the broken boat rises above them, looming like a skyscraper. The massive section of the ship pauses, almost perfectly perpendicular to the surface, before beginning its plunge to the depths of the lake. Icy water floods the engine room, the boilers explode, and a tremendous column of fire and scalding steam shoots out of the stack. The air fills with a haze of steam and acrid smoke. The last of the *Bradley* disappears, dropping slowly to the bottom of Lake Michigan.

The men on the raft have all the time in the world—and absolutely no time at all—to consider what just happened. They have no idea how long it will take for a rescue ship to arrive. Fleming informs the others that there is another boat nearby. It might take a while, Fleming cautions, for the ship to negotiate its way through the storm, but it will find them. Fleming rum-mages through the raft's storage compartment and pulls out a flare. He strikes it and holds it over his head. The sparks cut through the night and bathe the men on the raft in red.

The four men, drenched and freezing, are alone, huddled together on a life raft as they are tossed around like driftwood on the second-largest body of water in North America.

Hope is their only gateway to survival.

A TELEPHONE CALL INTERRUPTS LIEUTENANT COMMANDER Harold Muth's evening meal. It's the Charlevoix lifeboat station. The Coast Guard headquarters wants the *Sundew*, the boat Muth commands, to head to the site as soon as possible. It's just after 5:30 P.M.—minutes after Elmer Fleming's first distress call. Muth lives about five minutes from the Charlevoix station, and by the time he arrives there, the crew of the *Carl D. Bradley* has already been in the water for a few minutes. Of course, no one at the Charlevoix station knows the exact status of the *Bradley* or its crew, or if the men were even able to launch lifeboats. What they do know is that another boat—a German freighter—is in the area, and that it, too, is heading to the reported site of the sinking.

The Coast Guard moves quickly. In the brief time it takes Muth to grab a coat, kiss his wife, Doloras, good-bye, and drive to the station, the Charlevoix station's personnel have prepared the *Sundew* for its mission. The *Sundew*'s Charlie 12 status presents problems, not so much in terms of the time it will take to prepare the vessel, but for the time it will take for the executive officer to pull together a crew. Since the *Sundew* isn't technically obligated to leave port any sooner than twelve hours after a call, its crew, away on shore leave, might be out for the evening or otherwise difficult to locate. The men on the *Bradley*, if they have survived and are in the water, don't have twelve hours; they probably don't have even three.

It's already been a somewhat frustrating day for Captain Muth and his crew. One of the *Sundew*'s most important functions—pulling buoys before winter sets in and the lakes freeze over—had to be curtailed because of high winds. Muth had ordered the boat's return to Charlevoix early in the afternoon, knowing full well that the lost hours might come back to haunt him in the near future, if the fickle November weather brings ice to places where buoys haven't been removed. Still, it was the right decision. The *Sundew* tends to roll slightly during the buoy-removal process, especially when the crew swings the *Sundew*'s boom out over the side of the boat. Rough seas would cause it to roll even more.

Built by the Marine Iron and Shipbuilding Company in Duluth, Minnesota, and commissioned on August 24, 1944, the USCGC *Sundew* was constructed in the standard cutter design of the day—180 feet long and 37 feet wide, with a 13-foot draft and twin diesel engines. Primarily a buoy tender, the *Sundew* is also used for aid-to-navigation missions; lighthouse maintenance; and, when needed, as an icebreaker. This is the *Sundew*'s first year stationed in Charlevoix. Prior to 1958, the cutter was stationed in Manitowoc from 1944 to 1950 before moving on, first, to Milwaukee, from 1950 to 1953 and eventually to Sturgeon Bay, from 1953 to 1958. Its biggest mission before tonight occurred in 1947, when its crew rescued 28 men on the *Jupiter*, a disabled ore boat, and towed the 3,000-ton vessel to safety.

Harold Muth believes his boat is well suited for the kind of duty his crew will be up against tonight. The *Sundew* is sturdy enough to plow through ice, yet, at 180 feet, it's sleek and compact, "an ideal length for coping with those waves on the Great Lakes," Muth says, "because she can ride out those big waves because you're not getting the torquelike stress you get on the longer vessels."

Muth doesn't need coaching in how to prepare his boat for the night ahead. At two o'clock that afternoon, Lansing Shoals registered winds coming out of the south-southwest at forty-six miles per hour; a few hours later, winds were clocked at sixty-two miles per hour. Moving his ship the forty-seven miles from Charlevoix to the *Bradley* site will take hours— realistically, four or five—and Muth expects one hell of a pounding along the way.

With this in mind, Muth orders the personnel on hand to secure everything on board the *Sundew* to the fullest possible extent. He wants all buoys, chains, sinkers—anything on deck that can move around in rough seas—strapped or tied down, transferred to shore, or taken below. Water is added to the ballast tanks. Fuel tanks are topped off. The men work quickly, and by the time the *Sundew* has picked up its remaining crew, the boat is prepared to stay out for days on end if absolutely necessary.

Warren Toussaint, hospitalman second class on the *Sundew*, knows that this is no ordinary November blow. He's served on ocean and lake vessels for a decade, including time in the navy, and has a deep respect for the capabilities of nature—forces that inspired the Coast Guard saying "Regulations say you have to go out; they don't say anything about your having to come back."

Toussaint spent his day on the *Sundew*, and he'd watched the weather worsen as the sun went down. When he finally left the boat for home at 5:00 P.M., the thirty-two-year-old corpsman was glad to be away from the water for a while.

Warren, his wife, Norma, and their three children have just sat down for dinner when the phone rings. Warren immediately suspects that it's someone from work with bad news.

Norma answers the phone. It's the executive officer from the *Sundew*. Warren listens in on his wife's side of the brief conversation. The moment he hears her ask "Right away?" he understands that his evening meal has just ended.

As soon as Norma's hung up the receiver, Warren is on his feet.

The Toussaints and their kids toss on coats, head out to the car, and drive the eight blocks to the dock. Other than Norma's asking her husband if he really *has* to go out in the storm, neither talks directly about what's really on their minds—not with the kids in the car.

Warren has already said what he felt needed to be said, back at the house when they were preparing to leave.

"Don't believe anything you hear on the news or over the telephone," he instructed Norma. "Don't believe anything anybody tells you unless an officer in a uniform comes to the front door and tells you that I have been lost. Then you can believe it."

He addresses one other practical matter when they pull up to the Coast Guard station: "the insurance papers are in the metal box."

"I know that," Norma replies.

Toussaint kisses his wife and kids good-bye. He wonders—and not for the only time during the evening—if he will ever see them again.

The *Sundew* is ready to go at 6:20 P.M., some fifty minutes after the Charlevoix station first contacted Lieutenant Commander Harold Muth. Muth had hoped to recall enough deck and engine room personnel to stand watch for the customary four-hour shifts, but the final tally won't allow it. The *Sundew* usually carries a crew of thirty-three men—four officers and twenty-nine enlisted men. At Muth's request, Warren Toussaint conducts a head count. He counts three officers and twenty enlisted crewmen—not great, but sufficient. Muth wants as many capable men as possible for what will undoubtedly be a grueling search, but he's also conscious of the value of every passing minute.

The men on board the *Sundew* are quickly schooled on what lies ahead. To get from its mooring to Lake Michigan, the *Sundew* has to turn itself around. It must pass under a railroad bridge and enter Lake Charlevoix; turn around, backtrack through the bridge, and reenter Round Lake; pass through an open highway bridge; and ultimately proceed through a channel out to Lake Michigan. When the seas are calm, these maneuvers present little concern: a couple of toots to the bridge tenders, a relatively simple turn, and you are on your way.

Tonight, the strong winds out of the southwest make the maneuvers much more challenging. The winds are blowing the *Sundew* off course, and Muth has to calculate adjustments on the spot. ("You take a guess as to how much you're going to crab because of the wind effect," he'll explain later.)

He's especially cautious near the narrow railroad bridge. In making his adjustments, Muth tries to figure the different ways and directions his ship will be affected by the wind; rather than fight it, he lets the wind work in his favor.

"I gave her a good number of turns, to allow for the winds," he recalls. "We sailed through that bridge without touching either side. We had no trouble with the highway bridge."

A crowd gathered on the highway bridge watches the action below. Word about the *Sundew*'s going out to look for the *Bradley* spreads quickly, as people listening in on the radio calls transmitted all over the Great Lakes begin to gather the details surrounding the limestone carrier's sinking. Family members of the *Sundew* crew, curious Charlevoix citizens, customers from a nearby restaurant—all congregate on the bridge to watch the *Sundew*'s winding route out to the lake, "weav[ing] like a drunken sailor," as Norma Toussaint, one of the spectators, will remember.

"When they hit the lake," she says, "they really started to sway back and forth, tipping from one side to another. I was very apprehensive at that point."

Her husband shares her apprehension. He's been into and out of the harbor so many times that the maneuvers are almost automatic. In his two years on the *Sundew* he's never seen the boat roll in the channel, but it's rolling now.

Captain Muth takes no chances. He's stationed two crewmen at the bow of the ship, to stand watch and release the *Sundew*'s anchor in an emergency, but he calls them back inside when the *Sundew* approaches the end of the channel. From this point on, the deck is off limits. Muth anticipates a lot of green water sweeping over the deck when the *Sundew* finally moves onto Lake Michigan. Anyone on deck could be washed overboard.

The worst awaits them; no one on board the *Sundew* doubts it.

Massive waves hit the *Sundew* broadside and crash over the decks, sending the boat into a series of nasty rolls. Anything not lashed down belowdecks goes flying. The boat pops back up and waits for the next big one.

Warren Toussaint is not alone when he wonders what it's going to be like once they're out on the open water.

Other boats trying to reach the *Bradley* site find the going even tougher. *CG-4300*, a thirty-six-footer from the Coast Guard lifeboat station on Plum Island that deployed minutes after Elmer Fleming's first distress call, has already given up any thought of assisting in the search for *Bradley* survivors. Lake Michigan chewed up the small, four-man vessel as soon as it ventured out, tossing it around like a bathtub toy. The boat never stood a chance. Unable to steer or make any headway in the storm, the crew abandons its efforts, only to find their own boat in serious trouble when they try to return to Plum Island. They settle for the shelter of nearby Washington Island.

The *Christian Sartori*, which had set out to the site of the sinking at 5:53 P.M., barely manages to crawl along at one or two miles per hour. It's pointed directly into the storm, and at one point Captain Paul Mueller is astonished to discover his boat at a standstill in the waves, even though the ship is running at full speed ahead. The wind and sea act like a giant hand pushing against the vessel and holding it back. Mueller assumes that any wreckage— or lifeboat, life raft, or sailor in the water—will drift in the *Sartori*'s direction. He orders his men to keep a close eye out for anything caught in the ship's searchlight. It's a tall order, to say the least. Waves surge over the *Sartori*'s bow, and a blinding spray pelts the pilothouse windows. Still, a little while ago a watchman reported seeing a red light, something that might have been a flare. Mueller and the others, once alerted, had seen it, too. If there are any survivors out there, the *Sartori* has to reach them soon.

Farther southwest on the lake, the USCGC *Hollyhock*, a Coast Guard cutter out of Sturgeon Bay, Wisconsin, fares much better. She suffers some of the pounding the other vessels have experienced, but with the seas at her starboard quarter, she negotiates the lake at a better speed. The problem is distance: under optimum sailing conditions it would take three or four hours to get from Sturgeon Bay to Gull Island; under the present conditions its chief engineer has to check down its engines to avoid heavy pitching in the waves, which adds to the time to reach the site of the sinking.

CG-35329, the Coast Guard's thirty-six-foot motorboat out of Charlevoix, finds itself in the same predicament as the one out of Plum Island. It can't hold its course, and in the forty minutes since its launching, it has barely found a way out of the breakwater and onto Lake Michigan. When the *Sundew* edges out onto the lake, the motorboat tries to fall in behind it, with no improvement.

As he passes the motorboat, Harold Muth concludes that conditions are far too dangerous for the smaller vessel to continue.

"He told me he'd lost his steering, that the boat wouldn't answer the rudder," Muth remembers. "I said, 'I think you should get back to port and get out of the storm.' I didn't want another problem on my hands. I had enough on my hands now."

As if by its own will, the *Sundew* urges itself deeper into the storm. In the pitch black, the men on the Coast Guard cutter can't see the threat as much as feel it. Captain Muth has chosen a course, more out of necessity than option, that places the *Sundew* in a trough, putting the sea at the ship's beam. Waves, some rising higher than the wheelhouse windows, plow into the boat, burying its deck and rolling the *Sundew* at precarious angles.

Muth has to think back to his days on the North Atlantic during World War II to remember such imposing seas. He'd been a gunnery officer on the USS *Howard D. Crow*, a destroyer escort, and during his twenty-two convoy missions between the United States and Europe, he'd sailed through a few full-force gales. One in particular remains in memory. It's the only time, he confesses today, that he was ever frightened by a storm.

"We had a hellacious full gale up in the North Atlantic," he remembers, "and the convoy was just on steerage. Everybody was told to maintain steerage and ride it out the best they could.

"On a destroyer escort, you start your navigation watch—your deck watch—from the flying bridge, and you're out in the open. We told the gunners to stay inside the little ammunition shack and off the deck. I was one of only two people outside. We could pick our course, provided we kept up with the convoy, and I was trying to pick out the best heading I could to keep the ship from pitching and rolling too much.

"We started taking some big ones. We rolled over about fifty, fifty-five degrees, and on the way back up, I could see stars. I could also see the crest of the next swell, and it was way the hell up there. All I could think of was, 'Oh, Jesus, this is the North Atlantic. It's going to be damned cold if we go over.' Just about the time we got right, that thing hit us. Down we went, seventy-two degrees. It wiped out our boat and did a lot of damage on deck, but we had everybody inside.

"The Old Man had a sea cabin one deck below, and he came up that ladder, the hatch flew open, and he screamed into the wind, 'What the hell did you hit?' 'The biggest wave I ever saw, Captain,' I said. 'That's all it was—a big wave.' He looked around but couldn't see much because of the fumes and everything in the air. 'Well, goddamn it,' he said, 'don't do it again.' And down he went, back down the hatch.

"Fortunately," he adds with a chuckle, "we didn't have another big one like that. That was the biggest wave I've ever seen. After that, I don't think I've ever been scared by any storm."

That was well over a decade ago. Now, with other ocean and lakes storms behind him, Muth has enough experience to know two things. First, as a captain, he knows that if he shows any fear, it will be hard on the morale of his crew. Second, he doesn't feel the fear because he is in command of his ship. He knows how it will respond to various headings and shaft revolutions, and even though he also knows the *Sundew* is going to take a tremendous beating in the storm, he has faith in his boat and his ability to command it: "You get bounced around a lot, but if you come back and you don't hang over, you're going to beat the storm."

Jack Coppens, a deck officer on the *Sundew*, in reflecting back on the boat's rough ride that evening, sees things in much the same way: "When we first went out through the breakwater, the ship started rolling real heavy. It rolled so hard you thought the darn thing would roll over. But when you do that fifty or sixty times—it goes over on her side and comes back—you say, 'Well, it's a good ship. It ain't gonna roll over.' You get confident after an hour or so of those heavy seas."

Most of the *Sundew* crew, however, is belowdecks. The men have no idea what's going on, other than that everything on board the *Sundew* seems to have been launched to a new location. The galley pantry has been rearranged by nature: almost everything is on the floor and soaking wet. In one of the storage lockers, paint cans have burst open, leaving a couple of feet of gloppy mess on the floor. Gas canisters stored on deck are washed overboard. The entire crew, almost to the man, is seasick.

They're also extremely concerned. One of the rolls is so extreme that it sends spray and water down the stack, washing up dangerously close to the ship's main electrical switchboard. Water gushes down the intake ventilator behind the pilothouse and into the radio room, shorting out the *Sundew's* primary transmitter. The secondary transmitter remains functional, but the *Sundew* now has lost its ability to send long-range messages or to talk to anyone outside channel 51.

Concerned about the safety and morale of his crew, Captain Muth sends Warren Toussaint from the pilothouse belowdecks to check on them. Toussaint heads down to the mess hall, where a good portion of the crew is likely to be. The men, he discovers, have tied themselves to the tables and chairs. Toussaint decides to make the engine room his next stop. He lurches his way down the passageway and starts down a ladder leading to the room, but he has to stop. The chief engineer, frightened out of his wits, is standing at the bottom of the ladder, one foot on the first rung.

"How are you doing?" Toussaint asks.

The chief never takes his eyes off the inclinometer, which measures the angle of the ship's rolling.

"If that thing goes past fifty-five degrees, I'm out of here," he tells Toussaint.

The man the *Sundew* crewmen call "Doc" agrees with him on this point. "I'll be right behind you," he says.

Where they intend to go is anyone's guess. No one is permitted abovedecks unless he's on watch, and one place belowdecks is just as horrendous as another. The crew quarters are abandoned, mainly because no one's going to be getting any sleep with the *Sundew* rolling the way it is—unless you happen to nod off while you're tied to a table. In the mess hall there's comfort, if not safety, in numbers.

From the vantage point of *CG-1273*, a twin-engine Grumman HU-16 Albatross dispatched from the Coast Guard air station in Traverse City, there isn't much to see.

Visibility is surprisingly good, but the wind bops the plane around enough to spook all but the stouthearted. Fortunately, the aircraft's two-man crew has the kind of cowboy mentality necessary for the job: the high winds blowing the plane around might make them a little nervous, but the conditions also give them the kind of adrenaline push that thrill-seekers are always chasing.

Not that they're thrilled to be here. The men are exhausted, ready to go home. It's been a very long day, beginning in the morning when the Albatross was sent to look for a three-man fishing tug that had gone missing in the storm. The tug had been out on Green Bay yesterday, and when it didn't return to Oconto on time in the evening, the Coast Guard organized a search to commence at daybreak. *CG-1273* took off just after dawn and, by midmorning, the crew located the tug on the southern portion of the bay.

This was only the beginning. Rather than return to Traverse City, *CG-1273* was ordered to head to southern Lake Michigan, to assist in another search, this one for the wreckage of a navy jet that had crashed into the lake on its approach to the naval air station in Glenview, Illinois. *CG-1273* carried out that mission and was just returning to Traverse City when word of the *Bradley* sinking came in. Instead of returning home, the tired crew was ordered to head to the area near Gull Island where the *Bradley* was believed to have gone down.

Lieutenant Commander Louis Donohoe, coordinator of operations in Traverse City, really has no choice in the matter. He has one other Albatross at his air station, but it's under repair and not functional. It's too risky, Donohue decides, to send out helicopters in this weather, except as a last resort. Donohoe calls in a standby crew, which he'll deploy to the scene only in the event that survivors are spotted and cannot be picked up by any other method. In the meantime, *CG-1273* is to patrol the area, look for wreckage and survivors, and drop flares on the water to assist vessels heading to the site.

The Albatross, often described as a "flying boat," has been specially designed for rescue-at-sea operations. Designed shortly before the end of World War II, the aircraft features a long, heavy body and huge wingspan with fixed amphibious floats that allow it to land on water, if necessary, to pick up downed pilots or, in the case of those used by the Coast Guard, the crews of ships lost at sea. In the kind of storm it's facing tonight, however, it's doubtful that *1273* would even consider an attempt at a water landing.

When *1273* arrives on the scene at 7:15 P.M., there's nothing to see. The *Christian Sartori* is still off in the distance, about eight miles away, making very slow progress in its struggle against what the crewmen on the aircraft agree are the toughest conditions they've faced. From the plane, the seas are nothing but a mass of black waves cresting in white. *CG-1273* has all of two flares on board. The first is dropped from two thousand feet. The Albatross drops to five hundred feet, hoping to find something in the burning light. Nothing.

Lieutenant J. L. Sigmund, at the controls of *1273* with Lieutenant E. P. Baumann, radios the *Sartori* and, after a conversation with Captain Paul Mueller, drops his second and final flare near the ship. Neither the *Sartori* nor the plane find the slightest hint of wreckage or, more important, survivors. If there are men in the water, in either a lifeboat or on a raft, they're going to be next to impossible to locate.

The Coast Guard plane turns back to Traverse City, where it will pick up a larger supply of flares and refuel. The *Sartori* soldiers on, not realizing that four men on a raft are watching the action from a distance, hopeful that sometime in the very near future their ordeal will be coming to an end.

AS COLD AS THEY ARE, ELMER FLEMING, FRANK MAYS, GARY STRZ-elecki, and Dennis Meredith remain hopeful. They've already survived the *Bradley*'s sinking and found the life raft, which puts them in a much better position than thirty-one of their shipmates.

The pontoon-style raft is double-sided, with platforms of wooden slats mounted on large orange barrels. No matter how the raft might flip in heavy seas, it will always come up in a way that the survivors can climb back on board. Theoretically, the eight-by-ten-foot raft is supposed to hold fifteen men, although it's difficult to imagine how: the four men on it now, sprawled out the way they are, take up most of the room. A storage compartment in the center of the raft contains three flares and a cone-shaped sea anchor, designed to stabilize the raft in heavy seas. The anchor, dropped a short time ago, is doing its job. The raft holds the surface in the huge waves trying to flip it over.

Nearly an hour has passed since the *Bradley*'s stern disappeared beneath the lake's surface, but as they look into the distance, the four men can see a searchlight and two sets of running lights—red and green—on the horizon, heading in their direction. All they need do is hang on a little longer.

They huddle together and talk about the hours ahead, when they'll be out of the cold, in dry clothing and drinking hot coffee. Fleming takes the lead, repeating his story about calling in the Mayday message and seeing the approaching boat on the radar. He's reserved the raft's final flare for when the ship out there gets close enough to see it. He fired off the other two not long after the *Bradley* sank, and he has no idea if either had been seen by rescuers.

Gary Strzelecki also offers encouragement, exhorting his raftmates to hang on and warning them about any especially large waves heading in their direction. Gary and his wife, Ann, have a nine-month-old son, Benjamin, named after Gary's father. Gary, as almost everyone who knows him would admit, is hard to figure. He's as tough as shoe leather, with a wild side that's uncommon in a sleepy place such as Rogers City.

In high school he made friends from an unlikely source: his artwork. Strzelecki loved to draw, and he loved comic books. He'd buy as many comic books as he could afford, study them, and sell them used to anyone willing to come over to his parents' place and pay him a nickel apiece for them. He and Don Selke, the older brother of the *Bradley*'s Jim Selke, became friendly because they shared a talent that set them apart from their classmates.

"He was good at art in school," Selke remembers. "It was kind of a camaraderie type of thing because of our attachment to drawing. I wasn't all that good of an artist. I guess I had a little more control of my hands than some of the kids, but Gary was good."

If Elmer Fleming is the kind of guy you trust because of his experience, Strzelecki is the one you depend on because of his instincts.

The men fall silent as the *Sartori* draws near. It's rolling at a steep angle of nearly fifty degrees, leading Fleming to marvel at the "great seamanship and courage" he's witnessing. Mays, too, is taken by the *Sartori* crew's "nerve."

It's now or never, Fleming decides. He grabs the raft's remaining flare, pulls off its cap, and attempts to spark it. Nothing happens. He tries again and again, desperately trying to ignite the waterlogged flare. The *Sartori* is unbearably close, less than one hundred yards away. Its searchlight sweeps across the water, actually hitting the raft for a painfully frustrating split second, but just as it does, the raft drops over a wave and into a trough, out of sight. The men scream and wave at the *Sartori*, but they can't be heard above the noise of the wind and waves. In a last-ditch effort to ignite the flare, Fleming bashes it against his teeth. It's just too wet to light.

The men look on in mounting despair as the *Sartori*'s red lights disappear and all of the green lights on its starboard deck come into view. The *Sartori* is turning away from the raft and moving toward the area where the *Bradley* went down. Over the past hour, the raft has been swept away from the site by the wind and waves, and the men on board realize, almost all at once, that the raft is drifting from the area that rescue vessels will search. It's far too dark for anyone, even with the assistance of binoculars, to spot them from anywhere but up close. Their only chance now is to hold on until daybreak.

On the *Christian Sartori*, Captain Mueller and his wheelhouse crew look everywhere for the slightest evidence indicating that they're searching in the correct spot. Crews traditionally pull everything possible from the deck during a storm, but surely there must be some sign of a ship as massive as the *Carl D. Bradley*. Mueller and others had witnessed an explosion. Certainly something—a lifeboat, an oar, life jackets . . . *something*—should be floating on the water, provided, of course, that they are searching in the right location.

Then there was the red light Mueller and the others had observed following the explosion and disappearance of the ship. The red light had appeared only briefly before disappearing entirely. It was the kind of light a flare would make. If, in fact, there had been survivors, where were they now? Mueller had directed his vessel to proceed to where the light had originated, but survivors, like wreckage, are nowhere to be found.

As the *Sartori* pushes closer to the location of the *Bradley* sinking, its spotlight catches something shiny bobbing in the waves. The men strain to determine what it is, their efforts hindered by the glare of the spotlight playing off the thick mist in the air. It appears to be a beat-up tank.

The spotlight moves slowly over the area. The men peer out of the pilot-house windows in silence. Another object—what looks like a raincoat, twisted and carried along in the waves—appears for a moment and then is gone. Excited by their discoveries, the men scan the surface of Lake Michigan for something more revealing or promising. Nothing else turns up.

"My men lined the rail but we saw no one," Captain Mueller lamented later, in an interview with the *Detroit Times*. "It was not a pleasant feeling for us to find nothing but that floating tank."

The *Sartori* proceeds on. Mueller calls Ray Brunette at the radio station in Port Washington. He briefs the radio operator in a terse, sad statement.

"The tank appears to have been in a tremendous explosion," he says in his heavily accented English, offering no further description of what his crew saw. "Still searching. No survivors yet. No lifeboats visible. I believe all hands are lost."

ON MOST NIGHTS IN ROGERS CITY, THE PORCH LIGHTS GO OFF early. With the exception of a bar or restaurant here or there, businesses shut down early enough for shopkeepers to be home in time for dinner. Many homes don't have television, and evenings become family or homework time. Teenagers congregate at a place like the Cozy Corner or at the movie theater, but they're expected home at a decent hour—certainly before their parents go to bed, which, in these parts, is early enough. Outdoorsmen—or sailors, if they're in town—might get together at a watering hole and pick up the thread of a conversation from the night before, or if they're really lucky, brag about the day's catch or the deer they dragged out of the woods. They also know better than to stay out too late on a weeknight. Tomorrow is another workday, and it's prudent to let it arrive unaccompanied by a hangover or a short night's rest.

Tonight is different.

Word of the *Carl D. Bradley* shoots through the city. By the time the *Christian Sartori* finally makes its way through the storm to the scene of the wreck, and hours before the *Sundew* can expect to arrive there, everyone has heard the grim news. In no time, Rogers City is united in shock and confusion. No one knows anything for certain, including officials at Michigan Lime or the Bradley Transportation Company. The gatekeepers at the Port of Calcite hold firm in what they've been telling concerned callers, and they will remain so at least until the families of the *Bradley* crewmen are notified. The *Bradley*, they stubbornly tell callers or visitors, is due to arrive at about 2:00 A.M.

Porch lights stay on. Neighbors move from house to house, seeking information or commiserating about this crew member or that crew member—the guy who lives two doors away, or the guy whose wife you saw in the grocery store last Friday, or the kid who shouldn't have been on that damn boat in the first place. People speculate about lifeboats, rescue missions, the good swimmers among the *Bradley* crew, about all the islands near the area where the boat was at the time of its last distress call. People just need to talk.

It's the same at the businesses still open. Every establishment has a radio turned on. Customers listen, and when they speak, they do so quietly.

"We used to get there and it'd be noisy, with the kids talking and all this stuff," Rita Selke says of the Cozy Corner. A senior at Rogers City High School at the time, Rita was dating (and eventually married) Jim Selke's brother Don. She also had an older cousin, stokerman Paul Heller, on the *Bradley*. "There wasn't a kid in town that had any kind of music on. They were all hunting the airwaves, the radios. They had one set up at Cozy Corner, and we would go in there and listen. Or you'd turn on the radio in your car. Everybody was congregating and listening to anything they could."

Cash Budnick, an avid hunter, is out in a garage sandwiched between his house and a Chrysler dealership, skinning a deer, when he's interrupted by his wife's bursting in, a dishrag in her hand.

"The *Bradley* went down," she cries. "The *Bradley* went down."

Alvy Budnick, their twenty-six-year-old son, is a watchman on the boat. Their nephew, Frank Mays, also is on board.

Alvy has a three-year-old son, Kim, and two daughters, two-year-old Antoinette and two-and-a-half-month-old Candace Ann. His marriage is not going well, and his life in general has been difficult enough that his mother, a devout Catholic, has been praying that her son's troubles will somehow come to an end.

Alva Budnick had been named after one of his father's friends, though he had been christened "Alvin," probably after the Catholic saint. His teachers might have entered "Alvin" into their grade books, but friends and family would always refer to him as Alvy.

According to his younger sister Elaine, Alvy was an easygoing, "no-temper kind of person," but he never quite fit in, at school or at home. He wasn't an athlete, and he had no interest in hunting or fishing, his father's two lifelong passions.

"He was a very gentle person," Elaine remembers. "He didn't like killing things. *I* had to go hunting with my dad because Alvy didn't want to. He didn't get along with my dad because he wouldn't do what my dad wanted him to do, like the hunting stuff, so my dad was always on his case.

"He was the kind of person who took the blame for everything. I remember when my dad got a new car—during the war, when they were very, very hard to get—and he locked it. I wanted to get in the car and, of course, so did Alvy. We pulled on that handle and I broke it. My dad came out and said, 'Who did that?' I said, 'He did.' Alvy never said a word; he took the blame. That's the kind of person he was."

Elaine hears about the *Bradley* while she's in the shower, preparing to go out for the evening. Her husband knocks on the door, walks in, and announces, "The *Bradley* sank." Rather than go out, they head over to her parents' house and keep a vigil, waiting for further word about the *Bradley*'s missing crew.

Amelia Budnick prays for her son. She's no longer concerned about his other troubles. She just wants him back alive.

Cecilia Krawczak has just finished changing her baby daughter's diaper when a couple of her neighbors come down the hall and give her word of the *Bradley*'s sinking. Stunned, she almost drops the baby. She has never imagined a life without her husband. Joe had always been the family man, joking that they'd have to buy a two-story house for the twelve kids he hoped they'd have. Their happiest hours together had been during winter layup, when he worked on the boats during the day and was always home at night. But now here she is, on her thirty-second birthday, wondering if she'll ever see him again. Her kids, knowing that something's wrong, watch her for indications of how bad things really are. Two of her sisters come over to offer support.

But there can be no comfort in the face of such uncertainty, only hours of dread, each hour adding weight to a burden that Cecilia, like the families of thirty-four other men, must struggle to hold up.

At WHAK, Harvey and Janice Klann scramble to address a constant stream of unfamiliar tasks now demanding their immediate attention. Residents of Rogers City—friends and relative of *Bradley* crewmen—call for news and updates. The news wire services, assuming that the boat's home port might have updates they can transmit to newspapers and radio stations through-out the United States, do the same. Newspaper reporters from such cities as New York, Boston, and Chicago check in with questions of their own. The Klanns try to accommodate these callers while Harvey keeps the radio sta-tion on the air.

Harvey and Janice gather information wherever and whenever they can, but it's a process with few rewards. They talk to the Coast Guard and officials from the Michigan Limestone plant, but nobody seems to know much—or if they do, they're saying very little. The Klanns can understand this: these sources are overwhelmed themselves, whether they're trying to obtain their own reliable information, organizing search-and-rescue efforts, or notifying the next of kin of the *Bradley* crew. An anxiety, unfamiliar and intense, has wormed its way into Rogers City, leaving the community emo-tionally exhausted.

Keenly aware that misinformation can only add to the stress, Harvey takes a cautious approach to anything he says on the air or tells the station's callers. He'll adhere to this approach in the days to come.

"So many rumors start out when things like this happen," he'll explain at another time. "We tried to sift through this and not sensationalize it, but give information that would be of comfort and even insight to people. People wanted to know the facts, and we tried to get them as much information as we could when we were covering it."

Rogers City, he points out, is a religious community, and on the night of the sinking and over the following days he'll play inspirational music and religious programming that, he hopes, will offer comfort to the community.

Klann, an engineer, sets up a special feed line servicing the print media and other radio stations. He's heard more than he's getting off the teletype machine—but not much more—but he's reluctant to repeat anything he hears unless he can find a way to corroborate it, which only frustrates the station's callers.

"Other stations and the press were pressing us to pass along everything we had," he says. "We wouldn't do that unless we knew it was accurate. There were some conflicts of information. We wanted to get it straight."

Klann draws the line when other media outlets ask him to interview the families of the *Bradley* crew. He recognizes that he, as a newsman, is dealing with a legitimate news story of great interest and importance, not only in the upper Great Lakes region but also across the country, yet he refuses to take advantage of friendships and acquaintances. Families are dealing with enough, and Klann will not pursue a story that will only add to their emotional burdens. Besides, even if he were inclined to talk to the families, he is not currently in a position to do so. He's needed at the station.

Over the next few days, Rogers City will be overrun by reporters. They can file their human interest stories then.

To the outsider—and to the folks in this area, anybody not living in town is an outsider—Rogers City is little more than a wide spot in the road. This isn't a city that time forgot; it's a city that time never paid a whole lot of attention to in the first place. It's quaint, perhaps even fun to visit, but it will drive a big-city dweller stir-crazy in the time it takes to unpack your bags and settle in.

This, one senses, is fine with Rogers City residents. Its townspeople are unabashedly provincial. At a future date, writer/radio personality Garrison Keillor will invent Lake Wobegon, a fictitious small town in Minnesota, where, as Keillor describes it, "the men are strong, the women are good-looking, and the children are above average." In his books and radio sketches, Keillor will poke lighthearted fun at Smalltown, U.S.A, while at the same time he will pay tribute to a lifestyle that, in a way, is more wistful than nostalgic. Rogers City fits the mold. In a special 1950 edition of *Calcite Screenings*, W. H. Whiteley, publisher of the *Presque Isle Advance*, presented a history of Rogers City that might have served as a template for Lake Wobegon, had Keillor ever needed one. While describing the natural beauty of the area, Whiteley offers this aside regarding the women shown in one of the magazine's photographs: "All our girls are shapely and beautiful, intelligent and womanly. They could be nothing else, living in Rogers City."

Rogers City *is* a beautiful town. In 1958, it has yet to celebrate its centennial, yet in its relatively short time in existence, it has enjoyed healthy periods of prosperity, punctuated only by occasional downswings. The city's initial success stemmed from the lumber and commercial fishing trades. Later, the limestone business provided Rogers City with the kind of easygoing, self-contained environment that could be passed on from generation to generation. At a time when more Americans uproot and follow their hearts or jobs to other regions of the country, the people in Rogers City prefer to stay put.

In the beginning, Rogers City, officially incorporated in 1877, was defined by its lumber, as was most of northern Michigan. Massive forests of pine, cedar, and hardwood blanketed the area. The plentiful lumber was ideal not only for building homes in the newly settled towns springing up along the shores of Lake Huron, but also for exportation to the bigger cities that were constantly expanding and in need of building materials. William E. Rogers, a land speculator from New York, purchased the land now bearing his name, but he had no interest in it other than as an investment. His business partner, Albert Molitor, was another story entirely. He moved to the area; operated a sawmill and store; and, in general, laid the foundation for the tiny new town.

The early settlers in Rogers City and surrounding towns were largely German and Polish immigrants who started up homestead farms or worked in the lumber mills. These were hardworking, deeply religious Catholics—the ancestors of people living in Rogers City today.

The lumber industry brought Rogers City and neighboring Crawford's Quarry (later renamed Calcite) prosperity. It also led directly to the city's lucrative shipping industry. Since there was no railroad extending as far north as Rogers City, the lumber mills and farmers had to find a way to transport their goods to cities outside the immediate area—most notably Detroit. Lake Huron was the obvious answer. Docks were constructed. Rogers City became one of the busiest ports in the state.

By the turn of the twentieth century, however, the forests were largely depleted. Paul H. Hoeft, who earned his riches in lumber, had been interested for years in the area's limestone outcroppings, and he and a cement manufacturer bought a five-mile strip of land near Rogers City that, Hoeft believed, showed great commercial promise. The two men, along with other Rogers City civic leaders and businessmen, founded the Rogers City Land Company and looked for ways to develop the property.

Henry H. Hindshaw, a prominent Syracuse geologist, became the catalyst in that development. In 1908–09, Hindshaw surveyed the limestone near Rogers City and saw firsthand its commercial potential. He found an investor, W. F. White of White Investing Company in New York, to purchase and develop the land owned by the Rogers City Land Company. The Michigan Limestone and Chemical Company was born.

White served as president of the new company and, for a brief time, Hindshaw was its general manager. The company struggled in its formative years, but the arrival of Carl D. Bradley, who took over as general manager in 1911, signaled the beginning of significant growth. Bradley was an interesting study. Gregarious and engaging by nature, the fifty-one-year-old Bradley endeared himself to Rogers City when he moved to the city and became heavily involved in its civic affairs.

Bradley's biggest contribution was his development of a fleet of ships for transporting the different grades of limestone to ports throughout the Great Lakes. Massive limestone carriers bearing the names of important figures from Michigan Lime's early days, and featuring a distinctive self-unloading system, were constructed.

In 1920, U. S. Steel purchased the Michigan Limestone and Chemical Company, giving Rogers City a prominent role in steel production in mills near Great Lakes ports. As the plant expanded, so did the city. In its comprehensive history of Rogers City, *Calcite Screenings* noted that "a drowsy city of some 600 people in 1912 . . . [had] grown to a prosperous little city of 4,000 in 38 years." By 1950, the plant and shipping business employed more Rogers City residents than all other businesses combined. Six hundred people worked at the plant and quarry, and another 250 for the Bradley Transportation Company.

With 95 percent of the workers at the Michigan Lime and Bradley Transportation Company boats living in Rogers City, residents had little interest in affairs outside its own sphere of existence. It wasn't an issue of a community's animosity toward neighboring communities or other cities in Michigan, although there were grumblings that strangers weren't always welcome in Rogers City; it was more a case of the city's self-sufficiency. Rogers City was happy and sheltered. Its kids grew up, married locally, stayed in town, worked at the plant or on the boats, and eventually took care of their children's children. There was no reason to wander or stray. Everything you could ever need could be found in town.

And now, in the wake of the disappearance of the *Carl D. Bradley*, Rogers City is a community in crisis. Nature has torn a hole in its well-maintained fabric, affecting everyone in previously incomprehensible ways. The people of Rogers City lean onto each other for support, weathering the emotional storm, waiting for the first wave of shock to pass. Even though reason tells them otherwise, they allow themselves a sliver of hope.

John Enos has no intention of waiting around Rogers City for news about the *Bradley*. The Coast Guard is out there looking for survivors, and when they find them—and John doesn't doubt that they will—they'll be bringing them back to the station in Charlevoix. This, Enos figures, is where he needs to be.

John's older brother, Marty, is a stokerman on the *Bradley*. A big, even-tempered sort of guy, Marty has grown closer to John, seven years his junior, and his sister, Janet, five years younger, in recent years. Marty had worked in several jobs prior to joining the Bradley fleet. He and Janet had corresponded when he was out on the boats and she was away in nursing school, leading some of Janet's nursing school friends to comment on how tight the Enos family seemed. "Boy, I wish I'd been that close to my brothers," they'd tell Janet. "They wouldn't have anything to do with me."

According to Janet, Marty might have broken into the Major Leagues had he not gone blind in his left eye as a young boy. He'd been wheeling around in a wagon when a stick popped up into his eye. Marty had played baseball throughout his youth. He'd pitched for his high school team, and he actually tried out for a minor league team in St. Petersburg, Florida. His dream ended there: he had no peripheral vision, and runners on first base could easily steal bases on him.

Perhaps it's this athleticism that leads John Enos to believe that his brother has survived the shipwreck and the storm on the lake, even though Marty doesn't know how to swim. Marty would be strong enough to take care of himself. He'd find a way to the lifeboat and somehow make it to one of the islands.

After arriving in Charlevoix, John finds a spot near the dock and waits. Coast guardsmen, the families of the *Sundew* crew, reporters, curious residents of Charlevoix, and a few family members of the *Bradley* crew stand around, with little to do but try to find some reason for optimism. The wind makes it almost unbearable to be outside and, from time to time, those keeping vigil retreat to their cars or buildings for a brief stretch of warmth, or to listen for any morsel of news on the radio. As the hours pass, John Enos never flags in his belief that it's only a matter of time before his brother walks off the *Sundew* and the two of them drive back home. He's vocal about his feelings when a reporter notices him and asks what he's doing at the dock.

"My big brother Marty's out there," he answers. "He's a stoker on the *Bradley*. I was supposed to pick him up at two o'clock this morning over at Rogers City, but when I got the news I drove over to Charlevoix. This is the place to meet him now. He'll be coming in here.

"If anybody can make it, my big brother will," he continues. "Don't worry, they'll *all* make it."

It takes very little time for the *Bradley* reports to reach former Rogers City residents—people who have either moved away from town, or are attending schools in other cities, or are stationed elsewhere in the armed services.

Bob Crittendon, a freshman at Central Michigan University in Mount Pleasant, is in his dorm room when Jim Bison, a buddy from Rogers City, bursts in with news.

"Bob, you gotta come listen to this," Bison says. "Your dad's on the radio."

"What do you mean, my dad's on the radio?" Bob fires back. "He doesn't do that anymore."

Crittendon's father, also named Bob, was one of the founders of WLC in Rogers City. In the station's early days, the elder Crittendon performed any duties necessary at the station, including spending time at the microphone. Those days ended ages ago. He's now the station manager, and his duties are strictly administrative.

"Something's happened," Bison insists. "I think one of the boats has sunk."

Bob rushes into the next room, where Bison's roommate has set up a shortwave radio. Sure enough, the sound of Bob's father's voice is coming out of the radio's speaker. Bob listens carefully, trying to sort through the information he's hearing. Just a few months ago, shortly after graduating from high school, he'd worked at the Michigan Lime plant, picking up money from summer work to pay for his college tuition. He has no desire to work on the boats, but he knows a number of people, including high school classmates, who have taken jobs with the Bradley fleet. One of his closest childhood friends, a kid named Jim Selke, has been filling in as a replacement worker on the boats. Jim has talked about possibly enrolling at Central Michigan at the beginning of the second semester, once he's earned enough to pay his way.

Bob's father has all he can handle tonight. Every boat in the Bradley fleet is out somewhere, and everyone on these boats is demanding information—*anything*—on the *Carl D. Bradley*. Unfortunately, very little is known for certain. The details are out on the water, in a place no boat or plane has reached.

Flora Bellmore rereads a four-page letter, handwritten by her new husband, Doug, posted just three days ago, on Saturday, November 15. The *Bradley* was tied up in Cedarville at the time, and Doug had asked a fellow crew member, Wes Sobeck, to drop the letter in the mail when he got back to Rogers City. Sobeck's brother had passed away, and Wes and his nephew, both *Bradley* crewmen, had been excused from their duties on the ship to attend his funeral. The letter, postmarked from Rogers City on November 17; arrived in Onaway the next day.

The letter, full of the usual chitchat one might expect from husband and wife, was upbeat. Like the others on the *Bradley*, Doug Bellmore looked forward to the end of the shipping season.

"See you Tuesday if nothing goes wrong," he'd written, never dreaming that the final four words of his sentence would become permanently ironic.

Bellmore went on to suggest that Flora bring her sister and brother-in-law to the dock when she came to pick him up. He'd give them all a grand tour of the *Bradley.*

"I will take them up and show them all around," he volunteered.

It's a letter that will haunt Flora Bellmore for years, not only because of the mundane sentences that signify normal, everyday existence in the lives of husband and wife, but also for the occasional phrase, dropped here and there with no additional meaning intended, that would add weight to the message, moving it from the casual to the heartbreaking.

The return address, handwritten in two lines on the upper left corner of the envelope, originally meant as a kind of verbal shrug, has the effect of a dagger as Flora Bellmore rereads the letter:

> Somewhere in
> Lake Michigan.

LAKE MICHIGAN TREATS THE LIFE RAFT WITH DISDAIN, LIKE AN annoyance it can't quite shake. The raft rises and falls with the waves, each crest a hazard threatening to toss the raft over and pitch the four men back into the water. The men lay flat on their bellies, fitting their fingers through the raft's wooden slats, gripping as well as they can. They say very little to each other. From time to time one will offer a word of encouragement or hope, but mostly they struggle with their private thoughts. They pray, but all they hear in response are the sounds of the surrounding wind and waves.

They try to ward off despair. Their best hope, the *Christian Sartori*, hadn't seen them. How long ago was that? An hour? Two hours? Half an hour? There's no way of telling. Each man confronts his own faith in the future. Frank Mays believes it lies in the first light of the next morning. He has a mantra that he repeats to himself over and over again: "If we make it 'til daylight, we will be found."

The men know something of the enormity of Lake Michigan; they've sailed it enough to know that you can go a long time without a glimpse of land—or even another boat. With 22,300 square miles of surface area, the lake, carved into the land by glaciers during the Great Ice Age, has a greater surface area than any Great Lake other than Lake Superior. On the whipped-up waves of a body of water this large, a lifeboat is all but invisible. The *Sartori* hadn't seen them. Is there anyone else out there?

A giant wave pulls the raft upward. The men brace themselves. So far they've been dumped in the water only twice, and on both occasions they've surfaced near the raft. This is nature's terrible carnival ride, frightening the hell out of them as waves, some the size of two- or three-story buildings, pull the raft up to terrifying heights, only to drop it into another trough. The men hold their collective breath and wait.

This time the raft flips. Fortunately, no one is hit when it crashes back into the water near them. Frank Mays, Elmer Fleming, and Gary Strzelecki swim back to the raft and help each other aboard. Dennis Meredith, however, is struggling. His muscles are cramped from shivering; he is losing his resolve. He manages to find his way back to the raft, but he hasn't the energy to climb back on. Instead, he hangs on to the side, the lower part of his body submerged in the lake.

The others grab him and try to haul him on board, but he's soaking wet and unresponsive—deadweight. They implore him to help, but he doesn't seem to hear them. He's willed himself back to the raft, but he has nothing left to give. He's now on the clock: unless a ship arrives and rescues them very soon, he will succumb to hypothermia.

Gary Strzelecki grabs one of Meredith's arms, and Frank Mays takes the other. They hang on with all their flagging energy, to keep him from slipping away. The next wave is on them, pulling them up. The men hang on. If there's anything worse than the uncertainty, it's the reality that tags along behind it. They might not make it.

There are three basic stages of hypothermia—mild, medium, and severe— and Dennis Meredith is hovering between the last two. His body temperature has dropped dangerously low. He's exhausted, barely conscious. He's moved past the point of caring, beyond suffering, and he's now in a place where no one on the raft would blame him for just taking a lungful of water and drifting away.

By all rights, he should have lost his battle with hypothermia by now. Even in the heat of the summer, the Great Lakes are colder than the average swimmer can tolerate for any longer than a few minutes; divers need wet suits to withstand the water temperatures. By November the waters have cooled to such an extent that a person couldn't realistically expect to survive any longer than a couple of hours. In some respects, Dennis Meredith has already beaten the odds. In others, it's only a matter of time before they beat him.

In its simplest definition, hypothermia sets in when someone's body core temperature falls below 95 degrees Fahrenheit. Air and water temperatures play the most critical roles in establishing how quickly this occurs, but fatigue and a person's size, age, and physical condition also are factors. The three men on board the raft are all in danger of hypothermia, but since water cools the body up to twenty-five times faster than air, Dennis Meredith is in exponentially worse shape. He's barely dressed and partially submerged in water—a lethal combination. The fact that he's thin doesn't help, either. Fleming and Mays are a little huskier than Meredith and Strzelecki, and any extra insulation matters in times like these.

Every flip of the raft costs the men valuable energy. Heat escapes from their bodies just from the exertion of fighting the waves and swimming back to the raft. By huddling together on the raft, they conserve minimal heat, but even this has a limit. The elements are starting to get the better of them.

Dennis Meredith must have wondered, at some point earlier in the evening, before his thoughts turned entirely to survival, what he was doing out here, as far removed as he could ever imagine from a youth spent on a farm in Metz Township, a tiny, rural community about eleven miles south of Rogers City. Like many farmers in the northern part of lower Michigan, the Meredith family grew potatoes, and you couldn't be much more connected to the land than that.

George Meredith, Dennis's younger brother, would remember it as being a tough life. His parents had moved to Detroit, where most of his father's family resided. His father had taken a job at an auto plant, and when he found that Detroit didn't agree with him, he moved everyone back up north and purchased the farm. If the hardships and uncertainties of farming didn't test the family's mettle, tragedy surely did. Two of the Meredith kids died, one from spinal meningitis and another from pneumonia, one at age two and the other at three. "My dad had to ride on a horse to Alpena to get medication for the one little guy," George recalls. "That's a fifty-mile ride. By the time he got back, my brother had died."

According to George Meredith, youthful pleasures were simple or even silly, such as the time he and Dennis wondered what it would feel like to be shot. The two brothers did a lot of hunting together, and one day, while they were out hunting rabbits, they decided to check it out.

"We knew what guns would do, and we tested the distance," George says. "It was just fine shot from a twelve-gauge shotgun, and we knew at that distance it wouldn't really be dangerous. He sat on a stump and pulled an old navy mackinaw over his head. I went back so far and I blasted at him. I go, 'What did it feel like?' He said, 'It's like little pebbles falling on me.'" George laughs at the insanity of it all. "That was in our younger years," he says, "before we had to go to work."

For hours, Elmer Fleming has shouldered the responsibility of leading. He took command of the raft and encouraged the other three men, pleading with them not to fall asleep and leading them in counting exercises to see that they wouldn't. The others looked to him for strength, and he'd obliged to the best of his ability.

But he's really not that different from them. He's colder and weaker than he ever thought he could be, and while his resolve is still very strong, it's been tempered considerably since his first hour on the raft, when he was certain his distress message had been heard and rescue was only a short time away. Staying alive is becoming intolerably difficult. The last time the raft had flipped, he'd come back to the surface beneath the raft. The waves fought his efforts to swim his way out, but he'd found a way . . . but for what? The sight of Dennis Meredith, hanging on to what little life he has left in him, depresses him immensely. He's put himself through more than any-one should have to endure, with no assurance of anything but the crushing certainty that he would suffer more. And for what? To die in an hour? Two hours?

And what is his, Elmer Fleming's, obligation to this young man, or to the other two lying on the raft near him? When can he cease being a leader and concentrate solely on staying alive himself?

Fleming barely knows the three men sharing the raft with him. In this way, he's no different than other officers who don't make a policy of fraternizing with nonofficers. Fleming is old-school that way. He couldn't care less about his popularity, as long as his subordinates do their jobs. He might share a joke or shoot the breeze with the wheelsman on his watch, or have a word or two with one of the deck watches, but he prefers to keep to himself.

These men on the raft—this is another situation entirely. These are men fighting the same battle. As far as Fleming knows, these are the only survivors of the most harrowing experience of his life.

He will help them if he can.

Dennis Meredith's life ends as the other three men feared it would, with the young *Bradley* crewman still in the water, still clinging to the side of the raft. Any chance of his surviving ended with the disappearing running lights of the *Christian Sartori*.

Frank Mays notices first, when he sees Meredith's face still in the water after the raft has negotiated another wave. Mays reaches down to pull Meredith's face out of the water, but it's too late. Meredith's eyes are rolled back in his head; he is gone. Mays catches Gary Strzelecki's attention, and the two, without uttering a word, release Meredith's arms and let him drift away. His body will never be recovered.

Moments like these make you think about the others. Aside from the four on the raft, thirty-one men had either gone down with the *Bradley*, jumped when they'd had the chance, or been hurled into the lake when the ship started to plunge. How many, if any, are still out there? You want to believe that some of them made it, that, as unlikely as it may seem, they've been able to pass the minutes and hours the same way as you: staring ahead, marshaling every bit of energy into the difficult process of just staying conscious. Poor Dennis had given it his best, but it wasn't enough. How many others had fallen this way?

And what time is it, anyway? How many hours are left until dawn?

THE *SUNDEW* FINALLY ARRIVES AT THE SEARCH AREA—ABOUT TEN miles south-southwest of Gull Island—at 10:40 P.M., four hours and twenty minutes after its departure from Charlevoix and more than five hours after the sinking of the *Bradley*. To the men on board the Coast Guard cutter, the trip to the site seems to have taken much longer. Captain Harold Muth has plotted a course that placed the *Sundew* in a trough for most of the trip, exchanging comfort for a little added speed. No one on the crew underestimates the task ahead. It's too much to expect anyone to have survived in the water—not in the time it's taken the *Sundew* to reach the scene, not in these weather conditions. With any luck, though, some of the *Bradley* crew might have launched a lifeboat. Finding them in such a storm, in total darkness, is another matter altogether.

Muth can see the *Christian Sartori*'s lights in the distance. The vessel is patrolling an area dimly lit by red flares dropped on the lake by the Albatross, which has arrived back on the scene. The *Sartori* has been zigzagging around the area of the *Bradley*'s last radioed position, but Muth is skeptical that the German ship's efforts will yield any success. With the wind still blowing at sixty miles per hour out of the southwest, Muth figures that anything on the water should be drifting toward the small archipelago of islands to the northeast.

It's hard to determine the best place to search. The *Sartori* is combing the area where Captain Paul Mueller and others estimate they saw the flares, but from what Muth heard during one of the radio transmissions, there is some confusion over where the *Bradley* actually went down. Another ship, the *Harvey Brown*, although nowhere near the scene, disputes the unofficial coordinates. The *Brown* crew claims that radio transmissions stated the *Bradley* went down twelve miles *northwest*, rather than southwest, of Gull Island. If this is the case, any lifeboat would have drifted well north to northeast of the island. Muth prefers the coordinates supplied by the crew on the *Sartori*, who, after all, actually witnessed the sinking. Either way, though, as far as Muth can tell, the search should be somewhere north of where the *Sundew* is at the moment.

Muth assumes command—and the headache—of coordinating the search. He's been in touch with the *Sartori*, off and on, since the *Sundew* left Charlevoix, and also has spoken to Ray Brunette at the radio station in Port Washington. The search efforts are beginning to take shape. The *Robert C. Stanley*, a U. S. Steel ore boat originally waiting out the storm near Garden Island, has pulled up its anchor and headed south. It's now near the southern portion of Beaver Island, awaiting further orders. Other ships, including the Coast Guard cutter *Hollyhock*, are on the way.

The *Sartori* has been searching for hours, taking a horrible pounding in the process, and Captain Mueller is anxious to resume his trip to Chicago. The search has already cost him in time he doesn't have, and he can only guess at what his ship's rolling has done to his cargo. Muth hopes the *Sartori* will stick around a little while longer. Besides the benefit of having an additional ship engaged in the search, there's comfort in knowing that there's another vessel nearby, in the event that something goes wrong. The *Sartori* is under no obligation to stay, but Muth talks Mueller into assisting with the search until the *Hollyhock* arrives.

The *Sartori*, the two captains decide, will remain in the area while the *Sundew* searches in a pattern that, in time, will take it farther north.

"I conducted what we call a ladder search," Muth explains. "You try to figure out the drift line for anything that could be in the water—it's pretty much to the northeast—and make a ladder search, which is back and forth. We worked our way within a couple of miles of the sinking, and worked from there up in a line towards Gull Island."

Muth would later state that, by his estimation, the storm was reaching its peak about the time they were reaching the search area. The *Sundew* continues to take a lot of water over its decks, adding to the difficulty of the search, but the real trick, according to Muth, is in making turns on waters hitting the *Sundew*'s stern. Muth uses the same approach he took while guiding his boat out of Charlevoix: move the boat into the turn at normal speed, and give it a kick once in the turn, to get the boat turned around as quickly as possible.

As trying as conditions are for the *Sundew*, Muth is more concerned about the welfare of the Albatross. In this storm, the wind shear has to be incredible.

"I worried about those guys in the airplanes more than I did about the people on my ship," Muth says. "When I saw the conditions out there, I was glad to be on a ship and not in an aircraft. They were dropping flares. I could see the flares, but I didn't know where they were when they dropped them, because the wind would take them almost sideways."

Because he's working shorthanded, Muth has to improvise. Crewmen are pressed into services they don't normally perform. Finding men who aren't seasick is a priority. Warren Toussaint qualifies, as does Richard Selison, the *Sundew*'s cook. Muth assigns Toussaint to direct the searchlight while others gather at the pilothouse windows. The wind blows spray and spume almost horizontally, and the air is so thick with water that the lookouts can't tell if it's raining, snowing, or just blowing spray. Visibility is spotty, depending on where you're looking.

"It wasn't too bad if you were looking at a distance," Muth remembers, "but we couldn't see beyond the capabilities of our searchlight. You had a wall of water in front of you most of the time, and you're either going down or climbing up a wave. When you got on top of one, you could see beyond the next wave, but that's about all."

Toussaint finds manning the spotlight exhausting, edgy work. He's terrified by the ferocity of the storm. Most of all, though, he's frustrated by the futility of the search. "We didn't see a confounded thing," he says. "We didn't see bodies, we didn't see wreckage—we didn't see *anything* until daylight."

The *Hollyhock* joins the search at about 1:30 A.M., after seven very difficult hours in transit. Moving northeast from Sturgeon Bay, Wisconsin, to the search site involved sailing with a strong tailwind, which, under other circumstances, might have meant a smoother ride. In the mind of James Cropper, the *Hollyhock*'s skipper, the trip was like "a visit to hell."

"It was the roughest sea I ever saw, and I've seen quite a few," he'd tell the press the next day. "At times, the pitching and the rolling and the valleys were so deep it looked like the water had disappeared and was going uphill in front of us."

Harold Muth, for one, is relieved to hear from the *Hollyhock*. The *Sundew* is still working its way north but has yet to come across any sign of the *Bradley*. After talking to Captain Mueller on the *Sartori*, Muth dispatches the *Hollyhock* to the northeast, giving the search as broad an area of coverage as possible.

Convincing the *Sartori* to stick around takes all the persuasive powers Muth can muster. Captain Mueller had agreed to remain in the area until the *Hollyhock* arrived, but now that it's here, Muth is on him to stay even longer.

"He thought I was playing games with him," Muth remembers. "I said, 'Well, how about another half hour?' 'I'm sorry,' he said, 'but I'm really worried about getting to Chicago and getting back. I don't want to be locked in on the Great Lakes all winter long.'"

Muth persists, and despite his misgivings, Mueller relents. He agrees to stay another hour.

Elsewhere around the Great Lakes, from as far away as Cleveland to as nearby as Traverse City, plans are being made for an all-out search commencing at first light. The National Weather Service is calling for the storm to diminish by daybreak, and the Coast Guard is eager to send out as many aircraft, including helicopters, as possible. Naval and air force bases volunteer search planes, while commercial boats in the area, now at anchor, agree to venture out after the seas have quieted.

Bradley Transportation and Michigan Limestone officials, meanwhile, coordinate efforts to notify the families of the *Bradley* crew. Only eight months ago, in March, Bradley Transportation had thrown a gala party to celebrate the milestone of the company's going one thousand days without a disabling injury—a first in the history of marine transportation companies. Now the company is dealing with another first: prior to tonight, the fleet had never lost a ship.

Officials know, before they call or visit their first home, that families are likely to cite corporate greed as the reason for the *Bradley*'s loss. There will be resentment, anger, shock, and sadness.

What can they tell these families? That they should hold out hope when, realistically, there is little chance that the crew is still alive? That they should prepare for the worst when no one at the company has the slightest proof of a single loss of life? If they tell the families the truth—that at this point, they know nothing more than that the *Bradley* is missing—they will be suspected of withholding information or covering up the truth. This is a shipping community, and while nothing like this has ever happened before there, sailors and their families understand the risks involved in the work.

In most cases the crewmen's immediate families have already heard the news, either on the radio or from others. They know as much as company officials. Nevertheless, the personal calls must be made or, in the case of the out-of-staters—Roland Bryan, Ray Buehler, Richard Book, and John Zoho—someone has to go through the horribly impersonal process of notifying family members over the phone.

Even so, it's not a fail-safe procedure. Doug Bellmore, for instance, has remarried and listed his current wife as the person to notify in the event of an emergency. Bellmore's kids, however, live with his former wife, Alfrieda.

"I didn't know he was on the *Bradley* at the time it went down," Alfrieda says today. "I had no idea until later, when they started naming names. I think that's when my children heard about it—when it came on the radio. I wasn't notified because he was married to the other lady. She got the message, I didn't, although the kids should have been considered. They probably didn't even know the kids lived with me."

The officials cannot visit every single member of the different families, so they rely on word of mouth in the notification process. They will visit or call the person listed as the crewman's emergency contact and hope that that person, usually a wife, will spread the word.

Most of Paul Greengtski's family, for instance, live on a potato farm in Posen, and the fact that they live outside Rogers City isolates them from hearing about the *Bradley* right away. Greengtski was married and had a small child, and his wife is the person the company visits. The Greengtskis don't learn about their son and brother's fate until the next day. The delay affects thirteen people—Paul had six brothers and five sisters—close to the victim. When they finally do receive the news about the *Bradley*, the Greengtski family will join all the other families in hoping that he somehow found a way to one of the islands. His body, though, will never be recovered.

Norma Toussaint can't sleep. She lies in bed, listening to the radio and the sounds of the storm outside. Reports on the *Sundew* come in sporadically, but there usually isn't any new information to add to the previous report.

It's been this way all night. After dropping Warren at the Charlevoix lifeboat station, Norma and the kids returned home and finished their interrupted dinner. By the time they'd eaten and cleaned up the dishes, it was time for the kids to go to bed. Norma turned in early herself, but worry and the storm have kept her awake.

The storm is powerful enough on land. The wind howls relentlessly, snapping off tree branches and rattling windows. Intermittent rain pelts the area. Norma knows that her husband is facing much worse on the water. Realizing that she won't be getting sleep anytime soon, she brings the radio into bed with her. One by one, all three of her kids, frightened by the storm, join her.

The reports aren't encouraging. It seems to take all night for the *Sundew* to reach the site of the wreck, and then the man on the radio announces that the station has lost contact with the boat. This terrifies the children even more. At ages three, five, and seven, they aren't old enough to comprehend everything they are hearing, but they know enough to understand that their father is in danger. Norma finally sends them back to their own beds.

She maintains her vigil, dozing off from time to time, until she hears that the radio station has reestablished contact with the *Sundew*. Once she learns that the *Sundew* is holding its own and that the storm is expected to dissipate shortly before daybreak, she allows herself a few hours of sleep.

William Meredith, the youngest of the Meredith brothers, is waiting at the dock in his brother George's new Volkswagen when the *Munson* comes in. George hurries to the car, and the two head to their parents' farm to wait for further news about the *Bradley*. The wind, still quite heavy, nearly blows the small car off the road.

As residents of Metz Township, the Merediths are isolated from the activities in Rogers City. The personnel director at Michigan Lime had driven out to the Merediths to tell the family that the *Bradley* had sunk, that ships were searching for survivors, but that so far nobody has been found. The Merediths make coffee and, like families all over northern Michigan, sit by their radio and wait for the next report.

Back in Rogers City, Marlys Mays collapses when she learns about the *Bradley*. Her husband, she's convinced, would never last in the kind of storm that's been lashing the area. A doctor stops by and administers a sedative. The doctor has been so busy that the city has made a police department squad car available to drive him from house to house.

The Benjamin Strzelecki household deals with the possibility of the tragedy's affecting both of their children. Gary's wife, Ann, has been sitting with them throughout the evening. Ben Strzelecki's daughter Mavis is married to wheelsman Ray Kowalski.

Strzelecki, who sailed himself at one time, has been hoping that his son would go into business with him at the end of the current shipping season. Gary has been looking for a way to buy a house; move his family out of his parents' home; and, in the words of his father, "get his family on its feet." Ben Strzelecki knows now that there is a strong possibility that his five grandchildren will be losing their fathers tonight.

In still another household keeping a vigil, Mary Fleming tries to stay upbeat. Her husband, she tells some of the many people dropping by to offer support, is an outstanding officer and seaman. If anybody can survive a disaster of this proportion, he will be the man.

But she's also a realist. Earlier in the evening, after hearing about the *Bradley*, she pulled her fifteen-year-old son aside.

"Douglas," she told him, "your father may not be coming back to us."

TIME AND THE EFFECTS OF ENCROACHING HYPOTHERMIA STEAL Gary Strzelecki's resolve. Just a few hours ago, he'd been the life raft's tower of strength, boosting the other three men's spirits, watching for rescue boats, shouting out warnings whenever a massive wave rolled toward the raft, and helping Dennis Meredith in his final hours.

The loss of Dennis Meredith has chipped away at his morale. The *Sartori*'s not seeing them was bad enough, but that was only the beginning. The raft lost its sea anchor the last time it flipped, meaning a much rougher ride in the waves and a constant reminder of the prospects of another dip in the lake. At one point the Coast Guard Albatross dropped a flare near the raft, and on another occasion the men had seen a search ship in the distance. Neither means much now. No one was going to see the raft until after daybreak, and the presence of potential rescuers, rather than buoy spirits, seems like an especially cruel twist of fate. The air temperature has fallen into the twenties, and the men are still continuously doused with water and spray, which, in these temperatures, freezes on their clothing. Ice forms in their hair. The men squeeze together as closely as they can; they breathe on each other for warmth. They grip the slippery wooden slats and ride the waves.

No one has any idea what time it is. Frank Mays had grabbed his watch when he and Gary Price rushed to their quarters to retrieve their life jackets, but even if the watch was still running, there's no way Mays can read it now. It's too dark. Mays holds fast to his belief that everyone will be picked up if they survive until morning. It must be getting close to daybreak, he tells himself; they've been on the raft for hours.

Fleming and Mays work together in prodding Strzelecki to stay awake. They talk to him, encourage him to count along with them, and use some of their waning strength to massage him. "Don't go to sleep," Fleming tells him. "It won't be long."

Exhaustion has been beating down the three men for hours, but they now find themselves exploring an unfamiliar landscape: the treacherous terrain between falling asleep and losing consciousness. With sheer determination, Strzelecki might be able to fend off exhaustion and stay awake; he might not, however, be capable of fighting off hypothermia. Wherever he is, his world goes black. Mays, alerted by his snoring, shouts him back awake. Then it begins again, the process of Mays and Fleming's trying to keep Strzelecki conscious.

It's an exercise in futility. Shortly before daybreak, when the sky has lightened enough to outline the previously disappeared horizon, Strzelecki breaks out of his stupor and begins talking nonsensically about making a swim for shore. The other two try to reason with him, but Strzelecki, his face void of expression, hears nothing. He drags himself across the surface of the raft, flailing his arms and legs as if he believes he's already swimming in the water. Mays and Fleming lunge at him. They clutch his legs and clothing. They hang on to him as best they can, but neither is strong enough to hold him down. Strzelecki's adrenaline propels him to the edge of the raft.

Strzelecki slides off the raft and starts swimming. Mays and Fleming shout at him, but lost in the waves sweeping him away, he quickly disappears from view.

Land!

The sky is growing lighter by the minute, and Mays, peering out at the eastern horizon, sees what looks like a bump rising out of the water in the distance.

"There's an island over there!" he shouts.

Elmer Fleming struggles to his knees and strains to verify it for himself. It *appears* as if something is out there, but Fleming is wary of getting his hopes up. Only a short while ago, he and Mays had seen what Fleming thought was a plane. Mays believed it was a seagull. It had been at such an altitude that neither could tell for certain—until, that is, they spotted lights. It was a search plane, all right, but it was so distant that they could never have signaled it. It disappeared almost as quickly as it appeared.

The spot on the horizon grows larger as the raft drifts toward it. There's no doubting that it's a sizable chunk of land rising out of the lake. The men can make out the shapes of trees.

Seeing an island makes no sense to either man. According to Elmer Fleming's calculations, the *Bradley* had gone down about twelve miles southeast of Gull Island, and even farther from the other islands off to the east. They'd spent a night on some unbelievably turbulent seas, but could they have possibly drifted this far?

Fleming, familiar with the group of islands clustered in the area, tries to figure which island it could be. Looking around, he can see another small island behind them. The smaller island, Fleming believes, is Trout Island. The larger one they're moving toward must be High Island. Unfortunately, the way the raft is drifting, they're likely to move beyond the island and back onto open water.

The two men watch the island come painfully close—within sixty yards, as Mays would estimate later.

Mays wants to make a swim for it. All he wants is to get off the raft and on to dry land, where they can build a fire and wait for a rescue vessel. As he would admit years later, he "wasn't being realistic."

Fleming still has enough presence of mind to recognize the folly of leaving the raft. On a good day, in warmer water, with all their strength behind them, the two could easily swim the distance between the raft and the island. On this morning, however, they're now so weak they can barely pull themselves into a kneeling position, let alone push their cramped muscles into such a swim. God only knows how far Gary Strzelecki was able to go after jumping in the water a short time ago—and he was a much better swimmer than either of them. Besides, suppose, through some kind of miracle, they made it to the island. What would they use to build a fire to keep warm and alert rescue ships or planes? Neither of them has dry matches. How long would they survive without proper shelter? Would anyone ever find them?

No, it's getting light and rescue vessels will be looking for them on the lake, not on land. Hard as it is to believe, they're better off on the raft. With any luck, they'll have to hold on only a little longer.

RICHARD SELISON, STANDING WATCH ON THE *SUNDEW*'S BRIDGE, looks through his binoculars, out onto the horizon. There's something out there, though he's not sure what it is. The wind has died down measurably, but the seas are still at twenty to twenty-five feet, and whatever the *Sundew*'s cook is looking at rises into view with the waves, only to disappear when it drops back into a trough.

"Captain," he says to Harold Muth, standing nearby, "I see something up ahead."

"Where?"

"Almost dead ahead." Selison points to the spot.

Muth scans the area through his binoculars. Sure enough, something is out there, about a mile off the bow. But what is it? At first it looks like a small boat with two men. Muth figures it's probably just a couple of crazy deer hunters marooned overnight on High Island during the storm, now trying to make their way back to Charlevoix.

One could forgive the *Sundew*'s skipper for being cautious, if not skeptical. The boat's night on Lake Michigan has yielded very little other than a pilothouse full of exhausted, nauseous men. Once, in the early-morning hours, the lookouts spied what appeared to be a white life jacket carried on the waves, but it quickly moved out of the spotlight. Muth had ordered the wheelsman to turn the *Sundew* around for another look, but nothing turned up. The search continued. Later, with daylight approaching and more vessels joining the search, Muth decided to move the *Sundew* to an area between High Island and Gull Island. Muth still believed that this would be the direction any wreckage from the *Bradley* would have drifted.

Now the hunch appears to have paid off. Muth trains his binoculars on the object on the water in the distance. It's a little closer now. It suddenly becomes clear to Muth that he's looking at the orange barrels of a life raft, not a boat. Two men, wearing life jackets, are sitting on it. Muth orders the wheelsman to steer the *Sundew* in its direction.

He then sends a crewman belowdecks to summon Warren Toussaint. If the men on the raft are from the *Carl D. Bradley*—and Muth can't imagine where else they could have come from—they're going to need immediate medical attention.

Elmer Fleming sees the Coast Guard cutter first.

The raft has just drifted beyond High Island when Fleming spots a ship over Frank Mays's shoulder. It seems to be heading in their direction.

"There's a boat out there!" he shouts.

Mays turns for a look. After a night of disappointment and frustration, after dealing with the *Christian Sartori*'s coming so close, only to miss the raft and move on, after seeing other search vessels in the air and on the water, passing nearby and not seeing them, Mays guards his optimism like a precious stone. He has prayed to his God all night, as Elmer Fleming has prayed to his, but is this approaching vessel the answer to their prayers?

Mays can tell, from the boat's black hull and white lettering, that he's looking at a Coast Guard vessel. It appears and disappears as the raft rises and falls in the waves, but it's definitely moving toward them.

The men can only hope that the crew on the Coast Guard boat has seen them. There's no way to signal the boat—no flares or any other means—and Fleming and Mays are too physically depleted to even wave at it. They can only sit on the raft and wait.

"The Old Man wants you on the buoy deck immediately, Doc. We have two survivors."

It takes a moment for Warren Toussaint to open his eyes and grasp what the young *Sundew* crewman is saying. He'd been up most of the night, directing the *Sundew*'s spotlight, fighting the utter physical exhaustion brought on from handling the spotlight, bracing himself against a rolling boat, and battling the stress of an increasingly futile search. When Captain Muth finally sent him below for some sleep, Toussaint had stretched out on a bed in the *Sundew*'s sick bay. The brief respite, his aching muscles tell him, is not enough. It's shortly before eight thirty in the morning.

Toussaint moves to the buoy deck as quickly as his body will allow. The *Sundew* has substantially cut the distance between the raft and the rescue ship, and by the time Toussaint reaches the deck, the raft is about five hundred feet away. Captain Muth fills him in on the sighting and the *Sundew*'s rescue plans, predicting that Toussaint probably will have quite a job ahead. "If you need anything, just ask," Muth says.

Removing the men from the raft, Muth realizes, could be hazardous. The *Sundew* is still rolling heavily in the waves, yet it must maneuver close enough to the raft to allow Mays and Fleming safe transfer from raft to ship. Muth orders the wheelsman to position the *Sundew* parallel to the raft, a safe distance away, and let the raft drift up to the boat. Crew members, all wearing life jackets, lower cargo nets over the boat's side.

The raft eventually reaches the *Sundew*, but the two *Bradley* survivors are too weakened to leave the raft on their own. They can neither stand nor lift their arms over their heads.

A new plan is quickly drawn up, calling for two of the *Sundew*'s more agile crewmen to drop to the raft, secure it to the *Sundew*, and hoist Mays and Fleming to crewmen positioned on the cargo nets. Every man involved in the maneuvers has a rope tied around his waist, connecting him to the ship. With the *Sundew* rolling the way it is, it wouldn't take much to lose a man overboard.

Captain Muth has wisely placed the raft in the lee of the *Sundew*, easing the wave action on the raft, but there's still enough undulation to endanger the rescuers. The raft and the *Sundew* rise and fall in the waves but rarely move in unison. At times, when the *Sundew* is in a trough and the raft is riding the crest of a wave, the raft is almost at deck level with the *Sundew.* When the process is reversed, it looks as if the Coast Guard cutter might crush the raft beneath it. The men on the cargo nets run the risk of being caught in between.

Fortunately, the crewmen pull off the transfer without a glitch. Two men drop to the raft, tie it to the *Sundew*'s rail, and wait until the waves bring the raft almost even with the *Sundew*'s deck. They pass Mays and Fleming from the raft to the men waiting on the cargo nets, and from there they are hoisted on deck. For Fleming and Mays, what just happened won't make sense until later; at the moment, they are too cold and exhausted to do anything but submit to all the movement around them. The official time of the rescue is 8:37 A.M. The two survivors had been in the water almost exactly fifteen hours.

Warren Toussaint is ready to take over. He and several *Sundew* crewmen have been busy fashioning a makeshift hospital room out of the chief petty officer's quarters. Crewmen have brought stretchers and blankets to the deck.

Transferring Mays and Fleming from the deck to the room belowdecks involves a kind of awkward choreography. The *Sundew*'s deck is wet and slippery. This, combined with the motion of the boat's rolling, concerns Captain Muth. The two survivors have taken enough of a beating on the raft; the last thing they need is to be dropped on the deck. Muth assigns several crewmen to each survivor, to carry Mays and Fleming in a straddle position to the awaiting stretchers. Each man takes one of the survivor's limbs. They lift the two and shuffle gingerly across the deck.

Fleming and Mays, although conscious, are almost totally dazed. They realize that they've been rescued, but after fifteen hours of struggling to stay alive, they seem stunned by the fact that they actually accomplished the feat. Their eyes, Toussaint notes, are "dark," and they're speechless from exhaustion and the almost dreamlike quality of their rescue.

The two men, though, are in much better shape than anyone might have

On July 28, 1927, the *Carl D. Bradley*, newly fitted out and ready for work, made her first appearance, to great fanfare, at her home port near Rogers City, Michigan. (Presque Isle County Historical Museum)

Carl D. Bradley, founder of the Bradley Transportation Company and Rogers City benefactor, for whom the ill-fated ship was named. (Presque Isle County Historical Museum)

33 MEN WHO WENT DOWN WITH THE 'BRADLEY'

ERHARDT FELAX   JOHN FOGELSONGER   RAY BUEHLER   BERNARD SCHEFKE   WILLIAM ELLIOTT

FLOYD MacDOUGALL   ALVA BUDNICK   ALFRED BOEHMER   MIKE JOPPICH   DOUGLAS BELLMORE

KEITH SCHULER   EDWARD VALLEE   JOSEPH KRAWCZAK   RAYMOND KOWALSKI   EARL TULGETSKE

Crew mug shots. (Presque Isle County Historical Museum)

JOHN ZOHO

PAUL HORN

ALFRED PILARSKI

MELVIN ORR

GARY STRZELECKI

LEO PROMO

JOHN BAUERS

CARL BARTELL

CAPT. ROLAND BRYAN

RICHARD BOOK

JAMES SELKE

DUANE BERG

PAUL GREENGTSKI

PAUL HELLER

MARTIN ENOS

DENNIS MEREDITH

CLELAND GAGER

GARY PRICE

Aerial view of the Port of Calcite and quarry works of the Michigan Limestone and Chemical Company, 1961. (Presque Isle County Historical Museum)

The Bradley Transportation Company fleet, laid up on the Frog Pond: (left to right) *Calcite*, *W. F. White*, *Irvin L. Clymer*, *Carl D. Bradley*, *John G. Munson*, and *T. W. Robinson*. (Presque Isle County Historical Museum)

The Bradley Transportation Company boats were known for their huge A-frames and booms used to unload cargo. Pictured here is the *Carl D. Bradley* unloading into a hopper at Peerless Cement in Detroit, 1955. (Presque Isle County Historical Museum)

The *Bradley* was the first ship to pass through the MacArthur Lock in 1943. (Presque Isle County Historical Museum)

The *Carl D. Bradley* on the St. Marys River, near Lake Superior. (Presque Isle County Historical Museum)

The *Carl D. Bradley* (left) was the largest ship on the Great Lakes for twenty-five years, until the *John G. Munson* (right) was launched in 1952. (Presque Isle County Historical Museum)

Elmer Fleming, the *Bradley*'s first mate and one of the shipwreck's two survivors. (Presque Isle County Historical Museum)

Harold Muth, captain of the *Sundew*. (Harold Muth)

USCGC *Sundew*, a 180-foot vessel, braved the storm to search for survivors of the *Carl D. Bradley*. (Harold Muth)

Warren Toussaint, shown here with the *Bradley*'s recovered starboard lifeboat. (Warren Toussaint)

The crew of the German freighter, M/V *Christian Sartori*, witnessed the sinking of the *Carl D. Bradley* from a distance. Despite the fierce weather conditions and a tight shipping schedule, the *Sartori* stayed in the area, searching for survivors for more than nine hours after the loss of the *Bradley*. (Ralph Roberts Collection)

(*Presque Isle County Advance*)

Frank Mays, one of the *Bradley* survivors, is carried to a makeshift hospital room onboard the *Sundew* shortly after his rescue.
(*Presque Isle County Advance*)

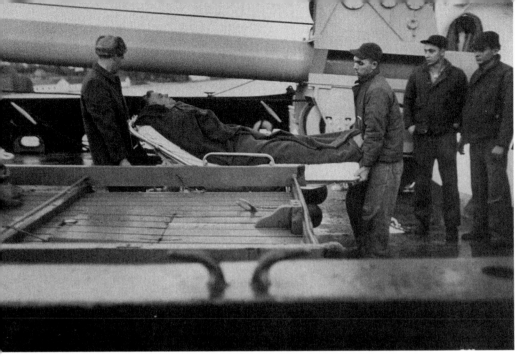

Elmer Fleming carried off the *Sundew* after the Coast Guard cutter's arrival in Charlevoix. Note the life raft in the foreground. (Art Shay, Getty Images)

The *Bradley*'s life raft, in Calcite a few days after the rescue of Elmer Fleming and Frank Mays. (Presque Isle County Historical Museum)

St. Ignatius Catholic Church was designed to look like the long limestone carriers that gave Rogers City its identity. (Dennis Meredith)

The center aisle of St. Ignatius, lined with nine caskets containing the bodies of lost crew members, on November 22, 1958. (*Presque Isle County Advance*)

In 2007, divers John Janzen and John Scoles removed the *Bradley*'s original bell and replaced it with a replica bearing the names of the ship's lost crewmen. (This page, all; and opposite, bottom: Alan Williams and John Janzen)

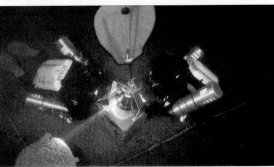

John Scoles, Frank Mays, and John Janzen with the recovered bell. (Alan Williams and John Janzen)

The wreckage of the *Carl D. Bradley*, in two pieces on the floor of Lake Michigan, as depicted by marine artist Robert McGreevy. (Robert McGreevy)

The pilothouse door of the sunken *Carl D. Bradley*. (Alan Williams and John Janzen)

A lakeside park memorial to the crews of the *Carl D. Bradley* and *Cedarville* lists the names of the lost crewmen and serves as a reminder of Rogers City's maritime history. (Top and bottom: Dennis Meredith)

A scene depicting the breaking apart of the *Carl D. Bradley*, engraved on Dennis Meredith's headstone, is a poignant memorial to a valiant crewman whose body was never recovered. (Dennis Meredith)

expected. Their faces are badly swollen and their lips are blue; they've suffered bruises and scrapes from their battering on the raft; they are all but encased in a thin layer of ice. Still, they show no evidence of frostbite. When Toussaint takes their temperatures, Elmer Fleming registers at 99 degrees, while Mays checks in at 99.4 degrees. Their extremities are swollen and they have no feeling in their hands and feet, but they have minimal control of them.

Toussaint requests the assistance of eight crewmen, who help him remove Mays's and Fleming's wet clothing and dry them off. The crewmen are then assigned to an arm or a leg, which they massage to stimulate circulation. Within minutes, Mays and Fleming have returned to the land of the living.

Meanwhile, up on the *Sundew*'s spar deck, coast guardsmen use the ship's boom to hoist the life raft—and, so far, the only remaining physical evidence of the *Carl D. Bradley*—out of the water. The raft has traveled almost seventeen miles from the site of the sinking.

Ten minutes after being carried down to the *Sundew*'s makeshift hospital room, Fleming and Mays insist that they're well enough to give Captain Muth a formal statement about the sinking and their travails on the lake. The two men are already alert, much warmer—and very hungry. Warren Toussaint, believing that anything, solid or liquid, will upset their stomachs, turns down their request for food, promising something hot to drink a little later. Fleming and Mays are adamant about another request: rather than return to Charlevoix for medical treatment, they would prefer to see the *Sundew* continue to search for their crewmates.

After making their statements, Fleming and Mays ask Muth to notify their wives of their rescue. They also repeat their request that the *Sundew* stay out and search rather than head back to Charlevoix. Muth confers with Toussaint. The men, Toussaint says, appear to be in good enough shape to stay on the lake.

Back in the *Sundew*'s wheelhouse, Muth considers the rash of recent events, how so many hours of frustration have culminated in good news for at least two families in Rogers City. Mays and Fleming had been on the bow of the *Bradley* when it went down. The stern had been equipped with two lifeboats. Maybe other survivors are still out there . . .

It's time, Muth decides, to let the Rescue Coordination Center in on the good news. His message is terse and to the point: "Picked up two survivors on raft, 71 degrees, 5.25 miles from Gull Island."

It's 9:15 A.M., nearly sixteen hours after the *Bradley*'s breaking apart, and fifty minutes after the *Sundew*'s sighting of the raft.

While the crew on the *Sundew* celebrate their discovery of two survivors, other search vessels move through the remnants of the storm. The storm's center has pushed into Canada, leaving behind winds of much lesser velocity. Coast Guard, army, navy, and private planes are in the air. It's finally safe to deploy helicopters. It seems that every boat or plane within radio distance is involved in the search.

At 9:17 A.M., two minutes after the *Sundew* transmitted its uplifting message about finding two survivors, a helicopter spots an overturned lifeboat about a mile south of where the *Sundew* had picked up Elmer Fleming and Frank Mays. As soon as the helicopter sends word of its discovery, the *Sundew* heads to the site. The *Sundew* edges its way up to the lifeboat, and crew members check beneath it for bodies or unconscious survivors. They see nothing. From the looks of it, the boat was never used.

Captain Muth wants the lifeboat brought aboard the *Sundew*, but his crew's efforts to pull it out of the water are cut short when a helicopter radios with bad news: a body has been spotted on the water just northeast of Gull Island.

DAWN BREAKS OVER ROGERS CITY WITH MOSTLY CLOUDY SKIES, diminishing winds, a hint of snow in the air, and heavy seas still breaking over Lake Huron's shores. Some of the town's residents have been up all night, waiting for further news about the *Bradley*. Others gave up and called it a night when they realized that nothing new was likely to happen or be announced until morning. It was best to try to catch a couple hours of sleep before getting up for work.

Rogers City has never been confronted by a disaster of this magnitude, and people aren't sure how they're expected to react to it. The town prides itself on its structured, principled lifestyle; there's an order to even the most mundane of activities. For instance, today is a Wednesday, which means the men and women go to work, the children to school. It's all very uncomplicated, which is exactly the way the citizens of Rogers City prefer it.

Despite the enormous emotional weight crushing the community, the residents try to bear up. The kids go to classes, as usual; their parents go to work. Some of the family members of the *Bradley* crew remain at home, but this proves to be more difficult than if they'd somehow been able to find a way to distract their thoughts with work. The *Bradley* story hangs in the air, in muted conversations, in the sounds of whispered prayer, in the silence of hope still holding despair at bay.

It also hangs in the heavy presence of the news media. Reporters and photographers began arriving last night, within hours of the news about the *Bradley*'s breaking apart. Rogers City, accustomed to receiving its local news in a weekly paper, suddenly finds itself at the epicenter of a huge, breaking national story, besieged by reporters from daily and weekly newspapers

from all around the country. Television and radio stations send representatives. Stringers and staff writers from out-of-state publications, including
Time and *Life* magazines, check in. A nation is now prepared to watch a
city's every reaction to every bit of news, good or bad.

A lack of a definitive conclusion to the story only makes it more compelling. Elmer Fleming's and Frank Mays's names aren't immediately released when the story breaks about the *Sundew*'s picking up two survivors,
leaving thirty-five families hopeful, first, that one of the two survivors might
be their loved one, and second, that more *Bradley* crew might be found
alive. Nor are individual names offered later in the day, when the Coast
Guard begins picking up victims. The uncertainty all but devours the town,
and the media take notice. Reporters are everywhere—in the bars and
restaurants, at City Hall, at Michigan Limestone and the gates of the dock,
on the street, in the *Bradley* families' homes, even on the sidewalks outside
the schools.

Richard Allgire, head of public relations at Michigan Lime, tries to accommodate the onslaught of reporters from a makeshift media headquarters in Rogers City, but he, too, is caught in the waiting game. Michigan
Limestone, U. S. Steel, and Bradley Transportation Company officials have
been arriving in town since late last night, but most of them have either
been visiting the families of *Bradley* crewmen or holed up, waiting for
news, in the "guest house" at the plant. The reports that Allgire does receive are confusing, incomplete, contradictory, or downright inaccurate.
Shortly after Captain Harold Muth's radio transmission about survivors, six
different stations around the Great Lakes reported the recovery of two survivors, leading to a short-lived misconception that *twelve* survivors had
been picked up.

The *Presque Isle Advance*, the weekly newspaper serving Rogers City,
helps handle the national media. The paper's offices have been flooded
with calls from New York, Chicago, Cleveland, and other cities across the
country, all looking for news or feature material. The publication's tiny
staff briefs callers on the search, information on the *Bradley* and its crew,

the Michigan Limestone and Bradley Transportations companies, and background on the city. Harry Whiteley, the *Advance*'s publisher, opens his offices to out-of-town reporters, giving them use of the paper's type-writers, telephones, and anything else they might require for filing their stories.

For Rogers City, the influx of reporters, photographers, and radio and television news stations presents a logistical nightmare. This is a town so small that it takes note of just a handful of new visitors—occasional tourists, out-of-towners passing through during hunting season, and recreational sportsmen and fishermen taking advantage of Lake Huron and the area's natural beauty. It's not a town brimming with a wealth of lodging facilities or rental car lots. The nearest cities capable of accommodating the kind of numbers Rogers City is now looking at are Alpena to the east and Traverse City to the west. One Rogers City car lot owner, in an effort to ease the transportation logjam, offers the use of his cars to the press and Michigan Limestone company officials coming in from out of town.

School-age children, from kindergarten through high school, sort through the confusion around them. Classes are interrupted by news reports and, later, the appearance of principals pulling students out of class to give them bad news about their fathers. Classmates of the children of the *Bradley* crewmen are stuck in the awkward position of trying to sympathize with their friends and slaking their unquenchable thirst for more details on the most dramatic local news story of their lives.

By midmorning, the dreaded news is finally starting to break: the Coast Guard boats searching out on the lake are beginning to pick up bodies of the crew of the *Carl D. Bradley*.

The city braces itself for the worst.

Marlys Mays is prepared neither for the news that her husband is one of the two survivors or for the rush of reporters turning up at her front doorstep. Before she'd met Frank Mays, the former Marlys Bush lived in Waterloo,

Iowa, a small town as far removed from the focus of national attention as one could imagine.

Being a sailor's wife and running a household eight or nine months a year are challenging enough for the mother of three kids under age five; dealing with the stress of the past day has taken her through every possible emotion, from the shock of hearing about the loss of the *Bradley*, to the despair of just knowing her husband had been lost, to the elation of finding out that Frank has been found alive, to the sadness she feels when she learns that others haven't been as lucky as her husband. A doctor's sedative helped her get through last night; it's likely she'll need another tonight.

Marlys and her kids—an attractive twenty-three-year-old mother and her cute little boys—are the perfect subjects for the type of news feature that reporters in these parts will wait for years to come around: they look good on camera; they are a heartening story in the midst of overwhelming tragedy; and they possess the kind of down-home innocence you most often found in a Norman Rockwell painting. Photographers corral the entire group for family pictures. One shutterbug lifts the baby out of his crib and plops him in his mother's arms for a picture. Flashbulbs go off from all sides of the Mays living room.

Marlys has her mother, who happens to be visiting Rogers City, and several friends around her for support, but none of these people knows how to handle the press. Marlys does the best she can in answering a flood of questions while she waits for someone from Michigan Lime to pick her up and take her to Charlevoix. The questions are as flat and predictable as any reader might expect, as are the answers. Interviewers and interviewee are anxious to get the business over as quickly as possible—the interviewers so they can file their stories on deadline for the next day's papers, Marlys so she can just put the experience behind her. Yes, she says, she's absolutely thrilled that her husband is alive. Yes, she feels horrible that other wives and mothers aren't getting the same good news. No, she doesn't want to see her husband going back on the lakes after all this has blown over.

"I never want Frank to go back to the ship," she declares. "I'll die if he does."

Mary Fleming, addressing the same questions a short distance away in her home, offers the same types of answers, although she isn't as adamant as Marlys Mays on the topic of her husband's returning to work on the stone boats.

"It's his life," she tells reporters. "His heart is in it. I'll do whatever he wants."

Like Marlys Mays, Mary Fleming has had plenty of support throughout the past twenty-four hours, with friends and neighbors dropping by to offer an encouraging word and sit with her. Two of Elmer's sisters have driven up from Detroit, and one of Elmer's brothers, Harold Fleming, a former steward with the Bradley Transportation fleet and currently a restaurant owner in Rogers City, is nearby. Mary's faith might have been bolstered by all the support, but what it ultimately boils down to, she tells the press, is her belief in her husband's abilities.

"I know how strict he and the captain were about boat drills," she says. "I knew if courage and seamanship could do it, my husband would survive."

By midmorning, Rogers City is contending with a crippling collective feeling of dread. Now that it's been revealed that the Coast Guard is picking up victims, the crewmen's families, a fairly tight-knit circle only a couple of days ago, find themselves in a horribly sensitive position—each family must hope that its loved one has survived, which, in the glare of brutal reality, ultimately translates into a need to believe that the victims are from other families. These are not people who, by nature, fall prey to denial, nor would they ever dream of wishing hardship on someone else, but hope and its bastard second cousin, desperation, leave them in a precarious emotional state. To those not directly related to the *Bradley* crew, the wait for official release of the victims' identities is less excruciating—but not by

much. As the hours go by and more victims are recovered, it becomes clear
to everyone, from the citizens of Rogers City to the press covering the
tragedy to those hearing about it in remote locations throughout the state,
that the entire town will be touched, in one way or another, by the loss of
the *Carl D. Bradley.*

"When you look at a boat as large as the *Bradley*, you get the feeling that
it's impossible for anything to happen," Mayor Kenneth Vogelheim says.
"then you look at the chance there will be more than twenty widows in
Rogers City, and you know the impossible has happened."

Years later, when describing the days following the loss of the *Bradley*,
people will remember thinking and worrying about the crewmen's children. What could their mothers and relatives have told them? What would
become of them? The older ones, of course, have a better understanding of
what's happening, but with such understanding comes another level of
suffering. The younger ones only know that their fathers are missing—if, in
fact, the issue has been addressed. All told, there are fifty-six children affected; two other *Bradley* wives have children on the way.

Eleanor Tulgetske, wife of *Bradley* wheelsman Moe Tulgetske, symbol-
izes what the families are going through. Elly is strong and intelligent, the
mother of four, ranging in age from one to six. The Tulgetske name is a familiar one on the stone boats: Moe, who joined the fleet on July 3, 1945,
has other relations working on the Bradley fleet.

Moe is typical of the men working on the stone boats. He's not particularly
enamored with the work, but it pays better than anything else available in the
area. He'd left Rogers City for a spell and taken a job at the Buick plant in
Flint, but it hadn't been a happy experience. Its only positive outcome was
meeting Elly. "I'm going back to the boats," he told her shortly after meeting
her, less than six months after moving to Flint. "I'd rather be on the boats
than in the factory any day."

One suspects that the work wasn't the only thing enticing Tulgetske back
to his old hometown. Flint has never been mistaken for a mecca for outdoor
sports, and aside from his wife and family, Moe Tulgetske loves hunting and

fishing above all else. His father taught him how to hunt, and he'll set out for the woods at every available opportunity. The same with fishing—if the boat is coming in, his gear had better be waiting in the car when Elly and the kids come to the dock to pick him up. When the *Bradley* was laid up over this past summer and Tulgetske was working as a watchman on the boat, he would even fish while he was on the job. He'd drop a line over the side of the boat and fish off the *Bradley*. "He'd come home with these wonderful filleted perch," Elly remembers.

As Elly recalls, Moe enjoyed bringing his family with him when he went fishing.

"We'd do it together as a family," she says. "It's funny. I said to him, 'You can't work all week long in the winter and then go hunting or fishing on Saturday and Sunday. You've got to spend some family time.'" The thought amuses her. "His idea of family time? Take the whole family and go ice fishing.

"But it was more than fishing," she continues. "We'd build a bonfire on the ice and race around. Then, when we'd see one of the tip-ups going, everybody would run for it and see what was on it. In the summertime, he'd take the kids to the dump. When they were in port, we'd always have our stuff ready and he'd take every single one of the kids to the dump. His kids were everything in the world to him."

Now she faces the obligation of telling these kids something about their father's fate. The problem is, she knows nothing for certain. Her frustrations began last night, when she placed repeated calls to the company gate, only to hear the same message—"We still have it coming in at two in the morning"—even though everyone in Rogers City already knew the *Bradley* had sunk. Things haven't improved today. She still hasn't heard from the company, and she's weary from the emotional ups and downs; from the knowledge that survivors have been picked up but not knowing who they are; or who, for that matter, the victims are.

Her frustrations reach a tipping point when the press finds her house. She's trying to busy herself with housework, catch the news updates on the radio, carry on conversations with well-wishers dropping by, and take care of her children. The unannounced arrival of a reporter, now standing in her living room with his notebook at the ready, frazzles her.

She hasn't even spoken to her children about their father, and now she is expected to share her story with a world that has edged its way into her life.

She talks to the reporter for a while. In the papers, she will be attributed with one of the better-known quotes to come out of the *Bradley* story, a quote that will be repeated for decades: "I always watched the boats, and I knew the town lived by them. Now the town is dying by them."

It's a nice quote, she'll admit, except for one major problem: she never said anything remotely similar to it. It makes good copy, but it's not correct.

It is, however, a strong practical lesson on how legends can spring from misconceptions or fabrications. The quote has now publicly connected her to the story.

ANY ELATION THE MEN ABOARD THE *SUNDEW* MIGHT HAVE FELT in finding two men alive on a raft is tempered by the discovery of the bodies of dead *Bradley* crewmen. As inevitable as this was from the onset of the search, it's still depressing work. Aircraft of all sorts, from military to civilian, have been searching since daybreak. When they spot a victim, they assist the *Sundew* by circling over the crewman and dipping a wing to indicate the body's location.

The men have drifted in a northeastern direction toward Gull Island. Most are floating fairly close together, in an area stretching out over a hundred yards. All are wearing life jackets, and all are in the same position in the water, their legs drawn up in a fetal position, their arms extended, their heads down. Some have drowned, either as the result of ingesting water from the huge waves or from inhaling water-saturated air. Others succumbed to hypothermia. A couple broke their necks as the result of whiplash when they hit the water. One suffered severe head injuries when he hit something—probably the raft—when he was thrown off the boat.

Retrieving the victims is difficult work. Once again, cargo nets are dropped over the side of the boat. Whenever possible the *Sundew* pulls up next to a victim, and the boat's crew, positioned on the netting near the waterline, pull the body from the water. When the boat cannot be positioned close enough for the men to reach a victim, a boat hook is used to snag the unfortunate *Bradley* crewman by the life jacket. With the added water weight, the victims are heavy and difficult to pull out of the water. The hard labor is matched only by the emotional burden attached to it.

Some of the bodies have drifted into water too shallow for the *Sundew,* so Captain Muth orders the lowering of the *Sundew*'s ramp boat. He places Warrant Boatswain Jack Coppens in charge of the operations.

"We had four guys in the boat," Coppens remembers, noting that while the wind had died down some, there still was enough heavy moisture in the air to make visibility limited. "The ramp boat was kind of like a landing barge, with a front end that drops down. We had a hard time lifting [the victims] over because we had to lift them over the side, which was about three or four feet. They were very heavy."

They recover five bodies before returning to the *Sundew*. It's Warren Toussaint's job to inspect each of the victims. He isn't authorized to legally pronounce someone dead, but he checks each man to verify that there are no signs of life. He then retrieves the man's watch, wallet, and other personal effects and places them in a large envelope.

The wallets identify each man, but to the crew on the *Sundew*, the victims' clothing provides clues to the lost lives of their fellow sailors. John Zoho's pockets, for instance, are stuffed with the $1,500 he'd retrieved from his room before heading to the deck of the sinking ship, and he is still in the white clothing he wore in the galley. Another of those recovered is wearing the kind of gray shirt worn by the engine-room crew. Several are dressed in light clothing, indicating that they might have been on watch at the time of the *Bradley*'s splitting in two and, as a result, had less time to prepare for the sinking than others. With nowhere to place the *Bradley* crewmen belowdecks, the men on the *Sundew* carefully line them up on the buoy deck, where they will remain until they are taken off the boat in Charlevoix.

The *Hollyhock* goes about the same dispiriting business, with a slightly different approach. A rescue swimmer drops into the water to assist with the recovery of a victim. While picking up the *Bradley*'s lost crewmen, the men in the *Hollyhock*'s pilothouse continue to scan the waves for evidence of the *Bradley* itself. Aside from the lifeboat spotted earlier, very little else has drifted into the area.

By one o'clock that afternoon, the *Sundew* is ready to return to Charlevoix. Frank Mays and Elmer Fleming have developed fevers, and Warren Toussaint, concerned that their rise of temperature might indicate the onset of pneumonia, advises Captain Muth to bring the *Bradley* survivors to a hospital. Mays and Fleming, although eager to see their families, would prefer for the *Sundew* to stay out a little while longer, but they're overruled. Muth calls the *Hollyhock* and puts its captain and crew in charge of the search.

A few minutes later, at 1:14, the M/V *Transontario*, a German freighter searching near the western shore of High Island, transmits a radio message that rekindles hopes of finding more survivors. A private plane patrolling the area has discovered a crewman floating face up and directed the *Transontario* to him. The *Bradley* crewman has been carefully brought on board.

"Man may be alive," the *Transontario* radios the Coast Guard station in Charlevoix. "Please rush a doctor!"

When they learn about the survivor, Mays and Fleming grill the *Sundew* messenger for more details. What does he look like? What is he wearing? The answers lead them to the same conclusion: it has to be Gary Strzelecki. Somehow he's managed to beat the overwhelming odds and stay alive after leaving the raft—an amazing feat given the fact that he'd been the water a good 4 to 4½ hours beyond the time when Mays and Fleming were rescued from the raft. Neither Mays nor Fleming would have doubted Strzelecki's toughness and resolve, or his swimming capabilities, but in surviving this long, he'd defied nature itself. He's barely alive, Mays and Fleming are informed, but they hold out hope for him.

The two survivors begin another round of serious praying.

The Coast Guard plots another rescue operation.

Dr. Frank E. Luton, a retired physician living in a remote resort area on Beaver Island, is the closest doctor to the *Transontario*, but getting him on board the German ship is going to take a great deal of skill, daring, and good fortune. He will need to be transported by helicopter to the *Transontario*, and then, like a scene out of a movie, be lowered by harness to the deck of a ship still rolling considerably in choppy seas. The doctor's descent to the deck will be further complicated by heavy winds. He could be dropped on the deck; dumped into the water; or, in an unlikely but possible scenario, blown into the helicopter's rotor blades.

The seventy-nine-year-old doctor volunteers for the duty as soon as he's contacted.

While the Coast Guard rushes a helicopter to Beaver Island to pick up Dr. Luton, the *Transontario* crew works desperately to keep Gary Strzelecki alive. His breathing is shallow and he barely registers a pulse; he's in shock from spending more than nineteen hours in the elements. The men on the *Transontario* follow the same procedures employed by Warren Toussaint when he began his initial treatment of Elmer Fleming and Frank Mays. They cut off the survivor's clothing, wrap him in warm blankets, and massage his extremities. They apply artificial respiration whenever Strzelecki appears to be drifting away.

A helicopter already out searching for *Bradley* victims is dispatched to Beaver Island, and Dr. Luton is ready when it shows up. During the ten minutes it takes the helicopter to reach the *Transontario*, Dr. Luton is briefed on the mission plans. He is fit into a harness and life preserver. The helicopter arrives and positions itself over the *Transontario*, hovering as close to the deck as it dares to go. Dr. Luton moves to the doorway.

Just as he's about to step through the doorway, a voice comes over the helicopter's radio, calling for the men on the helicopter to abort their mission. Gary Strzelecki has just passed away.

The *Transontario* moves on. When the ship reaches its destination—Milwaukee—Captain Walter Zeplin and his crew hold a brief on-deck ceremony and salute the last *Bradley* victim as he is turned over, wrapped in an American flag, to Coast Guard authorities. He'll be returned to Rogers City and his family for burial.

Captain Muth knows what awaits the *Sundew* upon its arrival in Charlevoix. People, he's been informed, started turning up at the docks last night, and hundreds more have been streaming in throughout the day. The *Sundew* has eight *Bradley* crewmen lined up on its buoy deck, and two survivors below, all subject of great speculation and concern. The press is going to demand every last detail of the search-and-rescue mission, at a time when all Muth would like to do is climb into bed and get his first bit of sleep in thirty-six hours. At this point he's resigned himself to whatever duty demands. He's just been through a series of events that, for better or worse, will follow him for the rest of his life.

Warren Toussaint, between monitoring the conditions of Elmer Fleming and Frank Mays, and overseeing the identification of *Bradley* victims, is emotionally spent. He's wept quietly at the sight of the lost crewmen, he's tried to allow himself hope for the discovery of additional living crewmen, he's rejoiced at seeing two survivors, and he's felt great relief in getting through his most fearful night in all his years of sailing. He wants sleep, but almost as badly, he needs a few quiet moments to take stock of everything he's just endured.

It takes the *Sundew* nearly three hours to reach Charlevoix. As the boat nears the channel leading to the docks, Toussaint approaches Captain Muth with a suggestion. The *Bradley* victims, he tells Muth, aren't covered; they will be in full view of those standing on the bridge and other elevated areas near the dock. Maybe they should be covered with a tarp. The onlookers will realize that there are bodies under the tarp in any event, but it's still better than having a family member of one of the victims looking down and seeing his or her loved one exposed on the deck. Muth agrees, and the men are covered.

Muth, the Charlevoix Coast Guard, and the city's police department officials have already conferred and decided that rather than tie up in its usual spot, the *Sundew* might be better off docking at the city pier, which normally services the ferryboats. This will provide better access to the ambulances and hearses already at the scene, and move things along more quickly in transferring the victims and survivors.

Hundreds of people watch as the *Sundew*, its crew lining the rails and its flag in tatters, pulls up to the dock. Police have set up barricades to block the media and onlookers from interfering with the work ahead, but the people standing dockside show no inclination to move. They are eerily quiet, stunned by the physical evidence of a tragedy that only a day or two ago seemed inconceivable.

"I have never in my life seen such a silence," Warren Toussaint would remark later. "Hundreds of people had come from Rogers City—plus the people from the community. They had listened to the radio and knew we were coming in. You could have heard a pin drop. For about an hour, the only sounds you could hear were our engines and the airplanes taking pictures from above."

Norma Toussaint, waiting on the dock to pick up her husband, also remembers the silence. "The families that were waiting said nothing," she recalls. "I was amazed by how silent all the children were. There were many small children there, but they were very silent."

It doesn't take much to pick the family members of the *Bradley* crew out of the crowd. Their anxiety and fears, the effects of a sleepless night, the hard shot of reality . . . all can be read on their faces, in direct contrast to the expressions on the faces of those with jobs to do. A temporary morgue has been set up in the Community Hall of the Charlevoix City Hall. The men responsible for transporting the victims stand silently beside their vehicles.

Dr. Lawrence Grate, Charlevoix's county coroner and a practicing physician, is first to board the *Sundew.* He is immediately escorted to the makeshift sick bay. Warren Toussaint, relieved to be turning over the two survivors to the medical authorities, briefs the doctor on the measures taken after the recovery of Mays and Fleming. Dr. Grate, like Toussaint before him, is surprised by the two men's general condition. He checks their vital signs, and notes their bruises and abrasions, and the heavy swelling of their faces and extremities, but aside from elevated blood pressures and slightly rapid pulses, the two are in remarkably good shape. They show no signs of frostbite, and they certainly don't require additional onboard medical attention.

Sundew crewmen prepare Mays and Fleming for the transfer from ship to ambulance. The two men are wrapped in blankets—Mays in a red one, Fleming in an olive-green one—and placed on stretchers. Meanwhile, other crewmen begin removing the victims from the deck. Using the *Sundew*'s boom, they lift the life raft off the boat and place it on the dock. The crowd gathered onshore, seeing the flurry of activity, presses forward for a better look, but vision is blocked by the tarp that the coast guardsmen hold up to shield the bodies as they are wrapped in blankets and removed.

Mays is the first one out. As they're preparing to move out of the *Sundew* and into public view, Dr. Grate advises him to shut his eyes until he's been loaded into an ambulance. Mays ignores the advice. He recognizes some of the faces in the crowd—family members of his crewmates. He is impressed by the number of onlookers, the reporters and television crews, and the relieved members of the *Sundew*'s crew. The crowd steps back, creating a path to the ambulance.

Within minutes, Mays and Fleming are whisked from the dock to the hospital. Their ordeal has ended, but as both already know, they will be asked to relive it, over and over, in the days—and years—to come.

Warren Toussaint scans the crowd until he locates his wife and kids. He flashes Norma a thumbs up before returning to his station to wrap up his work on the *Sundew*. The *Hollyhock* is now dockside, its crew going through the same grim process of removing the bodies from the boat. Between the two vessels, seventeen *Bradley* crewmen have been recovered. It's dark by the time the *Hollyhock* ties up, lending at least minimal privacy to the proceedings.

Toussaint's workday finally ends, but he won't be going home anytime soon. His wife, still waiting on the dock, is shocked when she sees the shape he's in. "He was exhausted," she recalls. "and I was worried about his general health. I had never seen him with big circles under his eyes, and his eyes were all red from weeping. I could tell he had been tearing up, but he was all business. He said, 'I'm sorry, I cannot come home. We must go out at three in the morning. I'll stay aboard and get some rest.' I was glad to know that he would get some rest, anyway. He gave the kids a hug and that was it."

The press, patient only to a point, clamors for an interview with Captain Muth. The two survivors were rushed off the *Sundew* without so much as a word with reporters, and no one from the *Sundew* is talking. As commander of the boat, it's Muth's job to brief the press on the *Sundew*'s search-and-rescue mission.

Given a choice, Muth could do without the honor. He'll be back in the boat's wheelhouse in fewer than ten hours, preparing for another day's search, and he'd much rather be spending the time at home, winding down and catching some sleep. He certainly doesn't want to be facing a horde of reporters shouting questions from every direction.

Muth provides details of every aspect of his boat's past twenty-four hours, including a description of the storm, the futile search at the site of the sinking, the daybreak fortune of finding two men alive, and the condition of the two men. He describes the way he allowed the *Sundew* to drift to the raft when his crew was rescuing Mays and Fleming. He tries to explain how the two men could have survived for as long as they did, under the conditions they faced, but he's at a loss for words.

"Survival depends on physical condition, the ability to stand exposure, courage, and faith," he says. "They'll tell you that a man couldn't have lived in the water of Lake Michigan yesterday for more than one and a half hours. I remember when I was on duty in Alaska, two men were pulled out of the water after three and a half hours. They lived, and that water's colder than our lakes. Who can say?"

Mays and Fleming, he adds, may have survived because of intangible factors that can't be measured by science.

"They had the will to survive," he states, "and someone was looking after them."

*   *   *

Neither Elmer Fleming nor Frank Mays would dispute the *Sundew* skipper's widely quoted assessment about divine intervention in their survival, although Fleming, deeply troubled by the loss of thirty-three of his shipmates, is cautious when he and Mays meet with the press a couple of hours after they've been brought to the hospital. Fleming, a Presbyterian, allows that he spent much of his night in prayer, and though he believes that his prayers were answered, he refuses to use his religious faith as an explanation for why two men are alive and thirty-three are not.

"The mysteries of religion are beyond me," he tells reporters. "You've just got to believe and that's it. When they say two wives' prayers were answered, what about the other thirty-three? Those other fellows in the water prayed just as hard as us, and their wives prayed all night, same as ours. Why my and Frank's prayers were answered is something we'll never understand."

Less than a day ago, time had been slow-moving and life-threatening. Now, in the warmth of the hospital, with medical personnel standing by and the two men's wives at their side, time seems to be flying by at blinding speed. Fleming and Mays had been examined by Dr. Grate immediately after their admittance to the hospital, and he had concluded the exam by offering the two a shot of whiskey. He'd no sooner left than Mary Fleming and Marlys Mays were brought in for a quick reunion. Before they realized what was going on, Fleming and Mays were whisked in their beds to the hospital's solarium, where a phalanx of reporters and photographers stood ready for firsthand accounts of the events surrounding the loss of the *Carl D. Bradley* and the two men's survival.

As is so often the case, the questions are much easier to ask than to answer. Fleming, in particular, struggles with his emotions, his thoughts weighed down by the grief he feels at the loss of thirty-three fellow crewmen. In time, Frank Mays will become the more vocal spokesman of the two, with Fleming preferring to stay silent on the topic of the *Bradley*, but at this press conference, Fleming does most of the talking. The initial questions, focusing on the breakup of the *Bradley*, require little more than a recitation of facts similar to the statement Fleming dictated to Harold Muth on board the *Sundew*.

"I was in the pilothouse on watch with the captain," Fleming begins. "We heard a thud. Then the alarm bell started ringing. Something spun us around. Then we looked down on the deck. It wasn't hard to see something was wrong. The stern was sagging."

Fleming, with an occasional assist from Mays, tells the press about how the *Bradley* sank and how they found their way to the life raft. When asked if others had made it to the raft, Fleming offers a fictional account that would be reported (and believed) until Mays eventually set the record straight forty-five years later.

"It was terrible," Fleming says of the loss of the two men, without mentioning their names. "We lost the first man about eleven o'clock when the raft was thrown right up in the air. It hit the water upside down and we had to swim to get back on. We lost the other man later, when a big wave hit us."*

Doctors keep the interview mercifully short, limiting it to ten questions. The press wants more, but reporters' protests are going nowhere on this night. The men are wheeled back to their room for their first decent sleep in more than thirty hours.

Ralph Przybyla parks his car and walks to the front door of the Charlevoix City Hall. The front door is locked, the blinds are drawn, and someone has taped paper to some of the windows. Przybyla, a thirty-year-old car salesman from Rogers City, raps on the door and waits.

Joseph Smith, Charlevoix's chief of police, answers the knock.

"I'm here to identify Alva Budnick," Przybyla tells him.

---

* "We had talked earlier and decided that this was not the time to tell the whole truth about Dennis and Gary," Mays would admit in his book *If We Make It 'til Daylight*. "We wanted to tell their families what happened before anyone else. We also knew we had to keep Dennis Meredith's and Gary Strzelecki's identities a secret until their families could be properly notified."

Frances Budnick, Alvy Budnick's wife, is Przybyla's sister.

Smith guides Przybyla to the room where the bodies of the *Bradley* crewmen are being held. The men, covered with olive-green Coast Guard–issue
blankets, are lined up in a neat row, each victim given a tentative ID until
he can be positively identified by a family member. The two men move
over to a body and Smith carefully lifts the blanket, exposing the deceased
man's face.

Przybyla can manage only a nod.

The past twenty-four hours have been extremely difficult for Lewis Patterson and George Jones. Patterson, a district manager for Michigan Lime, and
Jones, a district superintendent for industrial relations with the company,
are among a handful of company officials with the sad responsibility of
making in-person visits to the *Bradley* crewmen's next of kin. They can offer
no hope, no real comfort; they can only deliver news. They've had very little
sleep since receiving word of the *Bradley*'s sinking, and each visit to a new
household, with its horribly depressing scene, adds to a hefty emotional
burden.

This time they're at the front door of Al and Dolores Boehmer's house. Al
Boehmer, the *Bradley*'s second assistant engineer, had been one of the most
popular men among his crew—an easygoing guy with a crazy streak of humor. (One of his friends would recall how, after a night of drinking and
bowling, he'd returned to the ship and, for the sheer hell of it, walked the
length of the deck balanced on one of the ship's railings.) He also was a
top-notch sailor, well versed in engine-room procedures, and destined to
become a chief engineer. "He wanted to get to the top as fast as he could,"
Bob Hein, a good friend, remembers.

Bob had introduced Boehmer to the former Dolores Andrzejewski, a
pretty, vivacious young woman known as "Angie" by her friends. For all of
his bluster around the guys—Boehmer had put in a stretch in the army and
had worked on the stone boats for several years by the time he met

Angie—he could be very shy around women. One night, Bob and Al were hanging out in a hotel bar frequented by young people, and Al saw Angie standing with a small group of friends. Angie had been a classmate of Bob's, and when Al heard this, he told Bob that he wanted to meet her. "The girls slid over in the booth, and we sat down and had a real nice visit. And it took off for them. I was always kind of proud of that." He was amazed when he learned that Boehmer, a strong German Lutheran, was converting to Catholicism so he and Angie could be married. But then again, Boehmer probably would have converted to Hinduism if that's what she had wanted.

Patterson and Jones know none of this. All they know is that Al Boehmer's body has been recovered and brought back to Charlevoix, where it has been positively identified by a company official who knew him. They know that, besides leaving behind a twenty-nine-year-old widow, Al had two sons: a two-year-old and an eight-month-old.

Every visit begins with the same five words: "We have some bad news . . ."

No one takes it well.

Dolores Boehmer is no exception. Like others before her, she doesn't want to believe them. How do they know it's really him? Are they absolutely certain? What happened? Patterson and Jones provide the little information they have. Overwhelmed by the news, Dolores collapses, and Father John Rushman, an assistant pastor at St. Ignatius Catholic Church, is called. He'll stay a long time, trying to offer some sense of spiritual consolation, but in reality he is as much an outsider as Patterson and Jones.

He cannot bring Al Boehmer back.

THE *BRADLEY* STORY MOBILIZES THE STATE OF MICHIGAN. EXPEC-tations of finding missing crewmen alive have receded, and Rogers City now faces the prospects of an immediate future calling for more funerals than its limited facilities can possibly handle, not to mention a more distant future involving families who must go on without their husbands and fathers.

Thirteen of the eighteen recovered crewmen were from Rogers City, and eleven of those worshipped at the Catholic parish of St. Ignatius. Trying to coordinate a mass wake, funeral services, and burials requires an effort involving the families of the deceased, civic and company officials, the clergy, funeral directors, school officials, and a litany of other volunteer workers. All but three of the recovered victims will be buried in Rogers City. The others—Richard Book (Portsmouth, Iowa), John Zoho (Claireton, Pennsylvania), and Carl Bartell (Kalkaska, Michigan)—will be returned to their hometowns for private funerals. In Rogers City, the funeral and burial preparations are conducted under the intense scrutiny of an ever-expanding media presence, and overwhelming grief enveloping an entire community. Even as people scramble to pull everything together, boats are still out on northern Lake Michigan, looking for other crewmen. With fifteen men still missing, the potential for further preparations is very real—and daunting.

Funeral director Pete Gatzke, accustomed to a quiet but steady business, suddenly finds himself pressed into the most demanding task of his career. He's used to comforting friends and neighbors, guiding them through difficult times with a low-key approach that allows the grieving process to play itself out. The *Bradley* funerals, however, are different. There is no time for his usual personal touches. There are just too many dead crewmen.

"Extra caskets are coming in on a truck," he tells reporters, noting that he's already called in three embalmers from out-of-town funeral homes to assist him with the workload. "We've never handled nine bodies all at once before. We'll have to work all night."

A funeral home in Cheboygan pitches in as well. Florists work overtime to prepare flower arrangements for the caskets, churches, and a huge wake being planned for the high school gym. Churches plan their services. Dozens of households volunteer spare rooms to those coming from out of town with a need for a place to stay. A troop of babysitters is enlisted to watch the children of those attending funerals.

Elsewhere in Michigan, civic groups, banks, churches, newspapers, and businesses combine forces to create a number of fund-raisers devoted to helping the families of the deceased. The *Detroit News* establishes a *"Carl D. Bradley* Ship Disaster Children's Fund" and contributes $1,000 to set it up. In the weeks to come, the fund-raiser will collect individual donations as small as a dollar and as large as hundreds of dollars. Ships from all over the lakes take up collections and send in donations. The *Governor Miller*, an ore boat on the Pittsburgh Steamship Line, collects $110 from its crew, while the *Robert C. Stanley*, one of the ships searching for the *Bradley* the night it went down, chips in $712. Michigan Limestone contributes $10,000 to the fund, and the Presque Isle Bank another $1,000. Donations will pour in from across the country, many accompanied by letters of sympathy and support.

One, in particular, will stand out.

It is a homemade card, a single sheet of paper, divided neatly in half. On the left half of the page is a message, printed neatly in a child's hand and signed by four young kids:

Dear Children
We are sending this to you because we are so thankful for our Daddy, and we're so sorry you've lost yours. Love . . .

The contributors print their names below. On the right side of the page, carefully taped, are nineteen pennies and one nickel.

Lake Michigan is quiet. The storm, long gone, has left behind seas quite different from the ones that had racked the lake the previous two days. The waves are still choppy, but nothing in comparison to the walls of water that the *Sundew, Hollyhock, Christian Sartori*, and others had encountered on the night of the *Bradley* sinking. There's still a strong wind, with a dampness to the chilly air, but to Captain Harold Muth and his crew, this is more like the weather the *Sundew* is accustomed to seeing this time of year.

The sun hasn't risen yet when the *Sundew* and the *Hollyhock* leave Charlevoix for another day of searching. There is still an urgency to the work, but with little to expect but the recovery of more victims or the discovery of wreckage, the tension has dissipated. Resignation has replaced anticipation.

The Coast Guard expands its search to include the islands near the site of the *Bradley*'s sinking. A large group of volunteers—one newspaper account estimates 150—dropped off by helicopters and boats on Trout, Beaver, Garden, Squaw, Whisky, Gull, and High islands fan out over the islands, trudging along the shorelines, looking for anything that might have washed ashore, or for indications that someone might have survived the wreck. The searchers, bracing themselves against the raw weather, find no signs of anyone's making it to these desolate islands.

They do find signs of the *Bradley*. Small bits of wreckage and debris have washed ashore on Gull and Whisky islands; a single life jacket is picked up on Gull Island, but no sign of the man who had been wearing it. The southeastern tip of High Island yields better results: several life preservers and the *Bradley*'s capsized lifeboat. Aside from a small dent on its port side, the lifeboat is intact, complete with oars, life jackets, a lantern, a hatchet, and other survival gear. It doesn't appear to have been used.

Planes and helicopters spread out over the water, searching for wreckage, an oil slick—anything that might provide clues about the *Bradley*'s final resting place. So far no one knows where the ship is, other than the rough estimates supplied by Elmer Fleming's Mayday call and the coordinates provided by the *Christian Sartori.*

Very little turns up. For a ship that had been nearly two city blocks long and loaded with all sorts of machinery, tools of the trade, human possessions, and other gear, the amount of recovered evidence is maddeningly slight. The *Bradley* sank very quickly; by all indications, it took almost everything on board down with it.

For fifteen anxious families, awaiting final word on their loved ones' fates, this is the worst possible news.

Marge Schuler refuses to believe that her husband is dead, and she won't permit her three children to believe it, either. Keith Schuler's body is one of the fifteen still missing at sea. It doesn't matter to Marge that no other survivors have been found, or that it would have taken nothing less than an act of God for anyone to have survived in the elements for the past forty-eight hours. Marge believes that Keith must have found his way to one of the islands, and that he'll come walking through the front door again, just as soon as someone finds him.

"We're going to live as if your father is coming home tomorrow," she instructs her kids, and for years to come, that's exactly how it goes. She leaves the porch light on every night, and his clothes hang in the closet where they'd been the day he last left the house.

People around Rogers City would remember Keith and Marge Schuler as a storybook couple—good-looking, madly in love, lots of fun. Keith liked to kick back and strum his guitar. Marge, blessed with a better-than-average singing voice, would sit in with bands visiting the area. Both liked to go out dancing. According to the kids, Keith had an inventive nature that found him tinkering around the house, building the family's first television set from a kit—"the first channel we got was from Canada, but mostly we got the test pattern," DuWayne Schuler remembers—or making homemade fishing lures out of old spoons and Marge's tossed-out costume jewelry.

"I think my dad just wanted to be an up-north family guy, and that's pretty much what he was," DuWayne says.

The boats were not Keith's first choice of occupation. A decorated World War II vet, he'd worked in a lumber mill near Millersburg after the war, and he drove a milk truck for a while. With a young family and the need for a larger income, he'd moved everyone to Rogers City and taken a job on the stone boats. He worked in the engine room and, true to nature, he pushed himself into advancing in the engine-room ranks. He'd set a goal of becoming a chief engineer, and to achieve this, he attended classes during the off-season and learned as much as he could to move in that direction. As the *Bradley*'s third assistant engineer, he was well on his way.

Still, he made it clear to his sons that he didn't want them following his example.

"He wasn't crazy about working on the boats," DuWayne recalls. "He felt that it took him away from his family too much. He certainly told me that he would be disappointed if I didn't do something other than working on the boats."

Keith's uncle, Chick Vallee, had told his son, Barry, the very same thing.

Vallee's body had been recovered near Gull Island. On the night of the sinking, Chick's wife, Frances, had come over to the Schulers' house, and the two families sat together, supporting each other and fighting off despair. When Chick's body had been recovered and taken to Charlevoix, Frances's sister, Babe Chain, had been driven by a company official to identify the body. Reality had become constrictive enough to squeeze the life out of two families.

As the Schuler kids remember, it was a time of shaken faith. All three—DuWayne, Randy, and Jane—had gone upstairs after hearing the news about the *Bradley*, and all three had dropped to their knees by a couch and prayed, but their prayers had gone unanswered. Their uncle, one of the nicest guys they'd ever know, also was gone.

What's left, if you can't believe that your dad is coming home from work?

Jane, the youngest, cannot fathom the idea that she might never see her father again. In the months following the loss of the *Bradley*, her weight balloons, and she loses interest in school. She's always been proud of her schoolwork, and whenever her father's boat was coming in, she'd gather up her school papers and show them to him. He would praise her for her good work.

It doesn't matter anymore. From this point on she will tear up her papers before she gets home.

When Barbara Orr hears the initial reports about the *Bradley*, she briefly entertains the notion that her husband, Mel, might not have been on the boat. It's happened in the past. Mel was always the last one to board, and by Barbara's thinking, it's entirely plausible that he might have missed the boat and been left behind when the *Bradley* pulled out of Cedarville a couple of days ago.

When she learns otherwise, she turns her hopes elsewhere. Although he doesn't know how to swim, Mel has a knack for getting out of tight jams. He managed to survive having two ships shot out from under him during World War II, when he was serving in the navy in the South Pacific. What were the odds of something like that happening?

Mel didn't think much of it. "If it's my time, it's my time," he'd tell Barbara whenever the dangers of his job were brought up.

As it is, if it wasn't for his passion for hunting, Mel wouldn't have even been on the *Bradley* in the first place. It wasn't his boat. He'd switched ships so he'd be free to go deer hunting with a couple of buddies from Wisconsin. The original plan, before the *Bradley* received her last-minute orders to pick up another load in Rogers City, was for Mel to jump off the boat in Manitowoc, catch a ferry across the lake to Ludington, and meet Barbara there. Everybody's hunting gear would be waiting, ready to go at the house.

This time, though, Mel isn't going to survive a sinking ship. Barbara knows this. She knew as much last night, when her father heard the news on television and came running over to tell her about it, and then, a little later, when the minister stopped by. The Orrs have three kids—two girls and a boy—and since Mel's body hasn't been picked up, Barbara allows her children a little hope.

The reporters annoy her. They've been by the house, asking questions about matters that, in Barbara's view, are none of their business. Although she and Mel have lived in Rogers City long enough to know the way news and gossip travel, they've never gotten totally comfortable with it. Mel had worked in Detroit for a while, just to get away from a town that he felt was "too little for him," but he'd missed the laid-back lifestyle. If the circumstances were different, he wouldn't have stood for all the nosy reporters. Barbara is sure of that—so certain that she eventually hires an attorney to keep the press from her and her kids. There has to be a line between public interest and private grief.

The U.S. Coast Guard conducts formal inquiries into all major losses on U.S. waters, and the sinking of the *Carl D. Bradley*, the largest ship to go down in the Great Lakes, calls for an all-out investigation.

The process involves the establishment of an official, four-member Board of Inquiry, which seeks to determine, first, the cause of the accident, and second, what if anything might be done to prevent a similar accident in the future. In such investigations, witnesses called to testify usually include surviving crewmen from the accident, eyewitnesses, experts in ship design and construction, inspectors, company officials, sailors who had served on the lost vessel, dockside workers who loaded or unloaded the boat—anyone who can offer authoritative opinions on how or why the accident occurred.

It's a demanding process with numerous built-in pitfalls. Perhaps most daunting are the legal implications swirling around the board's hearings and findings. The hearings are crawling with lawyers waiting to hear just the right word or phrase necessary to assign blame and launch lawsuits. Conversely, officials from the company owning the vessel are not only hoping to avoid crippling litigation, but they also would like to find a way to recoup some of the company's losses. Family members of lost crewmen, desperately seeking explanations for how something like this could have occurred, follow the proceedings, if not in person, then through their attorneys. Reporters sniff around for new angles to a story that's losing its impetus.

The loss of the *Carl D. Bradley* is estimated at $8 million, making it the most costly shipwreck in Great Lakes history. The loss of thirty-three men—the greatest loss of life on Lake Michigan since the Armistice Day storm of 1940—adds another dimension to the investigation: to the layperson, there is no price that can be placed on a human life; attorneys, on the other hand, have no such limitations.

The Board of Inquiry feels pressure not only to get it right, but to get it right *quickly*. Investigators prefer to interview their witnesses as soon as possible after the accident, while the events surrounding the accident are still fresh in their minds, and before attorneys have the chance to coach or, in extreme cases, stash away the witnesses.

On Thursday, November 20, Vice Admiral Alfred C. Richmond, commandant of the U.S. Coast Guard, appoints a Board of Inquiry consisting of Rear Admiral Joseph A. Kerrins, Commander Charles E. Leising Jr., Lieutenant Commander Garth H. Read, and Commander Joseph Change. The panel will meet for its opening session the very next day, in the Presque Isle County Courthouse in Rogers City—the same day that the town begins its official mourning.

ON A TYPICAL FRIDAY AT CITY HIGH SCHOOL, KIDS GATHER IN the hallways between classes. They gossip or shoot the breeze, flirt with one another, talk about classes, or make plans for the upcoming weekend. It's a noisy place, with its own energy.

On this Friday, however, the halls are quiet. Classes have been canceled, and final preparations are under way for an event unlike anything the school has ever seen—a mass wake for the recovered victims of the *Carl D. Bradley*. A sense of disbelief still hangs over the place. A year ago at this time, Jim Selke, one of the missing crewmen, walked these very halls and starred on the basketball team. A few years before that, Gary Strzelecki played on the same team. Today, mourners will file by his body in a silent gym.

The crewmen's caskets, open for public viewing, are spread out in neatly spaced rows. Mourners snake their way through the gym to pay their respects. Flags decorate the caskets, and a beautiful white floral anchor, emblazoned with "Farewell, Shipmates" in red roses, stands on the stage, flanked by two American flags. The men will lie in state until early evening, and then the nine Catholic members will be transferred to St. Ignatius Church, where a similar showing and a holy hour will take place in the parish auditorium. This promises to be one of Rogers City's longest days.

People arrive early and, soon enough, the gym is filled with mourners of all ages and religious affiliations. Mourners appear stunned, almost unable to speak. When they do speak, it's to offer condolences to the families of the lost crewmen, or to quietly reminisce about the men in the caskets before them.

A few blocks away, on the second floor of the county courthouse, the Coast Guard's Board of Inquiry opens its initial hearing into the loss of the

Carl D. Bradley. The meeting is sparsely attended. An attorney representing Elmer Fleming is present, as are two Cleveland-based attorneys representing the owners of the ship. Norman Hoeft, general manager of the Bradley Transportation Company, opens the hearings as the first witness, and during his extensive testimony he provides a complete, detailed physical description of the *Bradley* from bow to stern, pilothouse to engine room. Such testimony tends to be dry, but crucial in an investigation of a ship downed as the result of structural failure. The board will take a very deliberate approach in examining the *Bradley* from every conceivable angle, from its construction to its performance history, from inspection procedures to day-to-day operations on the boat.

The unspoken issue is Captain Roland Bryan's culpability in the sinking, whether he jeopardized his vessel and crew by taking them out in the storm. The commerce vs. nature disputes are age-old, dating back to the old wooden boats that transported goods between ports in the nineteenth century. Sailors will tell you, somewhat cynically, that going out in a bad storm is never a problem as long as the ship doesn't sink, or that a quickly welded patch on a ship's hull is perfectly fine as long as it doesn't spring a leak. No one wants to go out in a nasty storm, but it's done all the time. The Bradley Transportation Company's safety record, until the moment of the loss of its first ship, was excellent. Still, both the company and Roland Bryan knew that the *Bradley* was ripe enough to require major repair work over the winter layup, which begged the question: Was the *Bradley* up to the task of taking on the storm on November 17–18?

Even as the Board of Inquiry works toward answering this and other questions, the *Sundew* and the *Hollyhock*, along with a helicopter and the Coast Guard Albatross, continue a search that the Rescue Coordination Center in Cleveland is all but ready to abandon. The searchers would love to find the missing crewmen and provide a sense of closure to their families, but from a realistic standpoint it's getting tougher and tougher to justify the costs and man-hours presently devoted to a mission that isn't going anywhere. Today is no different. No victims are recovered, no evidence of the

Bradley turns up. By the time the day ends and all those searching have returned home, the Coast Guard office in Cleveland will have decided to cut future air searches to one flight per day.

News about the loss of the *Bradley*, when delivered to crewmen's relatives living outside the state of Michigan, leads to quick, spontaneous travel arrangements.

Don Selke, stationed at a Marine Corps base in San Diego, hears about the *Bradley* after his mother calls his duty officer and leaves a message. Don's brother, Jim, hasn't been found yet, but after holding out throughout the night of November 18 and the better part of the next day, the Selke family has given up hope of seeing him again.

Don lets the news sink in. Like everyone else who's grown up around the stone boats, he never gave a thought to the prospect of one sinking.

"If you go for a boat ride, you come back," he states. "It's just like if you jump in the car and go to the grocery store this afternoon. It's never on your mind that you—or your wife or your brother—may not come back. It's one of those things. Everybody does it. You don't worry about it."

Getting from San Diego to Rogers City turns into an adventure. Don hastily arranges an emergency leave and catches a hop to Chicago. He then takes a train from Chicago to Detroit, and a Greyhound bus from Detroit to an out-of-the-way stop near Tawas City. It's four, five o'clock in the morning, and he's stuck at the side of the road in the middle of nowhere, wearing his Marine Corps uniform and carrying a seabag. He starts walking north and, a short time later, a truck driver, passing through the area, sees him and pulls over. He'll take him as far as Alpena. Don figures he'll hitch a ride in Alpena, with a truck heading west toward Rogers City.

His plans hit a snag when the police stop the truck just inside Alpena. The cop had observed a passenger in the truck, which is against the law. Don tries to explain his plight, but the cop isn't hearing any of it.

"You're going to have to get out," he demands, and once again Don is on

the side of the road with his bag, only this time he has company. The cop follows from a short distance as soon as Don starts walking.

"He paced me," Don recalls. "He followed me from like a block behind me until I walked out of the city limits. He was going to make sure I didn't get another hitch. When I got out where the hospital was, I was able to get a hitch. It wasn't fun."

Janet Enos is in Florida, visiting her grandmother, when she learns about the *Bradley* during a radio newscast. Her brother Marty was on the boat. She immediately packs and books a flight to Detroit, where she is picked up by her uncle. The drive from Detroit to Rogers City, long under the best of circumstances, drags on. Janet and her uncle speculate on Marty's chances of survival. He'd never learned to swim, and Janet relives a conversation she'd had with him earlier in the year, when the *Bradley* was laid up for the summer. He'd wanted her to teach him to swim, but she told him she didn't have the time. She tells herself that it wouldn't have mattered—not in those seas— but she's bothered nonetheless. Almost as heartbreaking is the knowledge that Marty was engaged to be married. The wedding was to take place in January.

Others travel long distances to get to Rogers City, but have an easier time of it. With the assistance of the Red Cross, Don Schefke and Jim Price return to Rogers City to join their families and attend their brothers' funerals. Barry Vallee, stationed in West Germany, hears the news, reports to his first sergeant, and winds up bumping an officer on a flight back to the States. Barry has just turned twenty-one, and only a few years earlier, he'd worked with his father, Chick, on the *Bradley*. He'd listened to his father's fears about the way the *Bradley* worked in storms. Chick didn't want his son working on the boats, and now, as Barry heads back to Michigan, he is forced to contemplate how his father's worst fears had come true.

The wake in the City High School gym is a physical manifestation of the city's grief, but it also serves as a reminder of the nature of sailing itself. You'd see these men around town, especially when the boats were laid up

for the winter, but most of the time they were always on the go, stopping in briefly when the boat was in port, but they were gone often enough and long enough that you spent more time talking to their wives and kids than to the men themselves. They were a different breed, as defined by their absence as by their presence.

Jobs on the stone boats dictate terms of separation, and these terms, under usual circumstances, are tolerable. The men living in and around Rogers City are in port often enough to keep separation anxiety at bay. For three of the four *Bradley* crewmen not from the area, the long periods away from home presented no difficulty at all: Roland Bryan, John Zoho, and Richard Book were bachelors, and they lived the lives of single men.

Ray Buehler was the exception. He and his wife, Frances, had been married for forty years, and they lived in Ohio. Frances would meet Ray whenever the *Bradley* was visiting Lake Erie and had docked nearby, but their separations lasted a lot longer than most other married couples in Rogers City faced, where the men were around every four or five days. Frances had last seen Ray when the *Bradley* visited Cleveland in September. They'd kissed good-bye and that was it.

It had been essentially the same for each of the fifteen men in the gym: they'd said good-bye and never returned. Some kind of spiritual contract— faith itself—had been violated.

It was tough enough when the men were away and an emergency cropped up at home, or a birthday, anniversary, or graduation came and went without a sailor being home to celebrate it with his family. These separations were accepted reluctantly, written off as part of the job.

A crisis, however, underscored the psychological price paid by those who staked their livelihoods in a line of work that kept them away from home.

Helen Berg remembers such a time all too well. Her husband, Jack, had gone to sail on the *Bradley* seventeen days after graduating from high school, and he worked on a handful of boats over the next thirty-seven years. He was away during the most critical time of her life.

"I was pregnant and I lost the child," she remembers. "My baby was stillborn and I almost died. My husband was out in the middle of the lake. The doctor told my sister, 'Call the boat and tell Jack that we can't save the baby, that we'll try to save Helen.' This was on a Sunday. He couldn't make a connection to get home until Monday morning. Can you imagine what must have gone through his mind all those hours? I was fortunate. I survived, but it was still touch and go and he was helpless. I'm not saying this to be gruesome. I was thinking about what *they*—the sailors—go through when something happens. There must be times when they're on that boat, pacing that deck, waiting until they can get off to make the connections to come home for some family emergency.

"When the *Bradley* went down, I said, 'Jack, I think it's time to get off the boats.' 'No, no, no,' he said. 'That's a once-in-a-lifetime happening.' Then, when the *Cedarville* went down in '65, I said, 'It's time.' He said, 'Helen, this is my life. This is the only thing I know.' He had no fear of the water. He loved the water."

Jack Bauers hadn't been in his Rogers City home all that long. A native of Cheboygan, he had been working for the Bradley line since 1950, and had been the *Bradley*'s first engineer for three years but he hadn't moved his wife, Aileen, and their two sons to Rogers City until just a few months ago. He already had his chief engineer's license and, by his thinking, he'd just have to wait his turn. That might take a while—chief engineers had a history of growing attached to their boats and hanging on a long time—but, at fifty-nine, Ray Buehler's best days were behind him, and he was already talking about retirement, maybe after one more season.

Not that Bauers had any special attachment to the *Carl D.*: he'd only been with the boat since August 15. The *Cedarville*, his old boat, seemed more like home, but Bauers had been bumped to the *Bradley* when the *Bradley* was being fitted out for her fall run. Bauers and his family had just moved into this small Hilltop Lane house—a move that seemed to signify a further commitment to the Bradley line.

Jack Bauers disappeared with the *Bradley*, and his family left Rogers City with the word of the boat's sinking. All that now remains is a note, written on the back of a blank check and posted on the front door: *Please do not leave any milk or papers until further notice. Thank you.*

As of Friday evening, twelve hours from the mass funeral services planned for St. Ignatius, fifteen men have yet to be recovered. Their families are suspended in a dark limbo between the living and the dead, between fading hope and outright despair. Even those who have faced the horrible truth that they will never see their husbands, fathers, brothers, or uncles again have to make important decisions about the near future. First and foremost, of course, is what to do about their loved ones. Do they assume these men are gone and, for the sake of closure, plan funerals of their own? Do they wait until the men are officially pronounced dead—a process that could take months? Should they purchase a headstone and place it in a cemetery?

They are like the families of soldiers missing in action.

There is also the issue of what to do about the funerals of those recovered. Should you go to the funerals if your loved one is still missing? At the very least, it's extremely awkward; at worst, it's unbearably painful. It's difficult enough, under the usual funereal conditions, to find something to say to the grieving, but what do you say under these circumstances, where all the deceased lost their lives as the result of the same accident, when you're still holding out for a miracle, or, at the very least, waiting for your own sense of closure? And what do they say to you?

Questions like these make one thing clear: Rogers City may be united in its sense of loss and grief, but when the day is done and the mourners have all returned home, each family of a lost crewman is left with an absence that isolates it from the others; it saps them of their present and leaves them looking at an uncertain future.

NINE CASKETS, DRAPED IN FLOWERS AND FLAGS, AND PLACED END to end, run down the length of the center aisle of St. Ignatius Roman Catholic Church. The caskets contain the mortal remains of Alfred Boehmer, Alva Budnick, William Elliott, Raymond Kowalski, Joseph Krawczak, Alfred Pilarski, Leo Promo Jr., Bernard Schefke, and Gary Strzelecki.

When it was built, St. Ignatius had been designed to look like a ship, in honor of Rogers City's maritime history. It now overflows with that tradition, with the families of the deceased, their friends and neighbors, fellow sailors, city dignitaries, and Michigan Limestone and Bradley Transportation Company representatives, all gathering to honor the souls of nine lost sailors. Father Adalbert Narloch, the parish pastor, estimates that 550 families—almost half the population of Rogers City—worship at St. Ignatius. All of them seem to be here today, along with people from other denominations and cities.

Bishop Stephen S. Woznicki, brought in from Saginaw to celebrate the Solemn Requiem High Mass, stands before the altar and begins: *"In nomine Patris, et Filii, et Spiritus Sancti."*

"Amen."

"Introibo ad altare Dei."

The mourners began assembling long before the Mass's scheduled 10 A.M. start. Mourners are clustered on the sidewalk outside the church in the sunny but chilly Saturday morning air, talking quietly among themselves and waiting for the ceremonial transfer of the caskets from the auditorium to the church. Nine empty hearses, flanked by lead funeral procession cars, wait in front of the church. Many of the vehicles have been borrowed from other funeral homes around the state, some from as far as a hundred miles away.

Rogers City is shut down, the townspeople's attention focused on the burial of their dead. By decree of Mayor Kenneth Vogelheim, the day, November 22, is a day of mourning. Flags fly at half mast on this day, and will continue to do so for the next twenty-nine. From this point on, according to the mayor, every November 18 will be a day of remembrance for the men who perished on the *Carl D. Bradley.* "Economically and romantically, we are proud of our marine history, a story unparalleled anywhere on the Great Lakes," Vogelheim declares. "The *Carl D. Bradley* disaster will forever be a terrible, heartbreaking part of our record."

The mayor's words are merely reflections of what an entire community is feeling. Businesses are shut down, the streets all but empty. Out on the Frog Pond, four stone boats are tied to the docks, abandoned and silent, their crews dismissed to attend the funeral services. Michigan Lime also is closed.

Two thousand people have crowded into the church and auditorium next door, spilling out onto the steps leading into the buildings and down the sidewalks along Third Street. The unseasonably warm temperatures are long gone, and wintry weather is setting in. The churchgoers wear heavy coats, and the women, as per Catholic Church tradition, all wear scarves or hats. The sky is robin's egg blue, but a cold breeze carries sparkling flecks of snow, as fine as tiny grains of sand, in the air. Loudspeakers transmit the sounds of the services for those unable to fit inside the church. Harvey Klann broadcasts the services over the radio for those unable to attend at all.

The services formally began forty-five minutes earlier, with a private closing of the caskets in the auditorium. The caskets, borne by sixty pallbearers and accompanied by the families of the lost crewmen, were then moved in a slow procession from the auditorium to the church. They passed beneath an arch formed by two dozen members of the Knights of Columbus, dressed in full colors and holding crossed swords aloft. The church bell tolled, marking the procession into the church.

"Kyrie eleison . . . Christe eleison . . . Kyrie eleison."

Although this is the largest single service for the *Bradley* crewmen, others will follow. Later in the day, separate funerals will be held for Paul Heller and Paul Horn in St. John's Lutheran Church. (Incredibly, this is the third Heller funeral in the past seven months. Paul's brother John Heller passed away in early April, and another brother, William, died at the end of July.) A private service for Edward Vallee will take place at the McWilliams Funeral Home. Tomorrow, Gary Price and Cleland Gager will be put to rest in Onaway. Other funerals, in Cheboygan and elsewhere, will follow next week.

"There was literally a funeral on every street," Mayor Vogelheim would recall. "The town just couldn't hold all the grief."

The Requiem Mass at St. Ignatius moves at a deliberate pace. The mourners follow along in missals, most unfamiliar with the special Latin prayers said for the dead. Children, dressed in clothes normally reserved for Sundays, follow their parents' leads in standing, sitting, and kneeling, though all but the oldest of them still struggle to sort out the events of the past several days. "Your daddy's in heaven," Eleanor Tulgetske had told her children as a way of explaining Earl's absence, and this is about as far as it goes for many of the kids.

Conspicuously absent from the services are Elmer Fleming and Frank Mays, who will not be released from the hospital for a couple more days. Some of the families of the unrecovered crewmen attend, while others cannot bring themselves to go. It's almost unbearably awkward, this division between those who can find closure with the burial of their loved ones, and those caught in the terrible limbo between vanishing hope and the horrific fear that their loved ones might someday wash up onshore somewhere, beginning an entirely new mourning process.

Bishop Woznicki's sermon, although sympathetic to the families of the deceased crewmen, cautions the congregation to avoid the kind of bitterness that might rise out of tragedies of this nature. He addresses the familiar man vs. nature issues, alluding to the new space exploration program on everyone's minds since the Soviets' launching of the Sputnik satellites over the past year.

"God is the master of the elements," he declares. "Is it possible that in our progress in science we are getting too proud? While reaching for the stars and moon, we have not yet mastered our elements of air, water, and fire."

"Requiescant in pace."

An hour and a half after it began, the Mass ends and the congregation moves out of the church and to their cars. Mount Calvary Cemetery, the town's Catholic burial grounds, is five miles southwest of Rogers City. All nine crew members in the St. Ignatius service will be buried here, and a funeral procession of more than three hundred cars, spread over a two-mile stretch, moves slowly over U.S. 23 toward the expansive cemetery which, with its rolling grounds and beautiful pine trees, truly feels like a silent place of rest. Once there, the mourners assemble on a hillside for a brief service of a few final prayers. Bob Centala, a former sailor on the *Bradley*, concludes the day's services by blowing "Taps" on a bugle, and the families move to the individual gravesites.

Meanwhile, memorials for the *Bradley* crew are held throughout the Great Lakes region. The bell tolls at the Mariner's Church in Detroit, once for each man lost. The four Bradley Transportation Company ships still out—the *Robinson* in Buffalo, the *Cedarville* in Port Huron, the *Rogers City* in Chicago, and the *Myron Taylor* in Conneant, Ohio—cease all operations at noon and hold onboard memorial services. Priests or ministers are brought on board, and prayers are offered on the decks or cafeterias of the ships. Wreaths of flowers are dropped on the water at the conclusion of the services.

Then it's back to matters of the living, both on the water and in the town.

The body of deck watchman Richard Book makes its way back to Iowa without any special notice. There will be a Catholic funeral Mass and he will be laid to rest beside his parents in West Phalia.

Book considered the *Carl D. Bradley*—or at least one of the boats in the Bradley fleet—his future. He loved sailing, and he believed that one day he would be on the bridge of a ship, in command of one of the stone boats. He even tried to convince his brother Mel, the oldest in the Book family, to leave Iowa and join him in Michigan.

"I was married and living in Portsmouth," Mel remembers. "I was trying to pay for a farm and raise a family. He was never married. He had nothing to bind him. I had an obligation, and it didn't sit too well with my wife."

A move to another part of the country, tied to a job that actually paid decent money, appealed to Mel as much as it had enticed his younger brother. Mel had devoted much of his life to working on farms—first, on his parents' farm in West Phalia, Iowa, and eventually on one of his own—and he'd spent too much time scraping to make ends meet. "Those were really, really tough times," he says with surprisingly little bitterness. "I don't give a damn if gas was ten cents, you still couldn't buy any because you didn't have any money."

For Richard, sailing represented a clean break with a very difficult childhood and youth. His mother died at age thirty-seven, while giving birth to her ninth child. His father died of a heart attack a few years later, at age forty, leaving the family farm to eight sons and a daughter. With Mel in charge, the brothers made a run at keeping the family farm going.

"We had two hundred forty acres, and a good bit of it was planted in corn that year," recalls Richard's sister Eileen, who, at fifteen, had to quit school when her father passed away. Richard, the fifth of the Book children, was too young and small to work in the fields, so he and Eileen were responsible for taking care of the house and preparing meals.

"It was just before the Second World War, and prices were just getting good for the farmer," Eileen says. "The thing that sticks in my memory is how all the guys went out. They did a hell of a good job. We were just starting to get a little rain. We'd had a drought before that, when my parents were alive, and my father almost lost the farm. Things were just starting to get better. I've always felt very proud of my brothers because, for as young as they were, they just worked like little demons. We had a pretty good corn crop that year, and I think they paid off all the bills before they separated us."

The kids were just too young to be left to fend for themselves. An uncle lived with them for a while, but that hadn't worked out, either. The family was split up, the kids sent to live in the homes of their baptismal sponsors, and for years they saw each other only occasionally. Richard wound up with an uncle and aunt. In high school, while riding his bicycle to school one morning, he was hit by a car and almost killed. The accident left permanent scars on his face and head. By the time he was finished with high school, he knew one thing: he needed to get out of Iowa.

The navy not only presented him with that opportunity; it also gave him his first taste of sailing. Richard heard about the Bradley Transportation Company while he was stationed at the Great Lakes Naval Base in northern Illinois, and he decided to check it out after he completed his duty. He started with the company on March 15, 1957. He enjoyed the work so much that he just stayed in Rogers City during the winter layup, working maintenance jobs on the boats and living in the International Hotel.

When remembering his brother, Mel Book thinks of a letter Richard had sent him shortly after he'd taken a job on the *Bradley*. Richard was elated. He'd finally reached some level of a dream.

"I am now on the Cadillac of the boats," he boasted.

◆

Dennis Meredith, like fourteen of his crewmates, will never be buried on land. Lake Michigan has became his burial place. His father, however, wants to make certain that his time on Earth is never forgotten. He sees that private church services are held for his son, and a headstone placed in the cemetery, in a spot where Dennis might have been buried, had his body been recovered. The headstone, specially crafted to specifications provided by Dennis's father, bears Dennis's name and the legend "Lost at Sea." It also features a carving of the *Carl D. Bradley* breaking apart on the surface of Lake Michigan.

AFTER DAYS OF SEARCHING WHAT SEEMS TO BE EVERY SQUARE mile of northern Lake Michigan in the Coast Guard Albatross *1273*, Lieutenant J. L. Sigmund finally scores a breakthrough in the discovery of the location of the wreckage of the *Carl D. Bradley* on Saturday afternoon, the same day that many of the *Bradley* crew members are being buried. With only a few hours of daylight left, Sigmund is flying about 5½ miles northwest of Boulder Reef, right in the area where the *Christian Sartori* had seen the explosion on the water on the night of November 18. Sigmund knows the area well. He's flown over it any number of times, day and night, since the evening of the *Bradley*'s sinking, but so far he hasn't seen anything remotely noteworthy.

Now, as he moves over the area, he sees a large spot of water that seems to be darker than the surrounding area. He turns the plane around and drops lower. After making several passes, he concludes that he's looking at an oil slick and, given its position, the oil might be coming from the *Bradley* wreckage.

Sigmund notes the oil slick's coordinates and relays them in to the Coast Guard station in Traverse City. A boat, he suggests, should come out and take a sample.

While Rogers City is busy putting many of its lost sailors to rest, the Coast Guard's Board of Inquiry conducts its second day of hearings, this time in Charlevoix. The board has moved proceedings to accommodate the crews of the *Sundew* and the *Hollyhock*, and to interview Elmer Fleming and Frank

Mays in the hospital. The eyewitness accounts provided by Fleming, Mays, Harold Muth, Warren Toussaint, and others promise to be the centerpiece of the board's written report.

The board sets up in the cramped quarters of the *Sundew*'s wardroom. Captain Muth testifies first. He gives a straightforward, unvarnished account of the *Sundew*'s search for the *Bradley* wreck and her survivors. He also tells of Frank Mays's and Elmer Fleming's rescue. He is all business, not inclined to play up the dramatics of the story that presently captivates the Great Lakes region.

Warren Toussaint follows with his account of Fleming's and Mays's conditions when they were picked up. He talks about the treatment he'd given them on the *Sundew*, and of his ideas about how the storm and water temperatures might have affected the other *Bradley* crewmen in the water. He also speaks of the deceased crewmen recovered by the *Sundew*—of the condition they were in, what they were wearing, etc., which provide insight into how much time the crew had to prepare for the sinking and, in some cases, how they died.

It's already 7:00 P.M. by the time the board opens its questioning of Elmer Fleming at Charlevoix City Hospital. The hospital staff has converted the solarium into an informal hearing room. Fleming and Mays, wearing hospital gowns and bathrobes, are taken down to the room in wheelchairs, and Fleming begins what will turn out to be the most riveting testimony of the hearings.

Aside from a tendency to mumble at times, or to talk too quickly for the stenographer to keep up with his frenetic pace, Fleming proves to be an excellent overall witness. He clearly takes the board through the sequence of events leading to the *Bradley*'s sinking, beginning in Gary, when the *Bradley* was preparing to head up the lake. As the officer in charge of overseeing the ballasting of the ship, Fleming recalls the preparations for the storm and the way the *Bradley* responded to it. The storm, he states, was serious, but the *Bradley* handled it well. The seas were high, but they weren't washing over the deck. "I was looking forward, and I was looking down at the side of the ship, and we still weren't working much," he tells the board, speaking of the *Bradley*'s final minutes before breaking in two.

His recollections of the actual sinking, as expected, are dramatic. He estimates that "approximately two minutes" passed from the initial "thud" to the sinking of the ship. He testifies about how, after the *Bradley* lost its electricity, he dashed to his room to retrieve a life jacket, and how he made his way back to the deck only moments before the bow section rolled over.

"She was going over fast," he says. "I do remember seeing Captain Bryan and several men working their way up to the high side, and I heard him say, 'Get to the high side! Get to the high side!' I could no longer get to the high side. Before I knew it, I was in the water, and when I came up I was about a foot from the raft."

Fleming's emotions surface while he talks about these events. He hadn't known all the crew members of the *Bradley*, but he agonizes over the memory of their efforts to get off the boat. The raft, he points out, was carried away from the scene very rapidly, and he had a good view of the *Bradley*'s final tortured moments: "The fore end went down and flopped, and the after end went down from the midsection, and when the boiler room hit the water there was a terrific explosion and we saw the last part of it going down in flames.

"We thought we heard voices, but in the dark we could not see. We lost practically everything on the raft. The only things we did not lose were the things that were in the little cabinets. There were four on the raft and it floated away fast. We could see nothing of the wreckage. There were a lot of ring buoys with lights and they were all lit."

Fleming has had plenty of time to reflect on these events, and he needs no prodding in recalling them for the record. He defends Captain Roland Bryan throughout, including his skipper's actions when the *Bradley* hogged and started to break apart. The loss of the *Carl D. Bradley*, Fleming makes clear in his testimony, was not a case of bad decision or poor seamanship.

Fleming testifies for two hours before Dr. Lawrence Grate, citing his patient's fatigue, halts the day's proceedings. Fleming—and Mays—will have to meet with the board on another occasion. Rear Admiral Kerrins, probably as exhausted as either of the two witnesses, agrees. They'll reconvene first thing in the morning.

Frank Mays's testimony is a stark contrast to Elmer Fleming's.

In years to come, Mays will write his own detailed account of the *Bradley* sinking; participate in commemorative services in Rogers City and elsewhere; grant interviews to journalists seeking information about his survival; give speeches about the *Bradley* at maritime and shipwreck conferences; appear in documentaries about the wreck; and, in general, become one of the most engaging witnesses historians could hope for.

However, when he's brought in front of the Coast Guard's Board of Inquiry, he has very little to say. Much of this is understandable. As the one who pumped water into the *Bradley*'s ballast tanks, Mays is quite naturally cautious—perhaps even suspicious—when addressing questions about the way the ship had been prepared for heading out into the storm. In absence of cargo to settle and stabilize the *Bradley* in heavy seas, ballast was really the boat's main line of defense against the storm. If the boat had been improperly or inadequately ballasted, it would have worked even more than usual, placing tremendous stress on the hull.

The Board of Inquiry, as one might expect, is very interested in all this, but rather than offer the kind of long, rambling, detailed answers characteristic of Elmer Fleming's testimony, Mays keeps his answers clipped and to the point, with little extra detail. He's not antagonistic toward the board; he's just not an easy witness. "Yes" and "no" answers are not uncommon, and a two- or three-sentence response makes him look absolutely talkative.

The board guides Mays through the events of the *Carl D. Bradley*'s final trip, including the ballasting of the ship, the way she rode in the storm, how she broke on the surface, and how Mays reached the life raft and survived. Mays is more forthcoming in his responses to questions about his survival, but he'd clearly prefer to be anywhere else than in front of the four-man panel. "I was happy to hear the words 'You are dismissed,'" he'd write later in his account of the hearing.

For the board, there's much more ahead, including a session with Captain Paul Mueller of the *Christian Sartori*. Piecing together the *Bradley* story turns out to be a mixed bag. It's not difficult to determine the timeline, or *what* happened, or *how* it happened. It's the *why* that leaves the panel at a loss.

RATHER THAN PROVIDE FINAL, DEFINITIVE ANSWERS TO QUES-
tions about the sinking of the *Carl D. Bradley*, the highly anticipated report
from the Coast Guard's Board of Inquiry only tweaks the controversy over
whether the accident was the result of an unavoidable force of nature, human error and bad judgment, or a state of disrepair of the ship itself. The
four-man panel considered and debated voluminous testimony from twenty-
four witnesses, including eyewitnesses to the sinking, participants in the
search-and-rescue operations, inspectors, shipbuilding authorities, and company officials, concluding that "the cause of the casualty was due to the
excessive hogging stresses imposed upon the vessel by reason of her placement in a ballasted condition upon the waves encountered at the particular
instant of breaking."

It's the only conclusion the board could have drawn. Elmer Fleming and
Frank Mays had testified extensively about the sinking and the events leading to it. Mays had testified that until the *Bradley* broke up, the boat was
working well in the storm—"normal for what the seas were." Since the
Bradley was known to twist more than the average bulk carrier in heavy
seas, the board was especially interested in learning about how much water
had been added to the ballast tanks to stabilize the vessel. Fortunately, in
talking to Mays they were speaking to the man who had pumped in the water on November 18; and in Fleming, they had the officer who supervised
the ballasting. The *Bradley*, Mays said, had been ballasted to capacity.

The board accepted Mays's and Fleming's testimonies. What the panel
still had to figure out was why its structure had failed. The limestone boats,
the Board conceded, took quite a beating in normal operations:

The trade followed by the self-unloading-type vessels is extremely hard on the vessels. The self-unloaders load and discharge many more cargoes per year than do the conventional bulk freighters engaged in the iron ore trade. Likewise, these vessels frequent out of the way places in shallow water and often ground and rub bottom while approaching docks.

The *Bradley* had dealt with all of this during its abbreviated final season.

The board relied heavily on the inspection records and the testimony of the Coast Guard inspectors who had examined the *Bradley* before the 1958 season commenced. In its report the board listed the numerous repair issues the inspectors had noted, as well as the repair plans for the 1958–59 layup in Manitowoc; the report even mentioned the two groundings and subsequent spot repairs that had not been initially reported, as required, earlier in 1958. Despite evidence of at least minor structural weakness, the board concluded that "the vessel was seaworthy at the time of completion of her annual inspection at Calcite, Michigan, on 17 April 1958, and that there is no reason to conclude from the testimony or from reasonable interpretation of other known facts that she was not in such condition upon departure from Gary, Indiana, on 17 November 1958."

If the boat was seaworthy and properly prepared for sailing light in a storm, only one conclusion could be drawn: the loss of the *Carl D. Bradley* could be attributed to the forces of nature. The focus now switched to the storm, and to whether the *Bradley* had any business being out in it.

In its report, the Board of Inquiry noted that Roland Bryan and Elmer Fleming were aware of the weather forecast warning of whole gale winds, and that sailing conditions had deteriorated to such an extent that "at least eight vessels were anchored or proceeding to anchor at the time of the casualty." The *Bradley*, however, forged ahead, and seemingly without difficulty:

Within one-half hour before the casualty, both survivors, Fleming and Mays, had occasion to traverse the length of the vessel from the forward

house to the after house on the weather deck, and neither one saw nor
heard anything out of the ordinary which would have caused them to
be concerned with the safety of the vessel . . . Up to the time of the casu-
alty, this vessel was riding easily, taking no water over the deck, and
with so smooth a motion that the sideboards were not necessary on the
mess table. Accordingly, persons on board were not aware of any rea-
son to be concerned for the safety of the vessel.

Despite this observation, and despite conceding that "there is no evidence that any licensed or certificated personnel of the CARL D. BRADLEY
committed any acts of incompetence, inattention to duty, negligence, or
willful violation of any law or regulation," the Board blamed the accident
on Captain Roland Bryan and his decision to sail in the storm rather than
drop anchor and wait for it to pass:

It is the stated policy of the owners of the CARL D. BRADLEY to give the
masters complete responsibility for the safety of their vessels and, there-
fore, complete freedom to anchor or postpone departure, if unfavorable
weather or other reasons dictate such action to be in the interests of
safety. In view of this, it is the opinion of the Board that the master of
the CARL D. BRADLEY, in making the decision to and in proceeding
across northern Lake Michigan from Cana Island toward Lansing
Shoal, exercised poor judgment. This decision was probably induced by
a zealous desire to hold as closely to schedule as possible, and because
of this, he gave less attention to the dangers of the existing weather
than what might have been expected of a prudent mariner.

Elmer Fleming's and Frank Mays's accounts of their harrowing night on
the raft, and Warren Toussaint's testimony regarding the condition of the
victims brought on board the *Sundew*, led to several recommendations in
the report. After hearing Fleming's testimony about how his last flare failed
when the *Christian Sartori* had drawn so close to the raft—a failure that

probably cost Dennis Meredith and Gary Strzelecki their lives—the board recommended that "each lifeboat and life raft on all Great Lakes cargo vessels be provided with a unit of at least six red parachute-type flare distress signals and the means to project them."

The style of life jackets on the *Bradley* also caught the board's attention. The life jackets used by the crewmen lacked the crotch straps found on the more recently designed ones, and in the fierce conditions on the lake, this could have been problematic, if not fatal, to the men in the water. The crewmen had to hold the life jackets down to keep them from slipping off, which added to the fatigue they experienced in trying to stay afloat in heavy seas. In addition, the jackets lacked any support for the wearers' heads, which meant, if a crewman lost consciousness, almost instant death. After reviewing all this, the board recommended that "all jacket-type life preservers be provided with a crotch strap to hold the jacket down on the body and with a collar to support the head out of water."

Before going public with the report, the board submitted it to Vice Admiral Alfred C. Richmond, the Coast Guard commandant, who had commissioned it. Richmond reviewed it and added his own thoughts on the *Bradley*, complete with his own remarks on the board's findings, in a separate document. Although not contentious in the wording of his opinions, Richmond wasn't completely satisfied with the board's conclusions.

Richmond disagreed with the board's thoughts on how unusual wave action probably caused the ship, running light, to hog and break apart. The two survivors, Richmond pointed out, had testified about how smoothly the *Bradley* was riding just minutes before it hogged and split. There was nothing unusual about the waves—or the storm, for that matter—that should have caused Captain Bryan to think he might be placing his vessel at risk by taking it out.

"Although in all probability the vessel broke in hogging," Richmond wrote in his remarks on the Coast Guard report, "the implication in the Board's conclusion that the fracture resulted because the vessel encountered an unusual wave condition while in ballast is not supported in the record. In the absence of any evidence of improper or unusual ballasting, such reasoning would necessarily require an assumption that the waves were unique in the vessel's twenty-one-year [*sic*] history of navigation in the Great Lakes."

Taking his logic one step further, Richmond could find no reason to blame Captain Bryan for his decision to sail if, as Richmond reasoned, the ship was properly ballasted and the wave action was nothing unusual. "The Board's conclusion that the Master of the BRADLEY exercised poor judgment in proceeding across northern Lake Michigan from Cana Island toward Lansing Shoal is also disapproved."

The problems, Richmond suggested, might have stemmed from an already weakened hull. In its report, the Board of Inquiry dismissed the previous structural problems (the hairline cracks found during the *Bradley*'s drydocking in 1957, the two groundings at Cedarville, the need for repairs and a new cargo hold) as factors leading to the accident; Richmond wasn't so sure.

"That the vessel broke up and foundered under conditions which, while severe, she should easily have been able to weather, leads inevitably to the conclusion that the vessel had developed an undetected structural weakness or defect," he wrote.

The differing opinions illustrate not only the difficulties of drawing conclusions on the causes leading to structural failure of a vessel, they also hint at the caution needed when issuing official statements in the face of potential lawsuits. During the hearings Victor Hanson, a Detroit attorney representing the widows of Raymond Kowalski, John Fogelsonger, Earl Tulgetske, and Gary Strzelecki, had requested permission to interview the survivors during their appearances before the board. Hanson's request had been rejected on grounds that the hearing wasn't a trial, but he was permitted to submit written questions to Elmer Fleming and Frank Mays. The presence of Hanson and other attorneys might have served as a warning that their conclusions might have serious legal consequences.

This, of course, isn't unusual. The initial shock and sadness following a tragedy such as the loss of the *Carl D. Bradley* are eventually replaced by anger and bitterness, which can be manifest in any number of ways, including finger-pointing; threats of lawsuits; or, in the case of Frank Mays and Elmer Fleming, cruel and irrational behavior by some townspeople who resented Mays's and Fleming's survival when they had lost friends or loved ones. Fleming would spend the remainder of his life suffering from a degree of survivor's guilt, and the cold shoulder he received from some of the people in Rogers City, along with the gossip that always seemed to find its way back to him, bothered him immensely. Mays, too, would be affected by the way he was avoided by his old friends and neighbors. "Had I done something wrong by surviving?" he'd wonder.

The legal issues are another matter. Michigan Limestone and Bradley Transportation officials, who had known the men on the *Bradley* and mourned their loss as they would the deaths of friends, and who had been through the trauma of notifying the families of the deaths of their loved ones, must face the realities of paying out financial settlements to the families and, more ominously, deal with pending lawsuits. The initial payouts had been quick, easy, and relatively inexpensive: the costs of the funerals, plus a flat $300 to each family to cover the loss of each crewman's personal effects. In addition, Michigan Lime donated $10,000 to the Disaster Fund.

What the company will not do is admit that the *Bradley* might have been in poor condition at the time of its final trip; any public concession to that effect would be an invitation to lawsuits. The company stands firm, pointing to the Bradley line's history and excellent safety record, and to the Coast Guard and *Lloyd's Register of Shipping* inspection records, as evidence of its devotion to the maintenance of its vessels.

The Board of Inquiry's report is further vindication.

"The U.S. Coast Guard testimony in the hearings verifies the fact that the vessel was seaworthy," Christian F. Beukema, president of Michigan Limestone, tells the press when the report is issued. "Certain repairs were recommended at the time of the annual inspection and were scheduled to be made after completion of the season. The portions of the ship covered by these recommendations were all in the interior and did not have any effect on the structural strength."

Beukema's statement is only one early move in a legal chess match to be played out over the coming months. The company's settlement offer would be countered with lawsuits, and the legal wrangling would further divide the community and the company that essentially supported it. Any goodwill built up between Michigan Limestone and Rogers City immediately following the loss of the *Carl D. Bradley* would be stretched to the point where there would be bickering between the current employees at the plant and the former employees and victims' families.

No one could agree on much of anything.

Matters might be less contentious if someone could locate—and explore— the wreckage of the *Bradley*. As of the July 7, 1959, issuing of the Coast Guard report, the exact location of the *Bradley*'s final resting place is still a mystery, and though there is no guarantee that exploration of the wreckage will yield significant insights into the cause of the vessel's sinking, the Coast Guard, Michigan Limestone officials, and the families and legal representatives of the *Bradley* victims are all frustrated that no one seems to be able to find the boat.

Not that there haven't been efforts.

Planes and helicopters, flying over the area in the days immediately following the *Bradley* sinking, had seen nothing other than an oil slick that disappeared the day after its sighting, though the oil slick's location did provide an important marker for future searches. In December, just a few weeks after the sinking, the *Sundew* had been back in the area, pulling buoys around Boulder Reef, and since he was already in the area, Captain Harold Muth decided to do a little exploring on his own. He directed the *Sundew* to the area where the *Christian Sartori* had witnessed the explosion, which happened to coincide with the spot where the oil slick had been seen. The *Sundew* passed over the area several times and, about five miles northeast of

Boulder Reef, the crew spotted what appeared to be a silhouette of something very large—perhaps a ship—on the bottom of the lake. Using a Fathometer, Captain Muth made a drawing of the object on the lake floor. Nothing conclusive could be ascertained from the drawing, but Muth was intrigued enough to note the coordinates of the object's position and send them, along with the drawing, to the Coast Guard headquarters in Cleveland.

Nothing happened for the next two months. Winter arrived, making further exploration of the site impossible. In February 1959 the Coast Guard dispatched two cutters, the *Sundew* and the *Mackinaw*, both ice-breakers, to look for the *Bradley*. The two vessels, moving through a field of drifting or solid ice—some of it fourteen inches thick—employed Fathometers in their search, with marginal success. The *Sundew* located a couple of "mounds" on the lake floor, but neither matched the *Bradley*'s dimensions. One of the objects seemed too long to be the *Bradley*, and the other didn't seem high enough. The ice on Lake Michigan made maneuvering extremely difficult, and after three days of searching, the two boats returned to their home ports without indisputable evidence of the *Bradley* wreckage.

The search efforts were vigorously renewed in the spring. There was still plenty of ice on the lake as late as mid-April, and the weather, as always, was unreliable enough to make extensive searching difficult, but the *Bradley*'s owners were growing impatient. On April 2, a plane chartered by U. S. Steel flew over northern Lake Michigan and discovered significant wreckage, debris, and personal effects from the *Bradley* washed ashore on Trout Island. A search crew was dispatched to the island.

"We had a whole party from the plant that went up there," Fred Dagner, a lifetime employee of Michigan Lime and the Bradley Transportation Company, remembers. "They flew us over on a plane. We stayed there for a week, searching that place, both shores. There were like eight or ten of us. We'd walk up and down the shores, looking for stuff. We'd stockpile what we found. We found some life preservers and some oars from the lifeboats—stuff like that. But we never found any bodies or evidence of anybody. No shoes—nothing. That was it."

The search party collected a significant assortment of items, including one of the *Bradley*'s pilothouse doors, a mangled portion of a lifeboat, a compass stand, and a helmsman's stool. Life jackets, their strings tied as if they had been in use, also were picked up, lending credence to the theory that other crewmen might not have been recovered because they had slipped out of their life jackets, either while fighting the waves or after they had passed away.

After examining the evidence, U. S. Steel immediately dispatched a thirty-eight-foot vessel, the *Penmanta*, under the command of Donald T. Nauts, master of the Bradley fleet's *John G. Munson*, to make another attempt to find the *Bradley*. Bad weather and mechanical problems plagued the boat's early efforts, but on the afternoon of April 29, after six days of delays and thwarted trips, the *Penmanta* scored a hit. Using a sonar device called a Sea Scanar, the *Penmanta* crew detected a large object 360 feet below the surface. The Sea Scanar recorded an image of the object which, U. S. Steel announced, was the *Carl D. Bradley*.

The discovery might have been greeted with more enthusiasm if not for an accompanying statement about the condition of the ship, published in the Fall 1959 issue of *ML Screenings*, the Michigan Limestone company publication distributed to its employees. "While it was generally believed that the *Bradley* sank in two pieces," the article read, "the sonar tracing showed that she appeared in one piece."

This, coupled with the Coast Guard's report and the company's official reaction to it, sets off a series of angry reactions. The families of lost crewmen are infuriated. In their minds, the Michigan Lime and Bradley Transportation companies are refusing to accept responsibility for the loss of the *Bradley*, and, in doing so, are refusing to offer a proper settlement to those who lost their loved ones and, on a practical level, their means of support. At the end of July—just weeks after the release of the Coast Guard report—attorneys representing ten families file lawsuits seeking more than $7 million in liability, which is more than ten times the $660,000 offered by the company.

Frank Mays and Elmer Fleming are justifiably upset by the implication that they were either mistaken or lying when they testified that the *Bradley* had gone down in two separate sections. Fleming, who has gone back to work for the Bradley line, avoids the controversy. Mays, who had taken a job at a company warehouse in Rogers City after his recovery from the accident, only to be dismissed after hiring an attorney to represent him, decides to go to Detroit and confront Christian Beukema about his firing and Beukema's statements about the *Bradley*'s wreckage being in one piece.

He gets nowhere. Beukema refuses see him.

Photographic evidence of the *Bradley* wreckage is needed to help settle the disputes, and in August 1959, a photographic survey of the wreckage, sponsored by the ship's owners, is completed by the Global Marine Exploration Company of Los Angeles. Unfortunately, the survey, conducted over a ten-day span beginning on August 21, only adds to the mystery and controversy.

For openers, there are no impartial witnesses to the survey. The Coast Guard, in particular, objects to being excluded. Rather than invite the Coast Guard or other observers to witness the exploration of the wreck, the Bradley Transportation Company maintains secrecy about the operation throughout its planning, until a few days before the beginning of the survey, when the company contacts the Ninth Coast Guard District Aids to Navigation offices to inform them of the operation. By this time it's too late for the Coast Guard to join and witness the proceedings.

Since the company is footing the bill for the survey, neither U. S. Steel nor Bradley Transportation is under an obligation to include witnesses. Still, in taking this approach the company risks having its objectivity and, ultimately, the results of its study highly criticized.

Which is exactly what happens.

The *Submarex*, a 173-foot vessel normally used for surveying offshore oil drilling, conducts the survey.

Equipped with sonar, television monitors, and cameras, the *Submarex* lo-cates the *Bradley* without a problem. However, the conditions for surveying and photographing the wreckage are less the optimum. A strong current stirs up sediment around the wreck, greatly reducing visibility and slowing the proceedings considerably. At a depth of 360 feet, the *Bradley* is in water too deep for free divers to move in for a closer, more detailed look.* Despite the obstacles, the *Submarex* gets what it came for: confirmation that the wreck is indeed the *Carl D. Bradley*, and the first look at the ship since its sinking.

The *Submarex* findings, published later in the year in *ML Screenings*, sup-port the earlier sonar tracings indicating that the *Bradley*'s hull is in one piece. Its deck is badly fractured from the hogging described by Frank Mays and Elmer Fleming, but the lower section of the hull appears to be un-damaged. By all indications, the *Bradley* planed to the bottom of Lake Michigan, settling in a southwesterly position roughly ninety degrees off its original course.

The findings ratchet up the controversy. Company officials are pleased with the survey's results. The findings, they believe, support their con-tention that the *Bradley* was brought down by an "act of God," as opposed to its breaking apart because of its poor condition. If this is true, it not only absolves the company from blame for the accident; it also translates into a much smaller settlement for the families of the *Bradley* victims.

The other side is skeptical. In the absence of independent, unbiased wit-nesses to the *Submarex* explorations, there is no proof that the Michigan Limestone and Bradley Transportation companies are doing anything other than making statements that support their own best interests. Bradley Transportation claims to have photographic evidence corroborating its claims, but the company refuses to share the photos. And even if the *Bradley* appears to be in one piece, there is no way of saying definitively that it didn't split all the way through.

---

* Within two decades, divers using mixed gases and other newly created equipment will be able to dive to the wreck. In 1959 this technology was not yet available.

Victor Hanson, the Detroit lawyer representing the estates of four of the *Bradley* crewmen, and the general counsel for the Maritime Trades Department, makes this point when addressing the press after the announcement of the *Submarex* findings.

"There may have been some continuity," he concedes, "but the ship must have cracked if the deck was cracked."

Nearly a year has passed since the loss of the *Bradley*.

It's time to settle.

The first anniversary of the *Bradley* sinking is marked by memorial services in Rogers City churches, and by a handful of newspaper articles rounding up comments from some of the *Bradley* widows, but with the passing months and another shipping season come and gone, the city has settled back into its old routine. The men are still out sailing, utterly convinced that the *Bradley* accident was a once-in-a-lifetime occurrence. Their wives and families, although more rattled now when the winds and seas kick up than they might have been a year earlier, also have moved on. In the months immediately following the loss of the *Bradley*, townspeople had talked quietly among themselves whenever they saw a *Bradley* widow moving up the sidewalk or walking in the next aisle at the grocery store, but this, too, has become a thing of the past.

"They don't talk about it much anymore in the bank," John Blasky, president of the Presque Isle Bank and secretary-treasurer of the Ship Disaster Children's Fund, tells the *Detroit News*. "After the big Christmas party we had here last year, the sad talk dropped off."*

But the reminders linger everywhere. For Cecilia Krawczak, the anniversary

---

*A month after the loss of the *Carl D. Bradley*, a Christmas party was held for the children of the shipwreck's victims. Toys and clothing poured in—literally by the truckload—the donations so great that some of the gifts were withheld for another time, leading Barbara Orr, widow of watchman Mel Orr, to note that "most of the youngsters probably had a bigger Christmas than they ever had in their lives."

falls on her birthday. In the absence of a settlement with U. S. Steel, she has been trying to support her six kids on a $254 monthly Social Security check. A year ago, she and her kids became kind of an unofficial poster family for the *Bradley* families when *Life* magazine published a photograph of them in its pages. The reality of 365 sunrises and sunsets has put some distance between the moment when she heard about Joe's death—so poignantly captured in the *Life* photograph—and today, but it still hasn't been long enough. She misses her husband terribly—enough so, she tells the press, that she feels as married now as she ever did.

"Forgetting isn't easy, even if you want to," she says on the eve of the first anniversary. "The children are always mentioning things the entire family used to do together."

Privately, however, she wonders how, with all these kids, she ever stands a chance of finding another husband. It doesn't seem likely.

Two of the *Bradley* widows—Ann Strzelecki and Frances Budnick—have remarried; two others report calls from total strangers proposing marriage. Four have left Rogers City. Economic necessity, along with the need to fill hours, have nudged some of the widows into finding jobs. Adeline Heller sells encyclopedias; Mary Promo, with a 7½-month-old baby to provide for, finds work in a variety store. Frances Vallee describes her new job at a drugstore as "a pathway out of my loneliness."

She would remember how her husband had the maddening yet somehow endearing habit of buying a new car without consulting her. It was his big surprise to the family. He'd come home with a brand-new car and, proud of his purchase, present it to his family with a big grin. "How are we going to pay for that?" Frances would wonder, and Chick would shrug. "I don't know," he'd say. "I bought it. *You* figure that out." They'd laugh because Chick knew damn well how they were going to pay for it.

The Vallee children have their own memories. Besides remembering the summer when he worked and bonded with his father on the *Bradley*, Barry Vallee remembers his dad's sense of humor, how he was the boat's

biggest practical joker. Barry's sister Sue hangs on to the small but significant memories, such as the times the family would sit around together and
eat popcorn or sundaes made with her mother's homemade hot fudge. Or
the times when Chick would take the family ice-skating, and how he'd fly
across the ice on long-bladed racing skates, pulling his daughters along behind him. Or of Sunday afternoon drives, when he'd pack the family into
the car and drive out to watch the construction of the Mackinac Bridge. Or
how they'd head out to a quiet spot behind Michigan Lime.

"We'd get in the car and ride behind Calcite," she says. You'd get behind
the quarry, in the wooded area, and see how many deer you could spot.
Once we came across a fawn that had just been born. We just stayed a moment and looked."

On Friday, December 4, 1959, one year and sixteen days after the sinking of
the *Carl D. Bradley*, U. S. Steel reaches a $1,250,000 lump-sum settlement
with the families of the lost crewmen. Following a brief but occasionally
chippy legal battle, the case ends in compromise, with U. S. Steel almost
doubling its original offer, while the lawsuits, once totaling more than $5
million, are brought down to a figure U. S. Steel finds more manageable.
U.S. District Court judge Charles J. McNamee, presiding over the hearings
in Cleveland, concludes the proceedings by appointing a commissioner to
determine how the settlement money will be divided among the victims'
survivors. The settlement, "one of the fastest in maritime history for a case
of its scope," according to one published report, will not guarantee lifelong
financial security for the *Bradley* families, but it offers relief.

The full effects of the shipwreck, however, won't be determined for
years. Some of the *Bradley* children, affected by a sense of abandonment,
will struggle with relationships throughout their lives. Frank Mays and
Elmer Fleming will watch their marriages fracture and fall apart. Mays will
never sail again. Fleming, on the other hand, will return to the lakes,

achieving his goal of attaining a master's position, but it won't last. He will retire from the boats, but not as a captain. His experiences on the *Bradley* have changed him—but as far as sailing is concerned, not for the better.

Tragedy exacts the price of its choice, in terms of lives lost and lives continuing, with no room for bargaining. The *Carl D. Bradley* story is no exception. And while, to many in Rogers City, it might seem unusual that Marge Schuler would burn her porch light every night long after it's clear that her husband is gone, it might well be that, in a simple porch light, she has found her own sentry in her battle against unimaginable loss.

It guards her heart against the night.

May 7, 1965

The early-morning air is foggy and chilly, with temperatures in the upper thirties. A light wind blows in from the southwest.

Shortly after 5:00 A.M., the *Cedarville*, a 588-foot Bradley Transportation boat constructed the same year as the *Carl D. Bradley*, pulls out of the Port of Calcite, loaded with 14,411 tons of open-hearth limestone destined for Gary, Indiana. The boat carries thirty-five men, including its commander, Captain Martin Joppich.

Like most boats its age, the *Cedarville* boasts a colorful history. Previously named the *A. F. Harvey*, the *Cedarville* had served as an ore carrier for the Pittsburgh Steamship Division of U. S. Steel prior to being transferred to the Bradley fleet in 1956. Originally a straight-decker, the vessel had been renamed and converted into a self-unloader during its layup over the winter of 1956–57. In nearly four decades of service it had suffered the usual indignities of heavy labor, the bumps and scrapes, the battles with nature, the need for occasional repairs. On the night of the *Bradley*'s sinking, the *Cedarville* had been on Saginaw Bay, running light and waging its own war against the storm that brought the *Bradley* down. Ironically, when Elmer Fleming had been awarded his first command of a ship, it had been on the *Cedarville*. Fleming's command was short-lived; he grew jittery whenever a storm blew in, especially at night, and he relinquished his command and resumed duty as first mate on another boat.

On this day, the fog on Lake Huron, a common enough phenomenon during the spring months, is thick, demanding constant vigilance in the

wheelhouse. If the *Cedarville*'s captain and crew need any further indication that they should sail cautiously, all they need do is look at the events of
less than half a day ago, when fog had been responsible for one of the most
unusual collisions in recent Great Lakes history. The *J. E. Upson*, a 504-foot
freighter bound for Silver Bay in Canada, had been caught in near-zero-
visibility fog and rammed into the base of the Gray's Reef life station just
west of the Straits of Mackinac. No one had been hurt in the collision, including the three baffled and frightened Coast Guard crew working at the
station, but it certainly should have acted as a warning to any ships sailing
in the area.

Captain Joppich, a thirty-year veteran of Great Lakes sailing, isn't especially concerned. The fifty-four-year-old skipper has sailed in all kinds of
conditions, including dense fog, and he's taken this particular course so
many times that he doesn't give it a second thought. Once he's cleared the
breakwater leading into Lake Huron, he has the *Cedarville* moving along at
the brisk speed of 12.3 miles per hour—the boat's maximum speed when
fully loaded. Visibility is about one mile.

The fog thickens considerably as the *Cedarville* moves westward. By the
time the boat reaches the Cheboygan-traffic-lighted bell buoy at 8:42 A.M.,
the earlier visibility has been cut in half. Joppich alters the *Cedarville*'s
course to allow for heavier traffic near the Mackinac Bridge. He does not,
however, order a reduction of speed. The *Cedarville* passes the *Benson
Ford*, a freighter headed in its direction, without a problem, in fog so thick
the men in the *Cedarville*'s wheelhouse cannot see the *Ford* when the two
vessels pass within half a mile of each other. Still no reduction in speed,
even though, at this point, the *Cedarville* is relying on radar and the sound
of other boats' fog signals, rather than vision, to know what's around it on
the lake.

Most captains, under these circumstances, would check down their ships'
engine shaft revolutions, reducing speed to half ahead. Len Gabrysiak, the
Cedarville's wheelsman, cannot understand Captain Joppich's decision to
maintain full speed. Gabrysiak has his first mate's license and usually serves

as third mate on the *Cedarville*. On this trip, however, he's been bumped by another third mate with more seniority.

According to his radar and ship-to-ship communications, Captain Joppich knows that there are five ships in the vicinity of the Straits of Mackinac: the westbound *Cedarville*; the *Weissenburg*, an eastbound West German freighter; the *George M. Steinbrenner*, a bulk carrier headed to Green Bay with a load of coal; the *J. E. Upson*, now anchored near Old Mackinac Point after its rude meeting with the Gray's Reef life station; and the *Topdalsfjord*, an eastbound, 423-foot Norwegian freighter loaded with 1,800 tons of cargo. Joppich, in a conversation with the *Steinbrenner*, learns about the presence of the *Weissenburg*, and in a conversation with the captain of the *Weissenburg*, he's informed about the Norwegian ship traveling ahead of him. The four ships register as blips on the *Cedarville*'s radar.

Joppich checks the ship's position and figures his course. The *Upson* is of no immediate concern, nor is the *Steinbrenner*, which is also heading out onto Lake Michigan, well ahead of the *Cedarville*. Joppich arranges a port-to-port passing with the *Weissenburg*. This leaves the Norwegian ship traveling ahead of the *Weissenburg*. The *Cedarville* tries to contact the ship, with no luck. According to the *Cedarville*'s radar, the ship is dead ahead. Joppich orders a change in course and reduces the *Cedarville*'s speed to half ahead.

The *Cedarville* is running blind. Lookouts can see nothing in the pea soup fog. Third Mate Charles Cook carefully monitors the radar, but the *Cedarville* has had some on-and-off problems with the radar; Cook knows it can't be trusted. Crewmen can hear fog signals from the other ship ahead, though sound carries in strange ways in the fog and there's no telling exactly where that other ship is. The only thing those in the *Cedarville*'s tense pilothouse know for certain is that there is a ship out there, somewhere near, and it's bearing down on them.

"She's pretty close," Cook informs Joppich.

Hoping to alert the other ship of the *Cedarville*'s presence, Joppich reaches up and blasts the passing signal on the ship's whistle. It's too late.

"There she is!" cries Ivan Trafelet, a lookout stationed on the *Cedarville's* port wing.

The massive form of a ship appears out of the fog, no more than a hundred feet away, directly in front of the *Cedarville*.

"Captain, we're going to hit!" Cook shouts.

Everything happens in a blur. Immediately upon seeing the *Topdalsfjord*, Joppich orders the engine room to reduce speed to slow, but when a collision seems inevitable, he orders the engines full ahead. He then directs Gabrysiak to steer hard right. Maybe the huge ships might still be able to avoid each other.

The *Topdalsfjord* takes evasive actions as well. In an effort to slow his ship by putting it in reverse, Caption Rasmus Hoagland orders his engines reversed to full astern and then he, too, orders his wheelsman to cut the ship hard right.

But it's far too late to avoid a collision. The *Topdalsfjord* plows broadside into the *Cedarville*, cutting into its hull on the port side near its seventh hatch. The *Topdalsfjord*, with a bow reinforced for ice-breaking, leaves a huge, deep gash, running from deck line to below water level, in the *Cedarville*. The two ships stay joined together, the bow of the *Topdalsfjord* buried in the *Cedarville's* side, until the motion of the *Cedarville* pulls them apart. No one is injured on either ship, and the *Topdalsfjord*, although sustaining substantial damage to its bow, is in no danger of sinking.

The *Cedarville*, however, is mortally lost. Water floods into its number two cargo hold. First Mate Harry Piechon desperately attempts to stave off the flooding by plugging the hole with the boat's collision tarp, but it doesn't work. It's now just a matter of time before the *Cedarville* fills with water and sinks.

No one panics. There should be plenty of time for the crew to launch lifeboats and abandon ship. Captain Joppich orders the engine shut down and the port anchor dropped. The crew, well versed in lifeboat procedures from their drills in the past, lowers both lifeboats to the spar deck. Joppich makes a series of calls, beginning with a Mayday transmission. He notifies the Coast Guard at the Mackinac Island station of the collision and calls the *Weissenburg* to ask the ship to stand by in the event that the *Cedarville* crew will need to be rescued when everyone abandons ship. He even places a call to the Bradley offices to inform them of the accident. He then assesses the ship's damage and makes a fateful decision: rather than abandon ship and wait for rescue, he decides to make a run for the beach near Mackinaw City. If he can ground the vessel, it can still be salvaged.

It doesn't get far—2.3 miles—from the spot of the collision to its final resting place. The *Cedarville*, burdened by the increased water weight, settles lower and lower in the water, slowing its progress to a mere six miles per hour in its dash for safety. The men on the deck, all in orange life jackets, prepare to launch the lifeboats. In the fog, it's impossible to see the beach, or even guess at how close it might be. The *Cedarville* lists heavily to its starboard side, and water washes onto the deck. The men manage to launch the number two lifeboat, but the other one is stuck on its cables. A few men jump overboard into the thirty-seven-degree water; the men on the lifeboat float free with it when the ship sinks. Others on the deck are tossed into the lake when the *Cedarville* rolls suddenly onto its starboard side. It disappears into 102 feet of water, marking the Bradley fleet's second loss of a vessel in less than a decade.

Len Gabrysiak is one of the men hurled into the frigid water. He's wearing a life jacket and he has a life ring, but neither offer much help when he becomes entangled in some cable on the sinking ship.

"I could feel myself being thrown," he remembers, "and it seemed like I had hit some cables—the port cables off the boom that ran back to the A-frame. The next thing I knew, I was in the water and I was going down. I closed my eyes to keep out debris—dirt or whatever—and it was light as I was going down, and then it was getting darker and darker. Finally, it was all black. I couldn't see anything through my eyelids. I was holding my breath. I said one "Hail Mary," and then another "Hail Mary," and then another one. I got about five in.

"While I was going down, when it was black, I lost that life ring. My hand just opened up. I couldn't hold onto it anymore, the pressure was so great. I was way down there. I don't know how far; but it was blacker than hell."

Suddenly, as if in answer to his prayers, he's released and he starts moving back to the surface. "Pretty soon, I could see light through my eyelids," he says. "But I was getting to the point where I couldn't hold my breath any longer. I decided to take a big swallow of water and maybe get a little oxygen with it and hang on. And that's what I did. When I broke the surface, I hit that big two-foot-square wooden collision block right in the chest. I shot right out of the water about two, three feet, and I finally settled on the water. I looked around, but I couldn't see a long way. I saw a raft, but it was a long way away and I wasn't that great of a swimmer. I would have never made it.

"I knew the water temperature was thirty-seven degrees because I heard it in the morning when I came on watch—they always call the engine room to get the water temperature—and I knew I had to keep my circulation going, so I started rubbing my arms and my legs underwater. I didn't know if it was going to help or not, but I did it anyway. I don't know how long I was in the water, but I was getting to the point where I was rubbing my arms and legs but couldn't feel anything anymore. I was looking around and I could hear some yelling, but I couldn't see anybody. All of a sudden, I could see a lifeboat way in the distance, and I started whistling and hollering, hoping they would see me or hear me. Pretty soon I could see that lifeboat coming toward me. They finally spotted me and came alongside me. I grabbed the gunwale with both hands and just passed out. I don't remember a thing after that."

Watchman Ed Brewster, from his vantage point at the stern of the *Cedarville*, hadn't been at all worried about the boat's status in the beginning. In fact, he'd been more curious about the potential of its sinking—so much so that he'd borrowed a camera and taken photos (eventually lost with the ship) of the water rushing into the *Cedarville*'s tunnel. When it became apparent that the boat was going to go down, Brewster moved to the starboard lifeboat and followed the standard lifeboat-boarding procedure.

"I was one of the last persons to jump in," he remembers. "I had to jump over the rail to get in. I was standing up right in the front, holding onto a line, when stokerman Casey Jones came running out of the fire hole. He hollered, 'Hey, wait for me!' I held out my left hand and said, 'Casey, grab my hand.'"

They never connected. The *Cedarville* rolled hard and, as Brewster recalls, water rushed up the deck.

"Our fingertips just touched," he says, "when a huge wave came washing down the deck and Casey disappeared. He's one person they never found."

The lifeboat stayed attached to the *Cedarville*, and when the boat rolled, Brewster was thrown into the water. Like Gabrysiak, he found himself fighting for his life while he was being dragged down with the ship.

"I must have gone down about forty feet," he says, "when whatever it was that was pulling me down let me loose and I came shooting up to the surface. Luckily, we had crotch straps on our lifejackets. Otherwise, that lifejacket would have come off. When I got to the surface, I looked over my left shoulder and I saw the stern of the ship going down. Then I looked ahead of me and the life raft was floating there. There were already quite a few people on it. I swam to the raft and they helped me on. I don't know how long we were on the raft, but the *Weissenburg* came alongside us a short time later."

Rescue vessels, led by the *Weissenburg*, rush to the scene. The *Weissenburg* combs the area, picking up twenty-seven crewmen from the water, the lifeboat, and a life raft that had broken free during the sinking. Eight men are unaccounted for, and despite exhaustive search efforts, they aren't found and are presumed to have gone down with the ship. Two of those rescued die shortly after they are picked up.

To Rogers City, the once-in-a-lifetime occurrence has happened twice in less than seven years. For Mac and Brenda Lamp, the *Bradley* and *Cedarville* tragedies are unbearably, inextricably connected: Brenda's father, Ray Kowalski, perished on the *Bradley*; Mac's father, Don Lamp, the *Cedarville*'s chief engineer, went down on the *Cedarville*.

Rogers City, barely recovered from the loss of the *Bradley*, prepares to mourn again.

Ten men lost their lives on the *Cedarville*.

Nine were from Rogers City.

EPILOGUE

IN THE DECADES FOLLOWING THE LOSS OF THE *CARL D. BRADLEY*, the ship's story assumes a place in Great Lakes maritime lore. Thousands of ships, from tiny boats to huge freighters, litter the bottom of the five lakes, in various stages of decomposition, many explored by sport divers drawn to the hulking presence of once-proud vessels now resting in dark, silent water. Their stories fill books or, in the case of those who lost loved ones in the accidents, scrapbooks and photo albums passed down from generation to generation.

Sadly, the *Bradley* and *Cedarville* stories are not the last. On November 29, 1966, the *Daniel J. Morrell*, a 603-foot ore carrier caught in a storm on Lake Huron, suffered a fate strikingly similar to the *Bradley's* when it broke apart on the surface and sank, at the cost of twenty-eight lives. Like the *Bradley*, the *Morrell* was running light, with no indication that anything was amiss until it hogged and sustained a fracture across its deck. Four men made it to a life raft, but only one, Dennis Hale, a twenty-six-year-old deckhand, survived. The *Morrell's* power lines had been severed before it could transmit a distress signal, and by the time the ship was reported missing and the raft was spotted by a Coast Guard helicopter, Hale had spent an astonishing thirty-eight hours on the lake, in high seas and subfreezing temperatures, wearing only his undershorts and a peacoat. He'd lost twenty-five pounds during the ordeal.

On November 10, 1975, the *Edmund Fitzgerald*, a 729-foot ore carrier loaded with just over twenty-six thousand tons of taconite iron ore pellets, became the largest, most recent, and, in terms of monetary cost, most expensive loss in Great Lakes history. Like so many ships before it, the *Fitzgerald* fell victim to a November storm, this one on Lake Superior, and its sinking continues to be one of the big mysteries in Great Lakes ship-wreck history. Fully stocked with modern communications equipment, the ship disappeared suddenly without sending a distress signal, even though its crew had been in contact with another freighter only minutes earlier. Its entire crew of twenty-nine went down with the ship.

Gordon Lightfoot's song "The Wreck of the *Edmund Fitzgerald*," an in-ternational hit, elevated the *Fitzgerald* to iconic status and, to a great extent, helped renew interest in Great Lakes shipwrecks. The survivors and rela-tives of lost crewmen of other recent shipwrecks would complain that the *Fitzgerald* received all the attention at the expense of other vessels, but there's no question that the Lightfoot song sparked an interest in exploring and understanding other wrecks. The *Fitzgerald*, in 530 feet of water, is all but impossible for free divers to explore. The *Bradley*, however, is not.

As the years added up and losses such as the *Morrell* and the *Fitzgerald* occurred, the *Carl D. Bradley* became known, at least among those who lost loved ones on the ship, as "the ship that time forgot." Rogers City hon-ored its memory, and that of the *Cedarville*, with annual memorial services, displays and artifacts at the city's maritime museum, and an engraved mar-ble plaque on its lakefront. An occasional book or television documentary would be released, spiking temporary interest in the ships, but overall in-terest declined with the general public's shrinking attention span and over-all disinterest in history.

Not so, however, among maritime historians and divers; the *Bradley* wreckage lay tantalizingly within reach, especially when technology and the use of mixed gases and rebreathers permitted divers to explore at pre-viously unimaginable depths.

Besides, there were still questions about the *Bradley* that needed to be answered.

*   *   *

Enter Jim Clary, a Port Huron marine artist highly acclaimed for his extraordinarily detailed paintings of Great Lakes ships and shipwrecks. Clary's interests in the *Bradley* run deep. He'd followed the story when it broke in 1958, and he had been, by his own description, "really touched" by the *Life* magazine photo spread and articles. He'd first met Frank Mays, via telephone, in 1975, and his first work on the *Bradley*, back in 1976, had been based on several telephone conversations with Mays.

"I thought Frank was a 'miracle man,' and always respected him," he'd say, "because I felt he was in that world beyond and back again the night of his ordeal."

Twenty years after his initial contact with Mays, Clary still has the *Bradley* on his mind. He'd agreed to do a series of paintings of the *Bradley* wreckage, but he'd like to see it firsthand, if at all possible. The problem is, no one has ever visited the *Bradley* wreckage.

Clary knows it's possible: others have visited storied shipwrecks, including the *Titanic* and *Edmund Fitzgerald*. A dive to the *Bradley* would be special.

"My main interest was to capture and write the last chapter of the *Bradley* in artwork," he'd remember. "No one had seen the *Bradley* for nearly forty years."

Clary relies on friends and connections to set a plan in motion. Josh Barnes, the former mayor of Charlevoix and a good customer of Clary's, shares his passion for the *Bradley*'s history and sinking. Barnes owns a pleasure boat, and he takes it out in search of the wreck site. It's hardly a high-tech venture, but by using "unsophisticated side scan equipment" he locates what he believes is the wreck.

Clary's next call is to Fred Shannon, a Mount Morris, Michigan, businessman and explorer who had arranged the expedition to the *Edmund Fitzgerald* in 1994. Shannon knows his stuff. He's not only an authority on Great Lakes shipwrecks and history; he also knows how to organize the type of complex dive required for an exploration of the *Bradley*. Shannon had used a two-man minisub called *Delta* when he visited the *Fitzgerald*, and he'd come away from the mission with stunning video footage—just the kind of material needed by Clary for his paintings.

Shannon is enthusiastic about the project, and he coordinates the technical aspects of the expedition. He contacts Delta Oceanographics, the California-based owners of the *Delta*, and arranges for its transfer to Lake Michigan. He also helps assemble the mission's crew and sets up the tug and barge operations for the dive. Clary directs the rest, from fund-raising and publicity to such finer details as picking up the needed provisions, paying for much of it out of his own pocket.

One person Clary would like to see involved is Frank Mays. As the *Bradley*'s sole remaining survivor—Elmer Fleming died of a heart attack in 1969—Mays is in a position to offer a unique perspective; as far as Clary knows, no one has ever survived a shipwreck and visited its gravesite later. Mays, now sixty-three years old, remarried, and living in Florida, jumps at the opportunity. With any luck, the mission will settle the long-standing dispute over whether the wreckage is in one or two pieces.

Clary and Shannon insist that Mays make a practice dive prior to his visit to the *Bradley*, mainly for reassurance that he won't grow claustrophobic or panic when the minisub is down in the darkness of the lake. Ironically, the practice dive is to the *Cedarville*, the ship on which Mays had served just prior to rejoining the *Bradley* after its summer 1958 layup. The *Cedarville*, lying on its side, the gash from its collision with the *Topdalsfjord* visible, fascinates Mays, who has no problems with the dive itself.

After months of intense preparations, the time arrives on August 15, 1995. Clary and Shannon enlist the talents of Ric Mixter, a Michigan-based videographer and documentary filmmaker, for the crucial task of capturing the images of the wreck on tape—in conditions that turn out to be prohibitive.

Shannon makes the first dive. The descent to the *Bradley* is uneventful, but the conditions around the wreck could be better. On Shannon's dives to the *Edmund Fitzgerald*, visibility had been good, and the men on board the minisub got a clear look at the sunken ore carrier. The *Bradley* is not as cooperative. Visibility, hampered by silt stirred up by a current, the minisub, and the remnants of a storm the previous day, is horrible—five feet at best. Shannon's dive nets very little other than glimpses of debris.

It's Clary's turn next, and his dive proves to be the longest of the expedition. *Delta* moves in for close-up views, occasionally scraping against the wreckage. Clary, like Shannon before him, struggles to make out much of anything in the murky water, though he does get a good look at the *Bradley's* stern.

Frank Mays finally gets his chance to see the ship for the first time since he watched it disappear beneath the waves. The poor visibility has reduced the wreckage to shadows and shapes, to such an extent that, while alongside the ship at the bottom of the lake, Mays can't determine whether the *Delta* is moving in the direction of the bow or the stern. He eventually sees the words CARL D. BRADLEY painted on the starboard side of the stern section, but after twenty-five minutes of exploration, the minisub heads back up.

The disappointing exploration, costing a reported $150,000, nets some rewards, but in the end, it fails to record evidence to settle the dispute over whether the *Bradley* is actually in two pieces, as Mays has rigidly maintained.

Clary organizes another trip, this one for May 1997. Frank Mays is back on board, though neither he nor anyone else will be diving to the wreck this time around. Rather than rent the minisub for this expedition, Clary and Shannon employ an ROV (remotely operated vehicle) to explore the *Bradley*. Tethered by cable to the mother ship and using video cameras linked to monitors on the boat, the ROV enjoys greater mobility than the larger *Delta*, and it's freer and safer to maneuver in tighter spaces.

The ROV delivers—and then some. It explores the entire ship, revealing the *Bradley* in remarkable detail. The ship, as Mays and Fleming witnessed and testified, indeed appears to have gone down in two pieces. The bow and stern sections, both upright but listing to port, line up almost perfectly but look to be separated by roughly ninety feet. By all indications, the back of the bow section hit the lake floor first. It is buried in mud, almost to the conveyor boom. To the amazement of those observing the monitors on the mother ship, the huge unloading boom is as intact and secured as it had been before the sinking. The stern is missing hatch covers, which probably were blown out during the sinking, and railings, which probably were pulled loose when the two sections separated. Debris and coal are strewn all around the wreckage, but no victims can be seen.

If funerals present closure to the families of the dead, seeing the *Bradley* wreckage represents a type of closure for Frank Mays. His life has taken a lot of turns since November 18, 1958, but it always will be defined by his final minutes on a sinking ship and his hours on a raft, staring down the odds and surviving a storm that tested his—and Elmer Fleming's—endurance. Seeing the *Bradley* wreckage is nothing less than a confrontation with his past, a vindication against his critics, and ultimately a settlement with history.

"I saw it go down in two pieces on the surface," he'd write in his account of the dive, "and now I've seen it in two pieces on the bottom of Lake Michigan."*

The Clary-Shannon expeditions mark an end to fact-finding explorations of the *Carl D. Bradley*. Barring the development of new technology capable of analyzing the wreckage and coming up with the cause of the ship's breaking apart, there isn't much more to learn. There is no chance of salvaging the wreck. It is a gravesite for those interred inside, and an important historical artifact to the Great Lakes shipping industry.

It might be assigned to the lakes if not for the interests of sport divers and deep-sea adventurers eager to take on the challenges of diving to one of the most fabled modern shipwrecks. This isn't for amateurs. Even the most ad-

---

* Even after this exploration, there's disagreement over whether there is a *total* separation between the two sections. The keel, a small but persuasive group argues, is intact, holding the two sections together. Those holding this position maintain that the forward section sank first, as maintained by Mays and Fleming, but instead of immediately sinking to the bottom of the lake, the bow portion disappeared from the surface and hung suspended below, held to the back of the ship by a small strip of the keel, until the stern section filled with enough water to sink. The two sections then dropped to the lake floor. The two sections might appear to be separated, but they line up so well because they are still joined.

It's a compelling, if unpopular argument, but since most of the bottom of the *Bradley's* wreckage is buried in mud and silt, it's impossible to prove—at least by visual inspection.

vanced divers would refrain from entering the wreckage, which promises many uncertainties to those relying on precision just to stay alive at these depths. As it is, the outside of the ship offers enough in challenges to hold an experienced diver's attention.

The *Cedarville* is a case in point. Compared to the *Bradley*'s final resting place in more than 350 feet of water, the *Cedarville*, at 103 feet at its deepest point, appears to be a much safer exploration. Divers can reach its superstructure at a depth of fewer than 50 feet, and much of this and the rest of the *Cedarville* can be penetrated by even inexperienced divers. Nevertheless, the wreck has claimed the lives of explorers, beginning in 1965, when, not long after the loss of the ship, a diver perished while trying to retrieve the ship's nameboard. Others followed, one suffering a heart attack during his dive, another after becoming trapped inside the wreckage.

The *Bradley* lies in totally dark water at 3½ times the depth, where visibility can be bad. Since it hasn't been explored by other divers, there is no research to guide explorers, and the information you might obtain from the earlier minisub and ROV dives is sketchy. Extra tanks and support divers are required. A diver would be burdened by a couple hundred pounds of equipment. The ascent time, from the wreckage back to the surface, would be lengthy, with divers having to stop at regular intervals and hover for long periods in the darkness. Finally, there's an issue of cost: you don't pull off a dive of this nature on chump change.

Of course, these are the kinds of obstacles that entice serious shipwreck divers—the more challenging the dive, the more attractive it becomes. In the world of deep-sea explorers, bragging rights carry extra currency.

Mirek Standowicz is the first.

His initial dive to the *Bradley*, on July 6, 2001, is more for history's sake than for a detailed study. Even with available technology, bottom time at this depth, and at this pressure, is limited, and Standowicz sets out with the goal of spending his short time on the *Bradley* videotaping the wreckage for a documentary being assembled by Jim and Pat Stayers of the Michigan-based Out of the Blue Productions.

Standowicz descends in pitch-black water, reaching the boom after ten minutes. In the darkness, he can't get his bearings, and he's not sure which way to go to reach the *Bradley*'s pilothouse. After only a few minutes on the *Bradley*, he abandons the dive when his ascent line becomes entangled between two sharp objects.

A second dive is planned for August 7. This one doesn't disappoint. Standowicz drops onto the *Bradley*'s pilothouse and, as he shines his light on the boat, he sees the white lettering CARL D. BRADLEY painted on the red paint above the wheelhouse windows. The glass is gone, blown out during the sinking, but otherwise the pilothouse is in very good condition. Standowicz videotapes inside, shooting the telegraph in the stop position and the wheel itself.

"Looking at the ship," he tells the Stayers afterward, "I had an overwhelming feeling that was like walking through a ghost town that used to be full of life."

Standowicz spends the entire dive exploring the *Bradley*'s pilothouse and bow, recording footage. He ascends from the wreckage with the same sense of awe that struck Jim Clary, Fred Shannon, and Frank Mays. Despite its tragic end and the loss of life, there is something beautiful about the wreckage and its history. It is now part of the lake that once defeated it.

As Standowicz would recall, "It seems like the *Bradley* is standing proudly on the bottom, ready to sail."

August 2007

Hundreds of feet below the surface of Lake Michigan, a torch is sparked and fire burns through the water, brightly illuminating the area around the stanchion holding the bell of the *Carl D. Bradley* in place.

This moment signifies the realization of a goal carefully planned by John Janzen and John Scoles, two Minnesota divers who intend to remove the *Bradley*'s bell and replace it with a replica bearing the names of the crew on the ship's last journey.

The two men recognize the solemnity of the task. In maritime tradition, sailors regard a ship's bell as the soul of the vessel. Removing the bell from a sunken ship is not just frowned upon, purists consider it a desecration. In replacing the original bell with a replica engraved with the lost sailors' names, Janzen and Scoles hope to create a memorial that honors the crew while bringing feelings of closure to their families.

Such a bell removal and replacement is not unprecedented. In 1997 a group headed by Tom Farnquist, the curator of the Great Lakes Shipwreck Historical Museum in Whitefish Point, Michigan, had organized a dive to the *Edmund Fitzgerald*—and not without protest from opponents who believed the bell should be left intact. Farnquist was supported by a consensus among the relatives of the *Fitzgerald's* twenty-nine lost crewmen, and the highly publicized dive was accomplished without incident. A replacement bell was affixed to the wreckage, and the original bell was restored and placed in the Shipwreck Museum, where it is tolled during memorial services every November 10—the anniversary of the *Fitzgerald's* sinking.

Scoles and Janzen have a similar aim for the *Bradley* bell. After they retrieve it, they will turn it over to the Great Lakes Lore Maritime Museum in Rogers City, where it will be housed after it is restored. Not surprisingly, Frank Mays is present at the bell dive. The two divers had met him three years ago at a diving and shipwreck show in Minneapolis, and the three quickly became friends.

Months of preparation preceded the dive. Scoles and Janzen designed a special battery system and underwater torch, and they made a number of practice dives in Lake Wazee, a flooded iron mine and the deepest lake in Wisconsin. The *Bradley* project involves three bell dives—one to cut off the bell, one to prepare the ship's stanchion for the replacement bell, and one to install it—plus what Janzen and Scoles hope will be additional bottom time to explore and videotape the wreckage.

They need—and are granted—permission from the state of Michigan to do all this. The *Bradley* is a gravesite, and some of the family members of the lost crewmen, like the families of the lost crewmen on the *Edmund Fitzgerald* before them, have petitioned the state to pass legislation prohibiting exploration of the ship or, at the very least, photographing human remains. The *Fitzgerald* has been declared a gravesite and off limits to future exploration by the Canadian government.* Divers are still permitted to visit the *Bradley*, but there are strict limitations on what can be removed or photographed.

Janzen and Scoles have visited the *Bradley* on several prior occasions, first in July 2004, when they became the first free divers to explore the stern portion of the wreck, and then again a year later, when Janzen explored the inside of the pilothouse while two other divers, Zach Demorest and Nick Shaffer, became the first divers to penetrate the wreckage when they entered the bow section and reached and videotaped some of the crew quarters. Then, in 2006, while awaiting formal permission to remove the *Bradley*'s bell, Scoles and Janzen began preparations for the mission by installing mooring lines and measuring the bell and its hanger.

The close-up explorations rewarded the divers in ways that were both exhilarating and humbling. Their first dive to the wreck, like any diver's first visit to a legendary wreck lying in dark, deep water, touched them in a sense that went beyond the thrill of discovery.

"You get goosebumps," John Scoles explains today. "When you come down to the wreck and your lights are shining on it, and it's so quiet you can hear the chain rolling on the mooring line, you get this eerie feeling. But it's peaceful. You can almost feel the souls on the ship. This is *their* place—their resting place. They're going to be there forever. And you can hear your heart beat."

Signs of the crew and their work are everywhere. A shoe sits on the deck. A work light, its cord still neatly wound, hangs on a hook in the after deck. Light bulbs, unbroken after sitting all these years at this depth, remain intact. One cannot see these things—not to mention the silt and layer of quagga mussels covering the wreckage like a coat of living rust—and not feel a sense of loss and passing time.

---

* The *Edmund Fitzgerald* lies in Canadian waters.

The men made their most significant discovery in the silt and mud on the *Bradley's* port side: the port lifeboat, never recovered and presumed lost somewhere in Lake Michigan, rests on the lake floor as if someone had pulled it from the *Bradley* and gently placed it there. Intrigued by their discovery, the divers examined the port and starboard lifeboat davits to see if the *Bradley* crew had been able to launch the boats, and they determined that the starboard lifeboat had been launched—or at least the crew had attempted to launch it. Its davits are out. On the port side, however, the davits are still locked in their cradle position, adding an air of mystery to how the lifeboat wound up separated from the ship.

The divers are reminded of the hazards they face each time they descend through the pitch-black water to the wreckage. At a depth of more than 350 feet, the water is bone-chilling, not much above freezing, and the pressure at that depth limits them to about half an hour of bottom time. To combat the cold, the men wear dry suits equipped with electric heaters, and, after each visit to the *Bradley*, they deal with the pressure by making an ascent to the surface that takes more than two hours. These issues are expected. It's the unexpected that concerns them. The wreckage's sharp and jagged edges pose all sorts of dangers. The icy temperatures could spell trouble for some of the equipment, as they discovered on a test dive, when one of the regulators sending oxygen to the torch froze up, cutting off the oxygen flow and necessitating the use of an "extra dry" grade of oxygen for future dives.

The bell retrieval dive presents its own challenges. An assortment of equipment, including the torch, the battery pack, and extra line and tanks, has to be hauled down to the wreckage, and setting up for the removal of the bell takes more time than anticipated.

"We shuttled all our gear down to the wreck, and then we had to shuttle it from the mooring line to the top of the pilothouse," Scoles remembers. "That was probably the hardest part of the whole dive. We were seventeen or eighteen minutes into the dive, and we'd just gotten our stuff there. I was thinking, 'Man, this thing's just not going to happen. We're falling behind here.' But about eighteen minutes into the dive, we split up. John did his thing, I did my things, and it all clicked and came together. The next thing you know, we lit the torch and *BOOM*, it was done. It went well after that."

Both men dread the thought of failure. During the couple of years that they spent jumping through the legal and political hoops necessary to gain permission to remove and replace the bell, Janzen and Scoles got to know not only Frank Mays; they became friendly with the residents of Rogers City, including some of the relatives of lost crewmen and the people running the maritime museum. It would have been one thing, Janzen says, if the mission had failed because they couldn't obtain permission to place the bell, or if the logistics of the dive prevented the dive; the divers could have lived with that. What they couldn't live with were the prospects of failing because of human error.

"We didn't want to let these people down," Janzen asserts. "We were afraid that something might go wrong while we were down there— something like our damaging or dropping the bell once we got it off. That would have been a sacrilege."

Fortunately, they encounter no resistance from the bell. It comes off much easier than they anticipated, and with their bottom time running out, they attach the bell to lift bags. They watch it move upward until it disappears from sight, and then they begin their ascent to the surface. Unfortunately, they won't have the satisfaction of seeing the bell actually pulled from the water: they'll still be in the middle of their decompression process when the bell has completed its ascent.

With Frank Mays watching, the bell breaks the surface, seeing the light of day for the first time in nearly forty-nine years. The relics from the *Bradley* story are few in number and are spread out in museums around the upper Midwest. The life raft mysteriously disappeared shortly after its return to Rogers City, only to surface later in an Ohio museum. The *Sundew* is now a museum ship in Duluth, Minnesota. The *Hollyhock* was sunk as a historical divers' reef. The bell, the most important artifact to be retrieved from the *Carl D.*, will not only reside in the town that suffered the greatest loss nearly half a century ago; it also will be tolled, beginning on the fiftieth anniversary of the tragedy, in poignant annual memorial services for men who, during the course of doing their jobs, wound up sacrificing their lives for a place in Great Lakes history.

The Great Lakes Lore Maritime Museum has a hall of fame honoring those who made significant contributions to Rogers City's nautical history. New members are inducted every summer during the city's annual nautical festival. Most of the inductees are from Rogers City or the northern part of lower Michigan, and most have a connection to the Bradley Transportation fleet. Captain Harold Muth and Warren Toussaint are members—not that they need a formal connection to the series of events that so deeply affected an entire community.

For Toussaint, like so many others, those events are brought into sharp focus at least once a year, and he doesn't anticipate that changing.

"Every November eighteenth, I kind of walk the floors," he says, "because I see the bodies again. My wife leaves me alone. I can finally get to sleep. But it's in my body, and it will be until the day I die."

THE CREW OF THE *CARL D. BRADLEY*, NOVEMBER 18, 1958

Carl Bartell, 25, Third Mate, Kalkaska, Michigan †

John Bauers, 30, First Assistant Engineer, Rogers City, Michigan ‡

Douglas Bellmore, 34, Porter, Onaway, Michigan ‡

Duane Berg, 25, Deckhand, Rogers City, Michigan ‡

Alfred Boehmer, 32, Second Assistant Engineer, Rogers City, Michigan †

Richard Book, 26, Deck Watchman, Portsmouth, Iowa †

Roland Bryan, 52, Master, Loudonville, New York ‡

Alva Budnick, 26, Watchman, Rogers City, Michigan ‡

Raymond Buehler, 59, Chief Engineer, Lakewood, Ohio ‡

William Elliott, 26, Repairman, Rogers City, Michigan †

Clyde Enos, 29, Stokerman, Cheboygan, Michigan ‡

Erhardt Felax, 46, Stokerman, Rogers City, Michigan †

Elmer Fleming, 43, First Mate, Rogers City, Michigan *

John Fogelsonger, 28, Second Mate, St. Ignace, Michigan ‡

Cleland Gager, 30, Oiler, Onaway, Michigan †

Paul Greengtski, 23, Watchman, Rogers City, Michigan ‡

Paul Heller, 45, Stokerman, Rogers City, Michigan †

Paul Horn, 21, Oiler, Rogers City, Michigan ‡

Dennis Joppich, 19, Wiper, Rogers City, Michigan ‡

Raymond Kowalski, 31, Wheelsman, Rogers City, Michigan †

Joseph Krawczak, 35, Wheelsman, Rogers City, Michigan †

Floyd MacDougall, 26, Oiler, Rogers City, Michigan ‡

Frank Mays, 26, Deck Watchman, Rogers City, Michigan *

Dennis Meredith, 26, Deckhand, Metz Township, Michigan ‡

Melvin Orr, 35, Watchman, Rogers City, Michigan ‡

Alfred Pilarski, 30, Second Cook, Rogers City, Michigan †

Gary Price, 21, Deckhand, Onaway, Michigan †

Leo Promo Jr., 21, Assistant Conveyorman, Rogers City, Michigan †

Bernard Schefke, 19, Porter, Rogers City, Michigan †

Keith Schuler, 38, Third Assistant Engineer, Rogers City, Michigan ‡

James Selke, 18, Porter, Rogers City, Michigan ‡

Gary Strzelecki, 21, Deck Watchman, Rogers City, Michigan †

Earl Tulgetske, 30, Wheelsman, Rogers City, Michigan ‡

Edward Vallee, 49, Conveyorman, Rogers City, Michigan †

John Zoho, 63, Steward, Clairton, Pennsylvania †

* Survivor
† Recovered
‡ Missing

APPENDIX

[The following is the report and findings regarding the loss of the *Carl D. Bradley*, filed by the U.S. Coast Guard's Board of Inquiry, beginning with the commandant's response to the report and followed by the actual report.]

UNITED STATES COAST GUARD

COMMANDANT'S ACTION
on
Marine Board of Investigation; foundering of the SS CARL D. BRADLEY,
Lake Michigan, 18 November 1958, with loss of life

1. The record of the Marine Board of Investigation convened to investigate subject casualty together with its Findings of Fact, Opinions and Recommendations has been reviewed.

2. The SS CARL D. BRADLEY, Official Number 226776, a self-unloading bulk freighter of 10,028 gross tons, built in 1927, departed Gary, Indiana, on 17 November 1958 en route to Calcite, Michigan, in ballast. At the time of departure the wind was 25–35 MPH from the south and the weather forecast was for whole gale winds, 50 to 65 MPH from the south shifting to the

southwest. The BRADLEY proceeded up the Wisconsin shore at distances varying from 5 to 12 miles. Although the wind velocity increased during the period, sea conditions were not considered severe and the vessel was riding smoothly. Sometime early in the afternoon of 18 November in the vicinity of Cana Island course was altered to 046 degrees True to cross Lake Michigan toward Lansing Shoal. While proceeding on this course the wind reached a velocity of 60 to 65 MPH from the southwest. The speed of the vessel was between 14 and 15 knots. The seas were slightly on the starboard quarter and according to the Chief Mate, who was on watch at the time of the casualty and one of the two survivors, the seas were estimated to be 20 feet in height with 50 to 75 feet between the crests. The vessel continued to ride smoothly, however, both as to roll and to pitch. At 1730 just at dusk while still on course 046 a noise described as a thud followed by a vibration was heard. The Chief Mate looked aft and saw the stern of the vessel sagging and it was immediately realized that the vessel was in serious trouble. The general alarm was sounded and the crew prepared to abandon ship. Distress calls on the radio-telephone were made by the Chief Mate who gave the vessel's position as 12 miles southwest of Gull Island Light. These calls were received by several radio stations, both commercial and Coast Guard. Within two or three minutes the BRADLEY heaved upward near No. 10 hatch, which is approximately amidships, and broke in two. The bow settled from aft, then rolled over and sank. The liferaft stowed forward which was being readied floated free. The stern settled from forward, then plunged with a flash of flame and smoke as the water reached the boiler room. Four crew members managed to board the liferaft immediately after the casualty but two were lost during the night.

3. A 254' German cargo vessel, the M/V CHRISTIAN SARTORI, was approximately four miles from the BRADLEY at the time of the casualty and observed the flash of flame from which she concluded the BRADLEY had exploded. Course was immediately altered for the scene but due to the ad-

verse sea conditions she did not arrive at the estimated position of the sinking until approximately one and one-half hours later.

4. Coast Guard air and surface units, assisted by the SARTORI until 0200, 19 November, searched the area throughout the night with aircraft providing flare illumination. Weather conditions and darkness severely handicapped the search and it was not until 0825, 19 November, that the raft carrying the only two survivors was located. After daybreak eight other merchant vessels joined the search. Later in the morning the lifeboat from the after end of the BRADLEY was located in an overturned condition. Of the thirty-five persons reported to have been aboard the BRADLEY there were, in addition to the two survivors, eighteen bodies recovered. Fifteen are still missing and are presumed dead. At the present time efforts to locate and identify the wreck of the BRADLEY are still continuing.

Remarks

1. Concurring with the Board, it is considered that the BRADLEY did not strike Boulder Reef but rather that she broke in two and the eruption of steam and combustible materials as she went down gave rise to the mistaken assumption on the part of the CHRISTIAN SARTORI witnesses that the vessel exploded.

2. Although in all probability the vessel broke in hogging, the implication in the Board's conclusion that the fracture resulted because the vessel encountered an unusual wave condition while in ballast is not supported in the record. In the absence of any evidence of improper or unusual ballasting such reasoning would necessarily require an assumption that the waves were unique in the vessel's twenty-one-year history of navigation in the Great Lakes. This premise and the conclusion must therefore be rejected, particularly in view of the survivors' description of how smoothly the vessel

was riding; a point of which the Board took special note and which was further supported by the statement of the Second Mate of the SS JOHNSTOWN. For this reason the Board's conclusion that the Master of the BRADLEY exercised poor judgment in proceeding across northern Lake Michigan from Cana Island toward Lansing Shoal is also disapproved.

3. The Board has offered no other conclusions as to the possible cause of this disaster and an exhaustive review of the record has likewise failed to yield any positive determinations in this regard. Contrary to the Board's opinions, however, the following factors may have had some causal connection and cannot be discounted merely for the lack of probative evidence:

a. The unexplained presence of the hairline cracks discovered in the vessel's underbody amidships during drydocking in Chicago in May 1957 strongly suggest the possibility of structural weakness.

b. The two unreported groundings experienced by the BRADLEY in the spring of 1958 and November of 1958 may have introduced unusual hull stresses. It is because such possibilities exist that 46 CFR 136.05-1 requires a Notice of Marine Casualty to be filed with the Coast Guard in all cases of stranding or grounding whether or not there is apparent damage.

c. The extensive renewal of cargo hold side slopes, screen bulkheads and tank tops planned by the company for the 1958–1959 winter lay-up is in itself indicative of wear and deterioration and raises the obvious question as to the general condition of the vessel's structure.

The possibilities raised by the foregoing coupled with the fact that the vessel broke up and foundered under conditions which, while severe, she should easily have been able to weather, leads inevitably to the conclusion that the vessel had developed an undetected structural weakness or defect. Due to the significance of such a possibility, particularly with respect to other vessels of similar design and vintage, consideration will be given to the initiation of an underwater survey of the BRADLEY depending, of course, on when and where the vessel is ultimately located and any other practical aspects which might limit the benefits to be derived from such examination.

4. Regardless of any other determinations, this casualty has emphasized the need for the program of technical evaluation to determine if there is any evidence of structural defects in other vessels of the Great Lakes fleet. Such a program has been initiated. In addition, a reappraisal of present inspection procedures as applied to Great Lakes vessels is indicated looking toward the adoption of such standards and methods that will increase the likelihood of early detection of possible structural weaknesses particularly in the case of older vessels. The Commander, Ninth Coast Guard District has been directed to adopt any reasonable procedure within the framework of present laws and regulations and to make further recommendations for any legislative or regulatory changes which appear necessary. Finally, it is considered that this casualty has dictated a need for owners and operators to re-examine their responsibilities to establish and maintain safe operating and maintenance standards.

5. The Board's recommendations concerning life jacket crotch straps, an additional liferaft, lifeboat mechanical disengaging apparatus, lifeboat painters and parachute type distress signals merit further consideration and will be made the subject of study by the Merchant Marine Council.

6. Subject to the foregoing remarks, the record of the Marine Board of Investigation is approved.

A. C. RICHMOND
Vice Admiral, U.S. Coast Guard
Commandant

[This is the full, unedited text of the Board of Inquiry's report.]

After full and mature deliberation, the board finds as follows:

Findings of Fact

1. The particulars on SS CARL D. BRADLEY:

Name: CARL D. BRADLEY

Owner: Michigan Limestone Division, U. S. Steel Corporation

Official No.: 226776

Tonnage: 10028 Gross; 7706 Net

Home Port: New York

Type Vessel: Self-unloading bulk freighter

Dimensions: 623' × 65' × 33'

Propulsion: Steam, single screw, turbo-electrical, two Foster Wheeler boilers 450#

Classification: Lloyd's Register of Shipping, 100A1 and LMC

Builder: American Shipbuilding Company, Lorain, Ohio, yard, 1927, hull number 797

Master: Roland Bryan, Loudonville, New York

Chief Engineer: Raymond Buehler, 1500 Cordova Avenue, Lakewood, Ohio

2. The CARL D. BRADLEY was given her last annual inspection at Calcite, Michigan, by Commander Mark L. Hocking and Lieutenant Frank Sperry, inspectors from the OCMI Office, St. Ignace, Michigan. This inspection started on 30 January 1958 and was completed on 17 April 1958, and a certificate of inspection was issued on that date.

3. The CARL D. BRADLEY had an established load line. The current certificate issued by Lloyd's Register of Shipping was last endorsed on 26 February 1958 by Mr. J. D. Wallace and R. S. Haugenson, surveyors.

4. During the 1957–58 winter lay-up, miscellaneous cargo hold repairs were effected. These included the replacement of deteriorated and loose rivets

by carriage bolts in the hopper side slope plates. Although the Coast Guard had not given prior approval to these repairs, they were considered adequate by Lieutenant Sperry when he viewed the work in progress. These repairs were later reported by the Master to be holding satisfactorily, and there was no report of leaking in the side tanks during the 1958 season.

5. The CARL D. BRADLEY was scheduled for extensive cargo hold renewal and replacement during the 1958–59 winter lay-up. This work was to be performed at Manitowoc Shipbuilding Company, Manitowoc, Wisconsin, and was to consist primarily of the reconstruction of the tank top, renewal of the cargo hold side slopes and screen bulkheads, and the installation of a centerline bulkhead between frames 32 and 170, as shown on H. C. Downer and Associates Drawings ID 411-59-3-1 (Appendix "Y") and ID 411-811-11-1 (Appendix "Z"), approved by the Coast Guard on 25 February 1958 and by Lloyd's on 11 October 1957. A comparison of the sideship section, as originally built (Exhibit 06), and that shown on H. C. Downer Drawing ID-411-811-11-1 (Appendix "Z") indicates that the above work would have increased the longitudinal strength by a moderate amount. It was also the owner's intent to dry-dock the vessel in Chicago after the completion of the work in Manitowoc for its five-year survey, the last five-year survey docking having been accomplished in Lorain, Ohio, in 1953.

6. The CARL D. BRADLEY was in drydock for period 9–15 May 1957 at Chicago, Illinois, to effect repairs incident to damages sustained on 3 April 1956 in a collision with M/V WHITE ROSE at South East Bend, St. Clair River. These repairs consisted of inserting one (1) new bilge plate 21 feet long to replace damaged sections of Plates E-14 and E-15 starboard, and minor fairing and riveting to shell plates K-8 and K-9 port side. In addition, hairline fractures in the transverse direction, located for the most part at the after edge of the riveted lap butts, were found in bottom plates B-16, D-16, D-18, D-19, starboard, and B-14, B-15, C-9, C-16, and D-12 port. These plates were repaired by cropping out the fractured sections of the plates

and the adjacent riveted lap butts and inserting a new full-width section approximately six feet in length. In effecting these repairs, the butts were flush welded and the seams were riveted. Satisfactory temporary repairs were also made to shell plate J-20 aft on the port side in way of the engine room forward bulkhead and internals in way of this plate and miscellaneous repairs were also made on the starboard side aft, exact location unknown.

7. On two occasions between the drydocking in May 1957 and the casualty, the CARL D. BRADLEY sustained bottom damage. In the spring of 1958, the vessel rubbed bottom while proceeding out of Cedarville, Michigan, and damage was incurred just aft of the collision bulkhead in way of No. 1 water bottom, port. The owners considered this damage to be of such a minor extent that no repairs were necessary. In early November 1958, the vessel again rubbed bottom while turning at Cedarville, and damage was sustained in way of No. 7 water bottom, port, in the A and B strakes. This damage, a transverse fracture approximately 14" long, was repaired afloat at Calcite, Michigan, by the owner's repair force by welding a channel bar over the fracture and blanking each end to form a cofferdam. The size of this channel is not known.

8. Neither of the above-mentioned damages was reported to the Coast Guard or Lloyd's, and the repair in No. 7 water bottom was neither reported to nor approved by the Coast Guard.

9. On 30 October 1958, a safety inspection was conducted on board the CARL D. BRADLEY by Lieutenant Sperry. This inspection consisted of a fire drill and a boat drill, during which both boats were swung out and No. 2 boat was lowered into the water and 28 crewmen exercised under oars to the satisfaction of the inspector. It was during this visit to the vessel that the Master reported that the repairs to the side tanks were holding up satisfactorily.

10. The CARL D. BRADLEY was of typical arrangement for self-unloading type vessels with a forepeak and a large cargo area, and having propulsion machinery aft. These areas were separated by two transverse watertight bulkheads, the collision bulkhead at frame 12 and the engine room forward bulkhead at frame 173. The cargo hold space was divided into five compartments by screen bulkheads above the tunnel and the unloading machinery was located in the conveyor room just forward of the cargo spaces. The entire 475 foot length of the cargo spaces was open longitudinally through the tunnel and conveyor room.

11. The CARL D. BRADLEY was engaged in the limestone and coal trade, operating primarily between the limestone ports on Lake Huron and unloading ports on Lakes Michigan and Erie. The 1958 season began on 22 April and the CARL D. BRADLEY had completed 43 round trips before the casualty. The vessel was not in operation for a period of about three months commencing about 1 July and ending about 1 October by reason of business lag. During this period, the vessel lay at Calcite, Michigan, with only a watchman on board.

12. Captain Bryan had been sailing as Master of the CARL D. BRADLEY since 1954. Chief Engineer Buehler had served on the CARL D. BRADLEY for almost the entire life of the vessel and as Chief Engineer since 1952.

13. The manager of the Bradley Transportation fleet is Mr. Norman Hoeft and he has held his present position for approximately two years. He has had no sailing experience, but has been in the employment of Michigan Limestone Division for some 33 years in various capacities. His last previous assignment was in the traffic department.

14. Present management knew of no company instructions issued concerning the sequence of loading, unloading, or ballasting of their vessels. They consider that the responsibility in these matters is vested in the ships' masters.

There were certain practices followed on the CARL D. BRADLEY which developed into recommended procedures as a result of the experience of vessel personnel and which were passed on by masters and mates to their successors.

15. The Master and Chief Engineer of the CARL D. BRADLEY were charged with the responsibility of keeping the management advised as to the repairs, maintenance and upkeep requirements. The management structure of the Bradley Fleet, which consisted of nine vessels, did not provide for a fleet captain or a fleet engineer.

16. The safety director of the Bradley Transportation fleet had not, in his four (4) years in his present capacity, received any complaints of unsafe or hazardous operating conditions on the CARL D. BRADLEY. It is noted that the safety program, as administered by the safety director for the Bradley fleet, was almost solely devoted to industrial-type safety conditions and did not encompass vessel material conditions. For success in this field, the National Safety Council presented an award of honor to the Bradley Transportation Line, Michigan Limestone Division, Rogers City, Michigan, for the world's record in having 2,228,755 injury-free man hours, 24 April 1955 to 31 December 1957. The present safety director had not at any time personally made a material condition inspection on the CARL D. BRADLEY.

17. The CARL D. BRADLEY departed Gary, Indiana, bound for Calcite, Michigan, at approximately 2200 on 17 November 1958. Prior to departure, the Master and Mate had knowledge of the weather forecast, which at 2000 warned of whole gale winds (50–65 MPH) from the south, shifting to southwest. At the time of departure, the wind was fresh (25–35 MPH) from the south and there was no sea.

18. When the CARL D. BRADLEY was secured for sea, special attention was given to the hatch clamps and boom stays, because of the impending

weather. The vessel was in a light condition with the forward tanks only partially ballasted. The ballasting of the after tanks (5, 6, and 7, and Trim) was handled by the engineering force, and the amount of water in the after tanks during this voyage could not be determined. However, normal practice was to have the vessel ballasted full aft to get the propeller down, and the vessel would, therefore, have had a draft between 17'6" and 18' aft. The forward draft was not measured at the time of departure. The above was the normal ballasting procedure for departing port without cargo.

19. At 0400 on 18 November 1958, the CARL D. BRADLEY passed Milwaukee at a distance of 11 miles, making approximately 15 MPH, and was abeam Sheboygan at 0700, a distance of seven miles. Two lake freighters, SS GOVERNOR MILLER and RICHARD TRIMBLE, were running parallel with the CARL D. BRADLEY, and closer to shore. The wind increased steadily after 0400, and during the 4–8 watch, the water ballast was increased to the maximum practical condition of 10, 16, 18, and 18 feet in tanks #1, 2, 3 and 4 respectively. The vessel remained ballasted in this manner until the casualty.

20. The CARL D. BRADLEY continued up the Wisconsin Shore at distances off varying from five to twelve miles. From a point off Cana Island, a course of 046° true was set across Northern Lake Michigan toward a point midway between Seul Choix Point and Lansing Shoal. Sometime prior to 1600 speed had been reduced by about 10 RPM so that the vessel was making approximately 14–15 MPH. At 1519 a fix was plotted by the Second Mate from visual bearings, and this position indicated the vessel to be slightly to the south of the line drawn on the chart for the route across Lake Michigan.

21. At 1600, when First Mate Elmer Fleming came on watch, the master was on the bridge and in charge of the navigation. The CARL D. BRADLEY was past Poverty Island on course 046° true and was riding comfortably with a heavy following sea slightly on the starboard quarter. The wind

had increased to whole gale force (60–65 MPH) and had shifted to southwest.

22. The SS JOHNSTOWN, ahead of the CARL D. BRADLEY by several
hours, passed Boulder Reef at about 1317, and had reported encountering
a very heavy sea there at that time. The only other lake freighter which reported passing Boulder Reef was the SS CHARLES L. HUTCHINSON, which
passed the reef at 0554 on the 18th, downbound and loaded. This vessel
reduced speed at 0700, because of heavy seas. All other lake vessels that
reported having been in the northern Lake Michigan area at this time reported that they had sought shelter, and at least eight vessels were anchored or proceeding to anchor at the time of the casualty, either in Green
Bay, at Garden Island, or in the Straits of Mackinac.

23. Sometime after 1600, the radar was placed in operation and was used
for all subsequent navigation, except for an RDF bearing of 051° true obtained on Lansing Shoal sometime before 1700. After the fix obtained at
1519 was plotted on the chart, no later positions were plotted. However,
radar observations indicated that on the course being steered (046° true),
the vessel would clear Boulder Reef and Gull Island by at least five miles. At
about 1720, radar ranges were taken on the north end of South Fox Island
and on Point aux Barques, which again showed the vessel to be slightly to
the right of the course line drawn on the chart.

24. Within one-half hour before the casualty, both survivors, Fleming and
Mays, had occasion to traverse the length of the vessel from the forward
house to the after house on the weather deck, and neither one saw nor
heard anything out of the ordinary which would have caused them to be
concerned with the safety of the vessel. In addition, Mays also went aft to
the engine room and returned to the fore part of the vessel through the tunnel, and, again, neither saw nor heard anything unusual. Up to the time of
the casualty, this vessel was riding easily, taking no water over the deck,

and with so smooth a motion that the sideboards were not necessary on the mess table. Accordingly, persons on board were not aware of any reason to be concerned for the safety of the vessel.

25. The bulkhead at the forward end of the engine and boiler spaces, "Blk #173" was fitted with a dogged watertight door which opened forward into the tunnel. This door was normally kept closed, although rarely if ever completely dogged. Just prior to the casualty, when Mays was aft to pump the water from the sump at the after end of the tunnel, he used this door, and when last leaving it, tightened at least one dog. The sumping of the water in the tunnel was a regularly assigned duty of the deck watch to be performed each watch, and on this occasion Mays found no more than the normal amount of water in the tunnel.

26. At approximately 1730, without warning, a sound described as a thud was heard on the bridge of the CARL D. BRADLEY. The thud, which Fleming could not more adequately describe, was followed by a vibration similar to that which is felt in a vessel pounding into a sea, with the propeller out of water, but the thud was such as to cause Fleming to instinctively realize that the vessel was in serious trouble. Looking aft, Fleming noted that the stern of the CARL D. BRADLEY was sagging.

27. After pumping the sump aft, Mays proceeded through the tunnel on the tank top to the conveyor room forward and was there when he also heard the thud which he was totally unable to describe. However, he, too, realized that the vessel was in serious trouble and ran immediately for the ladder leading topside. As he departed this compartment, he neither heard nor saw that section of the vessel being flooded.

28. Back on the bridge, the Master immediately sounded the general alarm and began to blow the whistle, while Fleming broadcast "MAY DAY" on channel 51 (2182 kc). This broadcast, which was immediately answered by

radio station WAD, Port Washington, Wisconsin, gave the CARL D. BRADLEY's position as 12 miles southwest of Gull Island. Upon request from WAD, the CARL D. BRADLEY verified this position. There had been just enough time to put out two "MAY DAY" messages before the power failed and the lights forward went out. There were no further signals heard from the CARL D. BRADLEY. The "MAY DAY" was heard and recorded by a large number of stations, including the Coast Guard Lifeboat Station at Charlevoix, Michigan, and primary radio station NMD at Chesterland, Ohio.

29. At 1730, the CARL D. BRADLEY was still on course 046° true, was riding easily and making about 14.5 MPH. The vessel was ballasted to the maximum practical extent with estimated drafts of 13'9" forward and 17'6" aft. The wind was southwest 55–65 MPH, and the sea was heavy, steep, and about 25 feet high from ½-point on the starboard quarter. The approximate air and water temperatures were 40° and 50°, respectively. The sun had set at 1710 and there was still 14 minutes of twilight which would end at 1744.

30. The German M/V CHRISTIAN SARTORI, a 254' general cargo vessel, was at 1730 about four miles distant from the CARL D. BRADLEY, and although the CHRISTIAN SARTORI did not hear the "MAY DAY," officers on the bridge witnessed the casualty. The CHRISTIAN SARTORI, southbound, passed Lansing Shoal at 1200. The JOHNSTOWN later reported sighting her at about 1400, one to two miles off her portside, when the JOHNSTOWN was abeam Gull Island light, distance three to four miles on course 050° true. This put the CHRISTIAN SARTORI approximately five miles off Gull Island. At about 1700, the CHRISTIAN SARTORI was on course 215° true making about two MPH when she sighted the CARL D. BRADLEY ahead 10–15° on her starboard bow. At 1720, the CHRISTIAN SARTORI came right to course 240° true to pass the CARL D. BRADLEY on her portside, and by 1730 the CHRISTIAN SARTORI was approximately six miles distant from Gull Island, bearing 260° true from Gull Island Light, with the CARL D.

BRADLEY 10–15° on her port bow. The only side light of the CARL D. BRADLEY seen at any time by the CHRISTIAN SARTORI was her red light, and at no time was the green light visible to the CHRISTIAN SARTORI.

31. When the alarm sounded, the crew responded quickly and sought to abandon ship. With the exception of the Second Mate, who tried to go aft toward the boat deck (body not recovered), those forward donned life jackets and went to the 15-person emergency life raft aft of the pilot house. Men aft were observed to be on the boat deck and lowering the starboard lifeboat. The two lifeboats were 25-person boats on the boat deck aft and were equipped with quadrantal-type mechanical davits, Manila falls, and common hooks.

32. Two or three minutes after the thud and after the stern had been noted to sag, the vessel heaved upward near hatch #10 and broke in two resulting in two sections approximately 300' in length, 65' wide, and 90' high, including the deck houses and superstructure. As the section parted, the forward end of the stern section, with the lights still on, swung to port, and the after end of the bow section swung to starboard. The bow section, maintaining an even keel, settled from the after end until the spar (weather) deck was completely submerged, then listed to port, rolled over, and sank. The life raft floated free.

33. The stern section settled from the forward end on an even keel and then plunged, still on an even keel, with the counter going down last. The starboard lifeboat swung forward on its falls. Whether the boat was completely launched before the sinking could not be determined. When recovered, it was upside down, and there was no evidence that it had been occupied. As the section plunged, there was a sudden eruption of steam, bright flame, and smoke.

34. The first indication of anything unusual about the CARL D. BRADLEY, as noticed by the CHRISTIAN SARTORI, was about 1730 when the lights in the

forward end were observed to go out. This was followed several minutes later by an explosion with considerable illumination and heavy smoke. When the smoke cleared, the CARL D. BRADLEY had disappeared from view and, whereas they had been getting a good image on the radar, there now was none. The CHRISTIAN SARTORI changed course to 195° true and headed toward the CARL D. BRADLEY's position and began a search for survivors which lasted until relieved at 0200, 19 November. Searching proved negative. Approximately one hour after the casualty, the CHRISTIAN SARTORI sighted flares on the water about one mile off her port bow between the ship and Boulder Reef Buoy and in line with the buoy.

35. The following Coast Guard units participated in the SAR emergency:

a. Plum Island Lifeboat Station—Heard "MAY DAY" at 1730 and dispatched CG-40300 at 1600. Due to heavy seas, this boat was unable to proceed and was recalled at 1900, arriving back at 2000.

b. Charlevoix Lifeboat Station—Heard "MAY DAY" at 1731 and dispatched CG-36392 at 1815. This small boat was recalled at 1855 on the recommendation of Commanding Officer, CGC SUNDEW, due to heavy weather.

c. Beaver Island Moorings—CG-36505 held in readiness and was not dispatched to the scene, due to the prevailing weather conditions and inexperience of the available personnel.

d. USCGC SUNDEW (WAGL 404)—Moored at Charlevoix, Michigan, in a 12-hour standby status. The SUNDEW was alerted at 1740 by the Group Commander, Charlevoix Group. The SUNDEW got underway at 1820 and arrived in the search area at 2240. The Commanding Officer, CGC SUNDEW, took over operational control of the search and coordinated the efforts of all units from this time on.

e. CG Air Station, Traverse City, Michigan—This unit had one aircraft, UF 1273, returning from an air search in southern Lake Michigan and one aircraft, UF 2135, in a maintenance status. In addition, the station had two helicopters ready for flight; however, these were held in readiness, due to the prevailing weather conditions. UF 1273 was directed to proceed to the scene and arrived at 1915. The ceiling in the search area was 2,000 feet, and this aircraft was used throughout the night in the search and also to provide flare illumination for the surface vessels. A total of 88 flares were dropped during the night of 18–19 November. At daybreak, three HO3S helicopters joined in the search, and the UF 2135 was dispatched to Beaver Island to provide gasoline for the helicopters.

f. CGC HOLLYHOCK (WAOL 220)—Moored at Sturgeon Bay, Wisconsin, in a 2-hour standby status. The HOLLYHOCK was alerted at 1815 by Operations, Ninth Coast Guard District, Cleveland, Ohio, and was underway at 1830. The HOLLYHOCK arrived on the scene at 0230 and reported to the SUNDEW.

36. The SS ROBERT C. STANLEY, anchored at Garden Island, heard the "MAY DAY," got underway at 1824, and proceeded to the search area, arriving at midnight. This vessel was joined by other lake vessels and numerous military and civilian aircraft as the weather moderated and daylight on the 19th commenced. CG-40561, from Beaver Island Moorings, and CG-40499, from Charlevoix Lifeboat Station, joined the search on 19 November.

37. Four crewmen, including Fleming and Mays, were able to board the life raft, which drifted rapidly away from the scene of the disaster. During the night, the other two were lost overboard as the raft flipped over several times in the heavy seas. The sea anchor also parted, leaving the raft completely at the mercy of the elements. At 0825 on 19 November, the SUNDEW sighted the raft with the two survivors, and Fleming and Mays were rescued at 0837 at a position 5¼ miles east northeast of Gull Island. An overturned lifeboat was sighted at 0930 at a position four miles east of Gull Island. This boat was not occupied and was later recovered off the southeast tip of High Island on the 21st. During the day, 17 bodies were recovered by Coast Guard

units in the area adjacent to and north of Gull Island. One body, that of Gary Strzelecki, one of the persons lost overboard from the raft during the night, was recovered by merchant vessel M/V TRANS ONTARIO at 1314 at a position close to the west shore of High Island. Each body recovered had an approved cork life jacket on, as did the two survivors.

38. a. The following men survived: Total 2:

  (1) Elmer Fleming, North Bradley Highway, Rogers City, Michigan
  (2) Frank Mays, 925 Linden Street, Rogers City, Michigan

  b. The bodies of the following persons have been recovered; cause of death—drowning: Total 18:

  (1) Carl R. Bartell, 357 North First Street, Rogers City, Michigan
  (2) Alfred Boehmer, 455 South 4th Street, Rogers City, Michigan
  (3) Richard J. Book, International Hotel, Rogers City, Michigan
  (4) Alva H. Budnick, Virgilene Trailer Court, Rogers City, Michigan
  (5) William T. Elliott, Virgilene Trailer Court, Rogers City, Michigan
  (6) Erhardt O. Felax, 685 South Lake Street, Rogers City, Michigan
  (7) Cleland E. Gager, Onaway, Michigan
  (8) Paul C. Heller, 1106 Riverview Street, Rogers City, Michigan
  (9) Paul Horn, 448 North 4th Street, Rogers City, Michigan
  (10) Raymond J. Kowalski, 1105 Dettloff Street, Rogers City, Michigan
  (11) Joseph Krawczak, 645 South Second Street, Rogers City, Michigan
  (12) Alfred Pilarski, 546 South Lake Street, Rogers City, Michigan
  (13) Gary N. Price, Box 76, Onaway, Michigan
  (14) Leo Promo, Jr., 419 St. Clair Street, Rogers City, Michigan
  (15) Bernard Schefke, 506 South Lake Street, Rogers City, Michigan
  (16) Gary Strzelecki, 234 West Michigan, Rogers City, Michigan
  (17) Edward N. Vallee, 206 Superior Street, Rogers City, Michigan
  (18) John Zoho, 853 Horton Avenue, Clairton, Pennsylvania

c. The following men are missing: Total 15:

(1) Douglas Bellmore, Onaway, Michigan

(2) Roland O. Bryan, Loudonville, New York

(3) John F. Fogelsonger, Medora Street, St. Ignace, Michigan

(4) Raymond G. Buehler, 100 Cordova Avenue, Lakewood, Ohio

(5) Clyde M. Enos, 410 Ball Street, Cheboygan, Michigan

(6) John L. Bauers, 316 Hilltop Lane, Rogers City, Michigan

(7) Keith Schuler, 314 North First Street, Rogers City, Michigan

(8) Duane Berg, 372 North Third Street, Rogers City, Michigan

(9) Dennis Meredith, RFD, Posen, Michigan

(10) Floyd A. MacDougall, 144 South First Street, Rogers City, Michigan

(11) Earl Tulgetske Jr., 1012 Dettloff Street, Rogers City, Michigan

(12) Paul Greengtski, RFD, Posen, Michigan

(13) Melville Orr, 1113 Third Street, Rogers City, Michigan

(14) Dennis Joppich, 457 South Second Street, Rogers City, Michigan

(15) James L. Selke, 795 South First Street, Rogers City, Michigan

39. All the persons reported to have been on watch in the engine room are among those still missing. Of the 18 bodies recovered, eight were from the forward end crew and ten were from the after end crew.

40. Radio station WAD, Port Washington, assumed the radio control on channel 51 (2182kc) in the SAR emergency and broadcast an order for radio silence at 1740. This initial order was repeated a number of times by WAD and other stations in the mideastern and eastern United States. The imposed radio silence was lifted at 1840 on 19 November, and the active search was discontinued on 21 November 1958 by Office of the Commander, Ninth Coast Guard District, pending further developments. Serious interference on channel 51 was reported. This interference was primarily from the unauthorized use of channel 51 by vessels on the Ohio and Mississippi Rivers, and partly from the failure of some Great Lakes area stations and vessels to

maintain silence. The interference, however, was not serious enough to interfere with the on-the-scene communications among the vessels and planes actively engaged in the search.

41. Boulder Reef lighted bell buoy (LL 2163) was on station and showing its proper characteristics at 1410 on 19 November when checked by CG SUN-DEW.

42. In the vicinity of Boulder Reef, shoal water of 60 feet in depth or less extends over an area which is approximately six miles long and three miles wide. The area circumscribed by this 60-foot depth curve runs mainly to the north northeast of Boulder Reef, which is marked on its southwest edge by Boulder Reef lighted buoy. The reef has a minimum depth of 15 feet adjacent to the buoy, and shoal area of 30 feet or less extends to a distance of about 1½ miles northward from the buoy.

43. Aircraft from Coast Guard Air Station, Traverse City, spent a total of 122 hours searching the casualty area from 18 November to 9 December. During this time, no evidence of the sunken hulks or large wreckage therefrom was sighted by the aircraft. Miscellaneous small pieces of wreckage were found, both by aircraft and searching parties, on the west shores of High and Beaver Islands. On 20 November, Coast Guard aircraft UF 2135 sighted an oil slick, resulting from oil bubbling to the surface from an underwater source. The source of this oil slick, which was feathering out downwind, was located 5½ miles distant from Boulder Reef Buoy on a bearing of 314° true. On 2 December 1958, the SUNDEW, sounding this area, noted on their depth recorder, type AN/UQW-IC, an irregularity in soundings which indicated a 25-foot pinnacle in 300 feet of water at the reported source of the oil slick. An immediate re-sounding of this area failed to again show the pinnacle, and later attempts to relocate it have likewise proven unsuccessful. Attempts to locate the hulks by soundings were made by CGC MACKINAW (WAGB 83) and the SUNDEW during January and February; however,

unfavorable winter conditions curtailed these efforts. Further attempts will be made when weather conditions improve.

44. The Board takes judicial notice of the following facts:

a. Records indicate that November is a month of severe storms on the Great Lakes. The storm of 17–19 November 1958 has been described by various shipmasters as the most severe they have encountered. The publication "Shipwrecks of the Lakes," by Dana T. Bowen, reveals that between 1900 and 1950, over one-third of the vessels lost by foundering were lost during November, and over one-half of all strandings occurred in November.

b. The trade followed by the self-unloading-type vessels is extremely hard on the vessels. The self-unloaders load and discharge many more cargoes per year than do the conventional bulk freighters engaged in the iron ore trade. Likewise, these vessels frequent out of the way places in shallow water and often ground and rub bottom while approaching docks. In addition, because of the short hauls between loading and unloading ports, the self-unloaders spend considerably more time at near maximum speed in the shallow rivers than do the conventional lake vessels.

c. The past inspection books, dry-dock examination books, and other official records of the Coast Guard were examined by the Board, and they revealed nothing of note concerning the CARL D. BRADLEY, except as mentioned elsewhere in the record concerning the last dry-docking in 1957 in Chicago, Illinois.

d. The official survey records of Lloyd's Register of Shipping were examined by the Board, and these records revealed nothing of note concerning the CARL D. BRADLEY. Extracts from the survey, in conjunction with the dry-docking in 1957 at Chicago, Illinois, are included with the record.

e. Section 726 of Department of the Navy Publication NWP-37, Search and Rescue, indicates that the wind current would be up to 30° to the right of the wind direction in direction of 045° true and 075° true.

Opinions

1. That the CARL D. BRADLEY did not strike Boulder Reef, but that she broke in half in deep water in a position about five miles to the northwestward of Boulder Reef.

2. That the vessel could not have proceeded for more than one mile between the time of the initial thud and the time she broke in half, and that the CARL D. BRADLEY continued on course during this period.

3. That had the vessel struck Boulder Reef, both parts of the hulk, by reason of their dimensions, would be visible in the water of less than 60-foot depth which extends for a distance of about three miles northeast of the reef along the track the CARL D. BRADLEY would have made.

4. And further, that, having in mind the manner in which the vessel broke and the way the stern section plunged to the bottom, the CARL D. BRADLEY sank in water considerably deeper than 60 feet.

5. Supporting the opinion that the CARL D. BRADLEY did not strike Boulder Reef are the facts established relative to the navigation of both the CARL D. BRADLEY and the M/V CHRISTIAN SARTORI.

6. That the cause of the casualty was due to the excessive hogging stresses imposed upon the vessel by reason of her placement in the ballasted condition upon the waves encountered at the particular instant of breaking. There were no facts disclosed by the testimony, or through examination of the files on the CARL D. BRADLEY maintained by the U.S. Coast Guard, or Lloyd's Registry of Shipping, which would lead to an opinion that there existed any defects in the area where the break occurred. However, it is felt that the appearance of hairline fractures in the vessel's bottom plating, as found in drydock, may be of significance in a technical study of this casu-

alty by the Ship's Structure Committee, or other technical body, although the Board could find no indication of a relationship between this casualty and these earlier-noted hairline fractures.

7. That the eruption of steam, flames, and smoke, noticed by the survivors and the CHRISTIAN SARTORI, occurred after the vessel parted, and was caused by water rushing into the combustion chambers of the boilers as the stern section plunged. The fact that all bodies from the after end that were recovered were victims of drowning, with no indication of burns or violence, supports the conclusion that the reported explosion was actually the eruption of steam and combustible materials from the boiler out through the stack.

8. That the vessel was seaworthy at the time of completion of her annual inspection at Calcite, Michigan, on 17 April 1958, and that there is no reason to conclude from the testimony or from reasonable interpretation of other known facts that she was not in such condition upon departure from Gary, Indiana, on 17 November 1958.

9. That the vessel was properly manned and equipped in accordance with existing regulations and properly secured for sea upon departure from Gary, Indiana.

10. That the temporary repairs to the cargo hold, made in the winter 1957–58 did not contribute to this casualty.

11. That the two unreported damages known to have been incurred during the 1958 season at Cedarville, Michigan, were minor in nature and of such location on the hull as to not have contributed to this casualty.

12. That the watertight door in bulkhead 173 at the forward end of the machinery spaces was not completely dogged at the time of the casualty, and

that the watertight integrity of the vessel was thereby impaired. It appears likely that the door became undogged by some reason unknown and then swung open, allowing the free entry of the water from the tunnel to the engine spaces. It is felt that, had the door been completely dogged and thus maintained bulkhead 173 watertight, additional buoyancy would have been provided, and the speed with which the stern section sank would have been materially reduced.

13. That the drownings of those crewmen whose bodies were recovered were caused by inhalation of the heavy spray. Because of the low water and air temperatures, and extremely rough seas, no type of life jacket could have enabled any person to have survived the 16-hour ordeal in the water. Further, that the type of life jacket worn by the victims caused fatigue by reason of the need to exert constant arm pressure on the jacket to keep it down on the body while in the water. It is the opinion of the Board that the cork life preservers are not a satisfactory type for sustained support in the water because of the way they fit.

14. That the drift and set of the life raft, lifeboat, and bodies carried them north of Gull Island and to the eastward. This drift and set is in fair agreement with what might be expected from the information contained in Section 726 of NWP 37, Search and Rescue Manual, although it is realized that the application of the theories developed in this manual to the relatively shallow waters of the area in question might not be unqualifiedly accepted.

15. That efforts made by the crew in attempting to lower the starboard lifeboat were thwarted by the short time the stern section remained on an even keel. With the prevailing weather conditions and the quick settling of the after section, it is considered extremely doubtful that a launching of a lifeboat in the vicinity of the vessel's counter by use of falls fitted with common hooks could have been successfully accomplished.

16. That the search and rescue operations in this casualty were thorough and well-directed. All Coast Guard units responded to the maximum of their ability under the existing weather conditions, and the major floating units were underway well within the period allowed by their standby status. The appreciation of the survivors and the representatives of the owners of the CARL D. BRADLEY for the efforts of the CGC SUNDEW is worthy of note. The decision of the responsible personnel attached to the Coast Guard Air Station to hold the available helicopters for actual rescue work in view of the weather conditions was based on sound judgment.

17. That the participation of the M/V CHRISTIAN SARTORI in the search was in keeping with the finest traditions of the sea. This vessel was immediately headed toward the scene of the casualty, and made every effort to assist under extremely adverse weather conditions. The fact that the searching of the SARTORI proved unsuccessful does not detract from the valiant efforts of the Master and crew to aid the crew of the CARL D. BRADLEY. The voluntary participation by other merchant vessels, as well as private, commercial, and military aircraft, and by the individual citizens of the various islands was also commendable.

18. That communications pursuant to this SAR emergency were adequate. All stations in the area maintained radio silence when so directed, and the interference on channel 51 that did occur did not impede communications on the scene.

19. That had the life raft been equipped with rocket or parachute-type distress signals, the survivors might have been located during the night.

20. That it is the stated policy of the owners of the CARL D. BRADLEY to give the masters complete responsibility for the safety of their vessels and, therefore, complete freedom to anchor or postpone departure, if unfavorable

weather or other reasons dictate such action to be in the interests of safety. In view of this, it is the opinion of the Board that the master of the CARL D. BRADLEY, in making the decision to and in proceeding across northern Lake Michigan from Cana Island toward Lansing Shoal, exercised poor judgment. This decision was probably induced by a zealous desire to hold as closely to schedule as possible, and because of this, he gave less attention to the dangers of the existing weather than what might be expected of a prudent manner.

21. That no aids to navigation or uncharted or incorrectly charted area of objects were involved in the casualty.

22. That no personnel of the Coast Guard or any other governmental agency contributed to the casualty.

23. That there is no evidence that any licensed or certificated personnel of the CARL D. BRADLEY committed any acts of incompetence, inattention to duty, negligence, or willful violation of any law or regulation.

Recommendations

1. That all jacket-type life preservers be provided with a crotch strap to hold the jacket down on the body and with a collar to support the head out of water. In this respect, the specifications for life preservers under 46 CFR 160.002-005 (Subchapter Q, Specifications) will require modification.

2. That a second additional life raft or other approved buoyant apparatus be mandatory on all Great Lakes cargo vessels of 300 gross tons and over, and that 46 CFR 94.10-40(a) and 46 CFR 94.15-10(c)(3) (Subchapter I, Cargo and Miscellaneous Vessels) be modified to require two life rafts and to specify that one of these rafts shall be in the forward part of the vessel and one in the after part of the vessel.

3. That each lifeboat on all Great Lakes cargo vessels of over 3,000 gross tons be fitted with mechanical disengaging apparatus. To effect this recommendation, the provisions of 46 CFR 94.10-5 (a)(4)(i) should be modified to include Great Lakes vessels and to require that all existing common hook installations be replaced with mechanical disengaging apparatus at the earliest possible date. Further, that the provisions of this recommendation be extended to include Great Lakes tank and passenger vessels of over 3,000 gross tons, and that the applicable sections of 46 CFR, Part 13 (Subchapter D, Tank Vessels), and 46 CFR, Part 75 (Subchapter H, Passenger Vessels), be so modified.

4. That each lifeboat on all Great Lakes cargo vessels be equipped with two painters as required for ocean and coastwise vessels, and that 46 CFR 94.20-10(a) and 46 CFR 94.20-15(a) be modified accordingly. Further, that the provisions of this recommendation be extended to include all Great Lakes tank and passenger vessels, and that the applicable sections of 46 CFR, Part 33 (Subchapter D, Tank Vessels), and 46 CFR, Part 75 (Subchapter H, Passenger Vessels), be so modified.

5. That each lifeboat and life raft on all Great Lakes cargo vessels be provided with a unit of at least six red parachute-type flare distress signals and the means to project them. This recommendation will require modification of 45 CFR 94.20-10(a), 46 CFR 94.20-20(a), 46 CFR 94.20-15(hh), and 46 CFR 94.20-25(m). Further, that the provisions of this recommendation be extended to include all Great Lakes tank and passenger vessels, and that the applicable sections of 46 CFR, Part 33 (Subchapter D, Tank Vessels), and 46 CFR, Part 75 (Subchapter H, Passenger Vessels), be so modified.

6. Inasmuch as the exact location of the hull of the CARL D. BRADLEY is unknown at this time and the possibility exists that reasonable efforts to locate the hull during this coming shipping season will be successful, which may or may not alter the findings of fact, opinions, or recommendations of

this Board, it is recommended that the Board remain in an adjourned status so that it may be reconvened should circumstances demand.

Joseph A. Kerrins
Rear Admiral, U.S. Coast Guard
Chairman

Charles E. Leising
Commander, U.S. Coast Guard
Member

Joseph Change
Commander, U.S. Coast Guard
Member

Garth H. Read
Lieutenant Commander, U.S. Coast Guard
Member and Recorder

GLOSSARY

aft (or after deck)—back, or stern, section of the ship

ballast—added weight, usually lake water, to lower the ship in the water and add stability

ballast pumps—pumps used to remove water from a ship's ballast tanks

ballast tanks—large, watertight storage tanks below the cargo hold, on the starboard and port sides of the ship, in which ballast is stored

beam—the breadth of a ship at its widest point

bow—front or forward section of the ship

bulkhead—partition used to divide sections of a ship's hull

capsize—roll onto a side and turn over

captain (or master)—commander, or chief officer, of a ship

chief engineer—crewman in charge of the ship's engine

conveyorman—crewman in charge of operating the boom in self-unloading ships

de-ballasting—the process of pumping, or expelling, water from a ship's ballast tanks

draft—depth of a ship's hull beneath the waterline

first mate—the second in command of a ship

fitting out—the process for preparing a ship for sailing after construction or a layup

fore (or foredeck)—forward, or bow, section of the ship

founder—to fill with water and sink

freeboard—distance between the waterline and the spar deck

galley—the area of the ship, usually aft, where food is stored and prepared

green water—solid water, rather than spray, washing over the deck

grounding—striking bottom, or running completely aground

hatches—openings in the ship's spar deck, through which cargo is loaded

hogging—the bending down of the front and back of a ship, with no support for the middle

hold—the large area of a ship in which cargo is stored

hull—main body of a ship, upon which the decks and superstructures are built

keel—backbone of the ship, running the entire length of a vessel, upon which the framework of the ship is built

lee—the side or area away from the direction in which the wind blows; shelter from the wind

list—a ship's leaning or tipping to one side

pilothouse (or wheelhouse)—enclosed deck in which the wheel and map room are located; the uppermost deck on a ship

port—left side of a ship when you are facing the bow

screw—a ship's propeller

shoal—shallow area of water, usually marked by a sandbar, reef, or area of rising lake floor

spar deck (or weather deck)—deck where the hatches are located

starboard—right side of the ship when you are facing the bow

steward—ship's cook

superstructure—structures and cabins built above the hull of a ship

wheelsman—crew member who steers the ship

working—a ship's twisting, springing, and flexing in heavy seas

BIBLIOGRAPHY

Books

Davenport, Don, and Robert W. Wells. *Fire & Ice*. Madison, Wisc.: Northword. 1983. (This is a flip book—two books in one volume; the book on the *Carl D. Bradley*, written by Davenport, is titled *Shipwreck on Lake Michigan*.)

Hancock, Paul. *Shipwrecks of the Great Lakes*. San Diego, Calif.: Thunder Bay Press, 2001.

Hopp, James L. M'aidez! *Tragedy at Sea: The Sinkings of the SS* Carl D. Bradley *and the SS* Cedarville. Author, 1981. (A revised, expanded edition of this book, *Mayday! Tragedy at Sea*, was published in 2008.)

Kantar, Andrew. *Black November*. East Lansing, Mich.: Michigan State University Press, 2006.

Mays, Frank, as told to Pat and Jim Stayer. *If We Make It 'til Daylight*. Lexington, Mich.: Out of the Blue Productions, 2003.

Micketti, Gerald F. *The Bradley Boats*. Traverse City, Mich.: G. F. Micketti, 1995.

Ratigan, William. *Great Lakes Shipwrecks and Survivals*. New York: Galahad Books, 1994.

Schumacher, Michael. *Mighty Fitz: The Sinking of the* Edmund Fitzgerald. New York: Bloomsbury, 2005.

Shelak, Benjamin J. *Shipwrecks of Lake Michigan*. Black Earth, Wisc.: Trails Books, 2003.

Stonehouse, Frederick. *Steel on the Bottom.* Gwinn, Mich.: Avery Color Studios, 2006.

Thompson, Mark L. *Graveyard of the Lakes.* Detroit: Wayne State University Press, 2000.

Newspaper and Magazine Articles

Alpena News. "A Few Minutes Changed Lives," November 19, 1958.

——. "View Bradley's Hull by Underwater Television," December 2, 1959.

Asam, Angie. "Bradley Bell Comes 'Home' to Great Lakes Lore Museum in Rogers City." *Presque Isle County Advance,* November 21, 2007.

Breslin, Ed. "They Wait in Fear for Knock at Door." *Detroit Times,* November 21, 1958.

Calcite Screenings. "Many Activities Take Place in Winter Shipyard," Spring 1953.

——. "Marine Inspection Service," Fall 1946.

——. "Repairs Made on Bradley Boats During Lay-up," Spring 1949.

——. "With the Boats from Layup to Fitout," Spring 1952.

Chicago Tribune. "Agrees to Pay 1¼ Million in Ship Disaster," December 5, 1959.

——. "Find Steamer Bradley Deep on Lake Floor," September 2, 1959.

——. "Hold Funerals for 12 Men on Freighter," November 23, 1958.

——. "Kin Offered $660,000 for Ship's 33 Dead," February 8, 1959.

——. "Sailor Tells Bradley Death 5 Miles Away," November 21, 1958.

Crittendon, Robert F. "WLF—WLC: Central Radio Telegraph Company." *Calcite Screenings,* Summer 1947.

Detroit Free Press. "Freighter Left Few Traces," November 21, 1958.

——. "Michigan Mourns Her Sailor Sons," November 19, 1958.

Detroit News. "Coast Guard Cutter Sundew Rescues Two from Floating Raft Wednesday Morning," November 20, 1958.

Detroit Times. "Overwhelming Response to Ship Disaster Children's Fund," November 27, 1958.

———. "Owners in Rogers City," November 20, 1958.

Giardin, Ray. "At First a Thud . . ." *Detroit Times.* November 20, 1958.

Giardin, Ray, Frank Morris, and Bud Goodman. "Sinking: The Grim Hunt Goes On for 15 Missing Sailors." *Detroit Times,* November 20, 1958.

Glynn, James. "Cutter Unloads Its Grim Cargo." *Detroit Free Press,* November 20, 1958.

———. "Only Survivors Tell How Freighter Sank." *Detroit Free Press.* November 20, 1958.

———. "Tells How 2 Missed Rescue." *Detroit Free Press,* November 20, 1958.

Glynn, James [with unknown coauthor]. "Two Drift for 14 Hours in Icy Michigan Waters." *Detroit Free Press,* November 20, 1958.

Great Lakes Shipwreck Historical Museum. "Frank Mays Visits Shipwreck Museum—Survivor of the *Carl D. Bradley,*" May 1, 2001.

Haseltine, Curt. "Seamen Rally to Aid Fellows." *Detroit Free Press,* November 20, 1958.

———. "Fury of Nature Spells Tragedy." *Detroit Free Press,* November 24, 1958.

Hoeft, Norman. "Early Shipping on the Lakes." *Calcite Screenings,* Spring 1942.

Life. "Newest of Lake Tragedies Sets Off a Desperate Search," December 1, 1958.

———. "Storm and Death on a Great Lake," December 1, 1958.

Lucas, R. H. "Winter Work." *Calcite Screenings,* Spring 1944.

Maher, Robert. "Letter Link to Love, Tragedy." *Detroit Times,* November 21, 1958.

———. "Rogers City Unites in Prayer." *Detroit Times,* November 21, 1958.

ML Screenings. "1927—Do You Remember?," Winter 1958–59.

———. "Bradley Found and Identified," Fall 1959.

———. "Children's Fund Established," Winter 1958–59.

——. "Coast Guard Spearheads Rescue Effort," Winter 1958–59.

——. "Let's Look at Michigan Limestone," Spring 1957.

——. "Michigan Limestone Aids Men's Families," Winter 1958–59.

——. "Shipmates Attend Services in Memory of Bradley Crew," Winter 1958–59.

——. "Steamer Bradley Named for Michigan Limestone Pioneer," Winter 1958–59.

——. "Steamer Carl D. Bradley Lost in Lake Michigan Storm," Winter 1958–59.

——. "Tragedy Strikes Safest Fleet," Winter 1958–59.

Mueller, Capt. Paul. "Rescue Skipper Tells Story of Sinking." *Traverse City Record-Eagle*. November 19, 1958.

New York Times. "Freighter with 35 Feared Lost in Gale on Lake Michigan," November 19, 1958.

——. "Inquiry on Liability Set on Shipbuilding," July 25, 1959.

——. "Only Two Survive Lake Shipwreck; Searchers Recover 17 Bodies—Hope Abandoned for 16 Others on Freighter," November 20, 1958.

——. "Testimony Set in Wreck," March 15, 1959.

Poulos, Nick. "Resume Search to Find Sunken Lake Freighter." *Chicago Tribune*. April 27, 1959.

Presque Isle County Advance. "Dead Are Laid to Rest as Community Mourns," November 27, 1958.

——. "Here Is What Happened," November 27, 1958.

——. "May 7, 1965: Cedarville Collides with Freighter and Sinks in the Straits," May 5, 2005.

——. "Str. Bradley Sinks with 35 Aboard," November 20, 1958.

——. "Survivor II: Stories of Survival on the Great Lakes," August 24, 2006.

——. "Survivor of Bradley Disaster Recounts Story at Library," September 2, 2005.

Sudomier, William. "Town Lives by Ships—and Dies with One." *Detroit Free Press*, November 20, 1958.

Thomis,Wayne. "Sailors' Shipwreck Story." *Chicago Tribune*, November 20, 1958.

Time. "The Death of the Bradley," December 1, 1958.

Toussaint, Warren. "May Day—May Day: Words No One Ever Wants to Hear." *Shipmates*, April–May 1997.

Traverse City Record-Eagle. "Coast Guard Starts Probe of Sinking," November 20, 1958.

———. "Heroic Doctor, 79, Was Ready to Risk Life to Save Crewman," November 20, 1958.

———. "Hope Dims for 15 Missing Seamen: Two Survivors Tell of Ordeal," November 20, 1958.

Underwood, Don. "Survivors Tell of the Break-up, Death, Cold and Fear." *Life*, December 1, 1958.

Whiteley, W. H. "Rogers City: The Limestone City of Michigan." *Calcite Screenings*. 1959. (Special edition of the magazine devoted entirely to the history of Rogers City.)

Documents and Reports

U.S. Department of Transportation, Marine Board of Investigation. "Foundering of the *SS Carl D. Bradley*, Lake Michigan, 18 November 1958, with Loss of Life. U.S. Coast Guard Marine Board of Investigation Report and Commandant's Action," July 7, 1959.

U.S. Department of Treasury, Marine Board of Investigation. "Commandant's Action on The Marine Board of Investigation convened to investigate the collision of the SS CEDARVILLE and Norwegian MV TOPDALSFJORD on 7 May 1965 in the Straits of Mackinac with loss of life," February 6, 1967.

DVD and Video

Carl D. Bradley: *40th Anniversary Remembrance*. DVD. Lexington, Mich.: Out of the Blue Productions, 1999.

Cutter Rescues. DVD. Saginaw, Mich.: Airworthy Productions, 2006.

Deep Adventure: A Dive to the Carl D. Bradley. DVD. Lexington, Mich.: Out of the Blue Productions, 2003.

Remembering the Carl D. Bradley. DVD. Hosted by Doug Petcash and produced and directed by photojournalist Corey Adkins. WWTV/WWUP-TV 9 and 10 News. Cadillac, Mich.: Heritage Broadcasting Company of Michigan, 2004.

The Wreck of the Carl D. Bradley. VHS/DVD. Kenosha, Wisc.: Southport Video Productions, 2001.

ACKNOWLEDGMENTS

MANY YEARS AGO, WHILE I WAS INTERVIEWING NORMAN MAILER FOR a magazine piece and we were discussing the differences between writing fiction and nonfiction, Mailer mentioned, only half-jokingly, that one of the big distinctions, as far as he was concerned, is that "God gives you the best plots." I believe that this is true. I'm certainly convinced that I never could have come up with a fictional tale of incredible loss, strength, and survival that compares to this story of the *Carl D. Bradley*, its crew, and Rogers City.

Early into my research, I decided that I wanted to tell this story in the present tense, not only because it helped bring a sense of immediacy to a fifty-year-old story, but also because it would give me the chance to write about the *Bradley*'s crew members in a way that made them more "alive" or "real" to readers. So often, in books of this nature, those who died in shipwrecks are assigned a place on a crew list posted at the beginning or the end of the book and, in my opinion, we somehow lose sight of the fact that these men were robbed of something that we take for granted. They lost years of their lives, they never realized their dreams, they left people behind. No, these were not men who aspired to greatness and high places; they were blue-collar working stiffs who labored in tough, occasionally dangerous jobs, and this, I think, speaks volumes about a lot of people sometimes forgotten, and often ignored, in our world today. In writing this book I wanted to bring these people back to life, even if for only a brief flash, and I wanted to honor them.

This became a tall task in that I was asking the crew members' families, relatives, friends, and fellow sailors to remember events of half a century ago—events, no less, that are still painful today when they are brought back into focus. All told, I conducted more than 150 interviews for this book. I interviewed a number of people more than once—some of them six, seven, eight times—and I was always moved by the generosity of spirit I encountered. Some weren't able to help me with their memories—so many of the children of the *Bradley* crew, for example, were very young at the time of their fathers' deaths, and they remembered very little, other than what they'd been told, about them—but they were nevertheless able to assist me by answering a few questions to the best of their abilities, or by referring me to others who could help. Others sat for long, and repeated, interviews. I owe all a debt of gratitude.

I'm also thankful to all the former stone boat workers, from captains to deckhands, who greatly aided this account by talking in detail about what it was like working, day to day, on the boats, enduring storms, and dealing with a tragedy that in some cases made them think twice about how they earned their living. My thanks to the coast guardsmen who went out to search for the *Bradley* crewmen, to other maritime writers who generously offered suggestions, and to all the others who helped with this book.

My deepest appreciation, then, to:

Jerry Badgero, Bob Bellmore, Terry Bellmore, Helen Berg, Mark Berg, Rolene Berg, Bob Bingle, Phil Boehmer, Eileen Bohon, Mel Book, Sharon Book, Edward Brewster, Kim Budnick, Viola "Babe" Chain, Barbara Chojnacki, Jack Coppens, John Czcerowsky, Fred Dagner, Cecelia Dembny, Jan Dullack, William Elliott, Janet Enos, Dave Erickson, Joseph Etienne, Michael Eustice, Chester Felax, Kenneth Friedrich, Leonard Gabrysiak, Art Gapczynski, Donald Greengtski, Teresa Greengtski, Bob Hein, Roger Hein, Sharon Hein, Mark Heller, Jim Hopp, Charlie Horn, Clarence Idalski, Michael Idalski, Bob Jess, William Joppich, Andrew Kantar, Geraldine Karsten, James Karsten, Marvin Karsten, Tess Kierzek, Harvey Klann, Janice Klann, Gerald "Kaiser" Klee, Elizabeth Kowalski, Michael Kowalski, Robert Kowalski, Ron

Krawczak, Mac Lamp, Laurie Leow, Elaine Lorenz, Ann Losinski, Jane Marshall, Alfrieda Martens, Sue McClure, Alice Meredith, George Meredith, Barbara Morrison, Priscilla Nensewitz, Ed Partyka, Donna Peacock, Richard Peacock, Clarence Pilarski, Alan Price, Charles Price, Duane Price, Gary Price, Eugene Promo, Norman Quaine, DuWayne Schuler, Randy Schuler, Donald Selke, Douglas Selke, James Selke, Rita Selke, Wayne Selke, Joseph Schefke, John Scoles, John Sobeck, Julie Soik, Eleanor Stevens, Fred Stonehouse, Linda Summers, Norma Toussaint, Paul Tulgetske, Bob Ware, Rich Warwick, and Harry Whiteley.

Captain Harold Muth was not only generous with his time, memories, and advice; he also contributed important photos for this book. Warren Toussaint, who still tells his story with flair and in unbelievable detail, also contributed a photo. Bob Crittendon sent a box of *Calcite Screenings* and *ML Screenings* dating back to the 1930s, which were invaluable in the researching of this book. Barry Vallee, son of *Bradley* conveyorman Chick Vallee, sent me his family scrapbook, complete with news clippings and a beautiful letter he'd written to his father while Chick was out on the lakes.

Many helped with the photo section for this book, and all deserve recognition. Mark Thompson (and the Presque Isle County Historical Museum in Rogers City) supplied the archival photos seen herein. Dennis Meredith contributed four photographs, including the picture of his uncle's headstone. Rich Lamb and the *Presque Isle County Advance* were gracious in permitting me to reprint materials originally published in the Rogers City newspaper. Ralph Roberts offered his image of the M/V *Christian Sartori*. Ric Mixter, the fine videographer and documentary filmmaker, sent me invaluable material, as did John Janzen, who contributed outstanding background about his dives to the *Bradley* and the bell retrieval. Videographer Alan Williams shot the underwater footage of the bell retrieval dives, and generously agreed to allow me to use previously unpublished stills of his work. Marine artist Bob McGreevy contributed the haunting painting of the *Bradley* wreckage on the bottom of Lake Michigan, and Jim Clary painted the stunning re-creation of the sinking of the *Carl D. Bradley* found on the cover.

Keith Dosemagen and Mike Gordon assisted with the photo scans, and Patrick McDonald created the map you'll find at the beginning of this book. I owe a huge debt to all of them.

The bibliography lists some of the books I consulted when researching for this book, but I'd like to single out several for being of special significance: Frank Mays's *If We Make It 'til Daylight*; Don Davenport's entry in *Fire & Ice*; Andrew Kantar's *Black November*; and William Ratigan's *Great Lakes Shipwrecks and Survivals*, the book that initially fired my interest in Great Lakes shipwrecks.

Thanks to Kathy Belden, Mike O'Connor, Gena Smith, and the others at Bloomsbury, who always help to make my books better.

Miles Doyle deserves special recognition and gratitude for his work on the manuscript. Miles was exceptionally helpful in his suggestions for improving the narrative, and his line editing was the best I've encountered in my career to this point. I feel very fortunate to have had him in my corner.

Finally, a tip of the cap to friends and family who help in all kinds of ways: Al and Diane Schumacher, Susan Schumacher, the "Back Room Boys" at Franks Diner (particularly "old-timers" Jim Sieger, Steve Paura, John Gilmore, and Lenny Palmer), the Diner Girls (especially the originals— Chris Schwartz, Lynn Groleau, and Kris Derwae), Ken and Karen Ade, Greg Bonofiglio, Peter Spielmann and Judy Hansen, and all the others who will be cheesed off with me for not mentioning their names here.

To my children—Adam, Emily Joy, and Jack Henry: all my love.

                                                          —Michael Schumacher

INDEX

Michael Schumacher, a biographer and Great Lakes historian, is the author of nine books, including *Mighty Fitz: The Sinking of the* Edmund Fitzgerald, and, more recently, *Mr. Basketball: George Mikan, the Minneapolis Lakers, and the Birth of the NBA*. He lives in Wisconsin.